echoes

echoes

nick bullock

VERTEBRATE PUBLISHING

Vertebrate Publishing, Sheffield
www.v-publishing.co.uk

echoes

nick bullock

First published in 2012 by Vertebrate Publishing.

VERTEBRATE PUBLISHING

Crescent House, 228 Psalter Lane, Sheffield S11 8UT.

www.v-publishing.co.uk

This book is a work of non-fiction based on the life, experiences and recollections of
Nick Bullock. In some limited cases the names of people, places, dates and sequences or
the detail of events have been changed solely to protect the privacy of others. The author has
stated to the publishers that, except in such minor respects not affecting the substantial
accuracy of the work, the contents of the book are true.

Photos: Bullock collection unless otherwise credited.

A CIP catalogue record for this book is available from the British Library.

ISBN: 978-1-906148-53-9 (Hardback)   ISBN: 978-1-906148-54-6 (Ebook)

10 9 8 7 6 5 4 3 2 1

Every effort has been made to obtain the necessary permissions with reference to copyright
material, both illustrative and quoted. We apologise for any omissions in this respect and will
be pleased to make the appropriate acknowledgements in any future edition.

Designed by Nathan Ryder, typeset in Arno Pro and Avenir by Jane Beagley, Vertebrate Graphics Ltd.
www.v-graphics.co.uk

Printed and bound in the UK by T.J. International Ltd, Padstow, Cornwall.

To Mum and Dad, who made me who I am and
looked after me in the ways that matter most.

To the memory of Jules Cartwright and Jamie Fisher –
climbing partners, but more than that; great friends.

CONTENTS

FOREWORD

Nick Bullock is a 'fucking nutter', or at least one could be excused for thinking him so. After all, here's a man who relishes the moniker of 'Psycho'. A self-proclaimed 'madman' who has fallen off and survived just about every dangerous route around. I mean, falling onto *The Bells'* peg! That is complete and utter insanity.

However, to aspire to being more than just another good climber you must have your head in the clouds and push the boundaries of your physical ability ceaselessly. And if you're going to do this then there comes with it a price – falls, obsession, relationship failures and, to a point, madness. And this is what these pages contain – an honest account of what it means to be an Alpinist.

After all, Bullock does join a long and distinguished line of glorious nutters across generations of British climbers – Crowley, Menlove, Whillans, Phillips, Dirty Alex, Dirty Derek, Johnny Dawes, Stevie Haston. All these climbers, I'm sure you will agree, are/were no mere slouches, just a few RPs short of a full rack. Besides, we need characters in climbing, as it was in danger of losing them all in the sport climbing 'purges' of the 1990s.

Having completely removed myself from the climbing scene since 1998, I had only vaguely heard of Nick Bullock. Back in 1997 he had attempted the Meru Shark's Fin in the Garwhal Himalaya a few years after myself, Johnny Dawes and Philip Lloyd made our attempt on this wondrous and only recently climbed mountain feature, but I never met him.

Then recently I was flicking through an Italian magazine in which he detailed his approach to writing about climbing. Even if there was no hope of getting published he would still write because he loved the added challenge of writing, of translating the intensity of the ascent into text. Here was a climber who I could equate with and I was intrigued to meet him. And meet him I did, very soon after arriving in Llanberis. We had a lot in common even though we had never met. We had climbed the same climbs, rocked over onto the same holds, clipped the same manky pegs and traversed the globe to many of the same boulder-strewn glaciers. That was as good a place to start from as I could wish for.

I had begun leading again after an eleven year hiatus due to injury, and had moved back to Llanberis for a while to hone my new one armed climbing technique. Nick was living in his van in the car park at Ynys Ettws and climbing every day. This prompted Adam Wainwright to mention with a giggle that we could be the only two full-time climbers in Llanberis. In the 1980s there would have been forty full-timers in the village.

Bullock is an amateur – I mean in the Olympian sense of the word – as we were all amateurs in Llanberis in the 1980s. He is a deep gasp of fresh air in this age of professionalism, this age of film deals and corporate sponsorship. Like an ascetic he simply goes climbing.

In *Echoes* Bullock is seeking his own voice. Under his guidance we are taken on a roller-coaster ride as Nick the all-round climber becomes Nick the all-round writer. His very irregularity of thought – one page he says grades don't matter when on the next page he is keen to onsight an E7 – is what makes this book so joyous to read. Those who don't change their mind regularly are at risk of being dishonest with themselves. There is no such risk in Bullock's writing.

However, it is the self questioning (sometimes self attacking) that makes this a rare climbing book indeed. Through his bold and adventurous climbs – often undertaken alone – he finds he has come to answer some important existential problems.

In fact, throughout *Echoes*, with its seemingly unthinking frenzy of ascents, Bullock comes to the realisation that he has answered some pretty tough questions.

Paul Pritchard
Tasmania

PROLOGUE – TRUST

I cradled the man's head in my hands. His hair was wet. Blood seeped between my fingers. Strings of cerebral fluid hung from his ears and nose. Grey sticky stuff dripped from my knuckles. Sprawled on the floor, the inmate writhed. He was short and stocky, a real powerhouse. I grabbed a blue prison vest, bundled it up, pushed the fabric into the hole in his skull. He was flapping like a fish.

Then, miraculously, the prisoner stood. Some kind of animal drive, some instinct for survival, forced him upright. He spoke, suddenly, in a strange bored monotone.

"Oh, oh, they tried to kill me … they tried to kill me … I'm dying."

He staggered forward, moaning unintelligibly, bumping into the weight-training equipment. It rattled. I held onto him, guiding him around stands, bars, and circular weights stacked in pyramids. Everything was streaked with blood and snot – and the grey fluid leaking from his head. He made a sound from the back of his throat, part growl, part cry.

We both slipped, leaving bright red skid-marks on the floor. For the second time he collapsed. Then he spoke again, very slowly.

"They've killed me."

I saw myself tangled up in cerebral string, red oxygenated froth soaking into my tracksuit trousers. I inhaled the smell of sweat and the metallic tang of blood. Then I slithered to my feet, screaming for help. The noise bounced back at me off the gymnasium walls. Thirty inmates stood quietly, like an expectant crowd at an execution. No one helped. No one except for John, an inmate entrusted with the job of gym orderly. He calmly picked up a short, blood-soaked iron bar, carefully wiped it clean, and put it back in its place on the rack.

I was too shocked and horrified to understand what had just happened. But I found out soon enough. A contract had been taken out on the inmate. The price for the hit was twenty quids' worth of crack cocaine paid by a dealer, who had often trained with the victim – until he found out he was a paedophile. The dealer had needed to save face.

The injured inmate was twice bludgeoned across the back of his head with the short iron bar, ordinarily used for bicep curls. The would-be killer held it in both hands like an axe and swung from behind the inmate's back as he leant forward to pick up his own weight bar. But the victim didn't go down on the first swing. The attacker – a crack-addicted coward – panicked. He lifted the bar above his head and swung again with even more force. This time the victim's skull popped and he crashed to the floor. The second swing had punctured his skull and saved his life by releasing the pressure from the first blow.

The police arrived almost immediately and began an inquiry. A clot dried on the gymnasium floor, large and jagged, like the outline of Australia, while I stood speaking to them. Two days later the police concluded I was innocent of taking a bribe 'to turn a blind eye'. It was ironic that I'd been accused of looking the other way. From our team of six physical education officers, I had been the one who most regularly complained to management about sloppy procedures causing us to leave inmates unattended. Maybe that's why the would-be killer chose to murder when I was on duty. It was retribution for my not trusting them.

The prison governors had been told this inmate was at risk, but they had ignored the warnings and so attempted to place the blame on me. The original paperwork proving my innocence had gone missing, but fortunately a photocopy was found, and the internal blame-shifting inquiry collapsed. I escaped prosecution either by a stroke of luck, or perhaps because of a methodical police investigation. I will never know.

I was thirty two and I had worked at Gartree Prison for ten years. I had spent eleven years in total working for the prison service at the time of this attempted murder, four and a half as a basic grade prison officer, and six and a half as a PE instructor. Over the course of my career, my opinions, my outlook, even my personality were transformed. At twenty one I had walked into a prison for the first time. I was impressionable, scared, desperate to be accepted and living constantly with doubt and uncertainty. At thirty two I was confident, prepared to give everyone a chance, be they paedophiles, murderers, rapists, gangsters, terrorists, drug dealers or fellow prison officers. It didn't matter to me the colour of a man's skin or his religion or from which country he originated. All I was concerned about was how people behaved and interacted with each other from day to day. Deep down I think I had always been like this, but in my early years of prison service it had been easier to fall in line.

I come from a working-class background, where black is black and white is white. As I matured I tried to bring this simple philosophy into my everyday life. But I have always struggled with inequality, with people receiving more than they deserve because of who they are or their upbringing. Inequality is largely what life is made of, and inside a prison inequality is rife. I find paedophilia abhorrent, but I also find pushing a shotgun into the face of a bank clerk or blowing up innocent people or pushing drugs to the masses just as abhorrent.

Yet for some complicated reason, in prison – and sometimes on the outside – it is deemed acceptable, even respected, for someone to destroy someone else's life – destroy a child's life by killing her father, to waste a life by pushing drugs. This was the type of hypocrisy among inmates I couldn't tolerate. The attempted hit in the gymnasium took place not because of the victim's crime. It happened because a drugs dealer trained with a paedophile and thought he had lost face. He needed to do something to regain his status.

As I sat cradling the man's head, with his blood and brains sticking to my hands, I heard a voice – my own voice. It was asking me something. Asking how I had ended up like this, desperate and lost among people who thought nothing of caving in a man's head and then standing back to watch him die, like a pack of jackals. I remember how the blood was everywhere…

…and as I write these words, blood brings to mind blood from my other life…

…I remember shouting over and over again.

"Watch me Michael! IGNORE WHAT'S GOING ON. Just watch *me*!"

Seventy feet below, my climbing partner stood holding my ropes. Looking down I knew instantly that his eyes were wired and wide but fixed on me, even though blood was splattering the grey rock, pooling in the polished folds of rhyolite just feet away from him.

I was on a difficult and scary climb called *Tess of the d'Urbevilles*, high up on the left wall of Dinas Cromlech's famous open-book corner in Snowdonia's Llanberis Pass. The walls are covered with routes of varying difficulty. *Tess* is one of the difficult ones – and most frightening. It has limited cracks for protection, and only those skilled at placing bits of fiddly gear can make the climb reasonably safe. Unfortunately, I don't fall into that category. I was climbing 'on-sight', knowing nothing about the route other than what I'd read in my guidebook description.

True to my character, I charged up the cliff with my usual why-bother-wasting-time-and-energy-fiddling-little-bits-of-pointless-brass-into-marginal-placements-when-forging-on-makes-more-sense philosophy. This approach works well unless outside forces intervene – or my arms get too tired.

The blood all over the rocks had not happened yet, and I was concentrating on my climbing. I had broken my kneecap a few weeks before in a fall from one of the slate quarries above Llanberis. Now I was forced to rock over onto my foot, twisting my knee into positions it didn't really like, and then putting immense pressure onto it as I stood up. It felt like an ice-cold nail was being driven into my leg. My eyes tried to focus on the sharp crozzled rock inches from my nose, but the sweat and tears provoked by all that effort and pain smudged my glasses and blurred my vision.

I was still on the sick from the prison, because of my knee, and I was now looking at a ground fall from seventy feet. My forearms ached from crimping my fingers onto edges no thicker than the tiles around a washbasin. I tried desperately to figure out a sequence of moves that would lead me to the comfort of the first good piece of protection since starting up the climb. What time and future I had left was contained in the puzzle of rock above me.

My trust in Michael was unquestionable. I knew I could forget about him and concentrate on the only thing that mattered, whether or not I could move just another ten feet to my right. This was everything climbing meant to me, this was what I loved doing best. I might have been in peril, but the situation felt normal to me – right on the edge, but enjoying it. Nothing odd was happening here.

The person climbing *Cenotaph Corner*, the climb to my right taking the centrefold of Dinas Cromlech's open book, was just a blur, an insect buzzing on the periphery. He was there, but only in the grey mist of my sub-conscious. I locked off. The muscles in my shoulder tensed. *Shake-out-chalk-up-study-plan-breathe-deep-control. Prepare.* Once committed to the next sequence of moves one of two things would happen. I would either climb methodically to the top, or fall in a heartbeat to the bottom of the crag. Reversing these moves, climbing back down, wasn't an option.

The insect to my right made a move. A move he will not forget for the rest of his life. A move I will not forget for the rest of my life. He stood up, making a move hundreds of climbers had made over decades before him, and in so doing dislodged a brick-sized block of rhyolite that had been wedged in the crack at the back of the corner for hundreds or perhaps thousands of years. The rock slipped from the corner crack and span off into space.

Suddenly, it seemed my heart was pumping something cold and crystal clear through my veins. My senses sharpened. I now saw everything. I watched with fascination as, end over end, the block spun. I heard the air it displaced whirring like the blades of a fan. The insect stopped buzzing, became human and screamed a warning. But his belayer took no notice. I went on watching, unable to pull my eyes away from the spinning rock.

The climber screamed again. The block closed on its target. He screamed for a third time, the block now just a few feet above his climbing partner's skull. The belayer looked up, jerked back his head. The block skimmed his brow before ripping into the bare arm gripping his leader's rope. Blood shot into the air and covered the rock around him. The belayer collapsed. His leader cried because now no one was holding his ropes. And the blood just kept on pumping out.

"Watch me Michael! IGNORE WHAT'S GOING ON. Just watch *me*!"

I made the moves to the right and finally reached the crack-system of a route called *Left Wall*. Here I was able to slot in two secure nuts that guaranteed I would not hit the ground should I fall. I was safe. And now hanging from big comfy holds, I looked down into Michael's massive owl-eyes. Not once had he taken them from me. Blood covered the rock just feet away from him. There had been screams and yells. The belayer's unconscious body had been lifted past him, and still Michael had faithfully watched me, utterly ignoring the body passing beneath our ropes. The poor leader had been lowered safely from *Cenotaph Corner*.

Half an hour later I finished *Tess* much relieved. But despite the nearness to death, the fear, even the damage done to another person, I was nevertheless still glad, even joyful, to be amongst the mountains. There was a big difference to my life in prison. The rock was blameless. Mountains are inanimate. And, of course, it was impossible for them to hate – or take revenge.

I found climbing five years after starting work for the prison service, and when I did it took hold of my life. Climbing changed me. It cradled me, allowed me to take hold of my own life.

I had been brought up to chase the security of working, the benefits of regular pay, sick pay, a mortgage, and a pension. Having got used to all that, it would be difficult to leave their security behind. But as soon as I became aware of the alternative and unfettered way of life climbing could offer, I began to nurture a dream of escape. The prison service was killing me. Even if I completed my service, I knew that the life expectancy of a retired prison officer was just two years. Every time I touched rock or whacked in an ice axe, my dream of freedom grew a little bit stronger. By the time I was thirty two, by the time I was holding an inmate's broken head in my hands, not a day passed when I didn't fantasise about standing outside the prison gates, taking one last look before turning and walking away – forever.

BRICK

I was born on Christmas Day 1965, in the front bedroom of 6 Brookhouse Road, a white-painted brick-built three-bedroom semi on the edge of Cheadle in Staffordshire. I was the second child to Maureen and Graham, my sister Lesley having arrived three and a half years earlier. Cheadle is a small market town on the edge of the north Staffordshire moors, an architectural mish-mash of red brick, blue brick, large sandstone blocks, ornate iron railings and black-and-white timber frames. The people of Cheadle were a mish-mash also, the working classes spanning rural and industrial occupations: coal mining, engineering, sand and gravel extraction, textile mills, farming and haulage.

Mum and Dad worked full time, so Nan, my mum's mum, would collect me and my sister from primary school. Nan also lived in Cheadle, having been evacuated from Sunderland during the war, in a rented three-bedroom semi surrounded by council houses. Having lost her husband, who had died at forty eight of a heart attack, and a daughter, who died of diphtheria, Nan lived on her own, addicted to the Valium she had taken

Left: Mum's mum and dad; my Nan and the Grandad I never met. *Right:* Dad and Mum with my sister Lesley's children. Clothile sat on Dad's knee and Jake with Mum. I reckon Dad is reaching for a roll-up or a cup of tea! *Photo: Lesley Stone*

since losing her husband. She stored sugar, tea and soap in case World War Three broke out, and only used two rooms of her large house while doting on her grandchildren.

Mum finished work at five and would pick us up before driving home and getting the tea on, usually sausage and chips or chips and fish fingers, or burger and chips, or egg beans and chips, the egg having been cracked and dropped into the chip-pan to come out brown and crunchy with a runny yoke. I loved chips. Lesley came home one day from school with an exotic new dish called spaghetti bolognaise, which was okay, but wasn't chips. On Sunday, because Mum had time to cook properly, we had a roast.

As a family we went on one holiday a year, always somewhere in Britain because of Tami our Golden Labrador. Dad would never have put her in kennels. Mostly we camped in Wales or stayed in the same guest house in Tenby. Dad worked full time at jobs he didn't enjoy: bricklaying, night shifts in the local textiles mill, driving, insurance sales, youth care in secure homes and social work. Social work – visiting old folk up on the moors – was the job he stuck longer than any before retiring and setting up a small printing company for computer stationery.

Mum worked full time also, first in accounting, then bank work and social work before returning to accounting and in later life she started a computer stationery brokering business called Diamond Forms, which just managed to pay her and Pam, her partner, a wage and nothing more. Mum was tall, slim and dark skinned and very conscious of her appearance. She would always make herself up before leaving the house but was a grafter, who always worked hard. One day after school, we arrived home to find Mum covered in oil under her Hillman Minx changing the starter motor on her own. No one else's mum did things like that.

She was also very much a full time mother. She drove my sister and me around, shopped for food on Saturday morning, cooked and cleaned the house with compulsive vigour and drank very strong instant coffee day and night while smoking Embassy Number 1 or Peter Stuyvesant extra-long cigarettes. My Dad was of his time. He didn't wash up, didn't cook, clean or shop, but he was always there, usually reading a book with a roll-up clamped between his index and middle finger and with a mug of strong tea with several sugars added. He worked on the house, the cars and the garden and was the person I would be sent to for a clip around the ear. Dad was also very astute and careful with money, something he learnt from his father, who was cautious through necessity.

Dad's parents had no savings. They lived in rented property and survived on a state pension. Grandad was quiet but caring and good fun.

Before he retired, he'd been a mechanic and a long-distance lorry driver. He often told the story of a fellow lorry driver – Jacky Oil – driving his lorry with strings of snot hanging from the wing mirrors after he had cleared his nose out of the window. Grandad loved the reaction from telling that story. Dad told me the story of how Grandad had suffered toothache as he drove south on a job, so called into the dentist and had the whole of his top-set of teeth removed. When he drove back north he called into the dentist and had all of the bottom teeth taken out as well. I think I probably learnt my black-and-white attitude from Grandad. He always had a Silk Cut hanging from his mouth but was dead-set against alcohol, having taken the horse and trap as a boy to the pub to collect his dad, who was drunk most nights.

Dad worked for every penny and watched every penny with reverence. At home we only had a phone for short periods when he needed one for work. Even then it had a bar so you couldn't make outgoing calls. Mum had to hand over wages and was given an allowance for food and the kids. She used to say Dad was so tight he squeaked when he walked, but if the money had been left to her, we would have been destitute. She would have given away her last. I remember Mum hiding bills or invoices from Dad so he didn't know she had spent money.

Wallowing in mud, wading and damming the dirty brook near our house, collecting birds' eggs, scrumping, hanging out, setting fires, tree climbing, hunting newts among the reeds, this was how I spent my time, a normal childhood growing up in Cheadle. When I was nine, long before the smart new gyms came into fashion, I joined Cheadle Health and Strength Club. This comprised a few old weight-training stations, a cable machine, skipping ropes, dip bars, blue mats and an exercise bike, all contained within the walls of a dusty, run-down former chapel. Monday, Wednesday and Friday, I would run the four miles from home to the old chapel where I followed a programme written by the local keep-fit guru. Afterwards I would run home. Through the Cheadle Health and Strength Club I became friends with Alan Johnson, a farmer's son from Huntley and it wasn't long before my main interests outside keeping fit were shooting and hunting.

In my final year of primary school, an enthusiastic teacher, Pip Owen, found I had a talent for gymnastics. Pip was a gymnastics instructor at a large club in Stoke-on-Trent and he got me enrolled. I was soon training four times a week. Mum found herself spending a lot of time driving me the thirty-mile round trip to and from Burslem after a day's work but she never complained and always appeared happy to dedicate her life to her kids.

When I was eleven I moved to Cheadle High School, a comprehensive recently created under the Labour Party's reforms by the merger of the local grammar and secondary modern schools. After the first year I was placed in the upper band, meaning I was studying for O-levels. My sister Lesley was already there and studying hard, but I hated school and didn't really try. Looking back, I can see clearly the path my life took and the people I chose to call friends. I was from a skilled working-class background, and so were most of my mates. Their parents owned their own houses and worked hard for what they had, just like mine. The parents of a few friends were from the professional classes and quite liberal and open-minded. Dad struggled with this kind of outlook. He was a staunch Conservative with strong right wing views. He called anyone who was liberal and open-minded "wishy-washy".

Before I was born my parents lived in Birmingham, off the Hagley Road in Harborne where at the time many new immigrants were living. This was long before racism in Britain became unacceptable. Such rapid change was difficult for many ordinary white Britons to absorb. I can still hear Mum telling me how there wasn't a bed in hospital when she gave birth to Lesley because they were full to capacity with immigrants. But I can also remember Mum and Dad talking about white people crossing the road as Mum walked toward them because her skin was so dark. Growing up, I would regularly hear Enoch Powell's 1968 'Rivers of Blood' speech quoted over the dinner table and the Labour leader Harold Wilson called 'Billy Liar'. Immediately after Powell's speech, made in a Birmingham hotel, the whole country was in turmoil. Workers marched with banners in support of Powell, a member of parliament in nearby Wolverhampton. Many people were carried along by the force of his words.

Even now, I find some of Mum and Dad's attitudes and politics from their earlier life difficult to understand. Dad was the eldest of three children but he didn't speak to his sister or his brother, David, who was twenty years his junior. Uncle David had long ginger hair tied in a pony-tail and was caring, liberal and good fun. He lived in a caravan on Cheadle common and had been arrested for growing cannabis around it. David was the ginger sheep I didn't know existed until I joined Cheadle Health and Strength Club, where he was also a member. Instantly, I connected with my soft-speaking uncle. He seemed different, being rather Bohemian and peaceful without the air of aggression that characterised many others in the town. I suppose Uncle David was the first person I met who didn't appear to want to live 'normally'.

Dad was conscripted into the army and served in the Korean War, driving a breakdown truck that was used to rescue other trucks or tanks that had broken down or slid into ditches. He didn't talk much about the war, not to me anyway, and when he came out of the army he took a bricklaying apprenticeship. From appearances, Dad was the archetypal Labour supporter, but he voted Tory and hated the unions for most of his adult life, a hatred born from an accident he suffered while working for Ansell's Brewery in Birmingham. Dad opened a large vat full of boiling cleaning fluid, which registered empty. But the gauge was faulty, and he was submerged in red hot liquid. He suffered second and third-degree burns to his whole body.

His union used the accident as a lever against the company, eventually making a deal with the bosses to get more power for themselves, but in doing so the shop stewards agreed not to push for the correct amount of compensation for Dad. They even visited Mum while he was still in hospital and threatened her when she suggested employing an independent solicitor.

Mum was the well-educated one, although this was still only a state education which culminated at eighteen. Yet Dad read avidly. He sucked in facts and information, listened to classical music and followed politics. Throughout my childhood my parents hardly drank alcohol. Dad would drink a bottle of Scotch over Christmas and then nothing for another year. Later in life, in his mid-fifties, he decided to become an alcoholic and began drinking half a bottle of whisky every day. Until recently I thought I inherited my obsessive genes from Mum. Now I'm not so sure.

I didn't really mix with kids from the council estates or with kids from broken homes. In fact, divorce was almost unknown in my circle of friends. I went through secondary school looking down on kids from the council estates, feeling I was something better, even though I wasn't. I was always up for a bit of an adventure – thieving, smoking or drinking – but only as long as I thought I wouldn't be found out. One day, aged eleven, I rolled up at home drunk, after the local pub's landlady gave me several ciders in payment for helping her move some boxes. Mum, normally the placid one, was furious although since I passed out soon after, I don't remember much. A few years later I helped myself to several bottles of barley wine through a broken window in the pub cellar. I got smashed and was caught by the police. They cautioned me and took me home to my furious mother and embarrassed father, who was then working at a secure home for young offenders.

I suppose I was of average intelligence, but while growing up I used my average intelligence for trouble and excitement – not education. I was a teacher's worse nightmare. I would learn if I wanted, but if a teacher couldn't prove the worth of what they were teaching, I couldn't be bothered. In which case, all my efforts would be put into working out how to do as little as possible. My English teacher told me I was worse than the real troublemakers. At least she knew what they were. But, she said, I was sly because she never knew what I was thinking. At the time I took this as a compliment.

On the surface, I was a confident teenager, into punk rock and hunting. In reality, I was shy and easily hurt. Uncle Dave moved to Brighton, where he became the road manager of a successful ska punk band called the Piranhas. Parked one night by the side of the road, Dave was killed by a drunk driver who ran into the back of the band's vehicle. Several members of the Piranhas were also injured.

Dave's death made me look at life differently. For the first time I experienced loss. Life was no longer safe. After Uncle Dave's death I became quite rebellious and mixed up. I thought a lot about death. My time was spent catching rabbits with ferrets in Huntley Wood or moodily stalking the sandstone flags between the two record shops in Cheadle's town centre. Initials were carved into Cheadle's sandstone paving flags and a worn runnel ran down the middle. Shit-covered Wellington boots, painted Doc Marten's, high heels, brogues, blue-crepe-soled brothel-creepers, platforms and torn work-boots with rusty steel, all writing their history into Cheadle's pavements. I would catch rabbits or buy records, doing both dressed in red jeans, a pink, green and black striped mohair jumper, Doc Marten boots and a green combat jacket covered in the names of punk bands – The Slits, The Vibrators, The Sex Pistols, The Ruts – and on the back I added a large encircled 'A' – the symbol for anarchy.

The farmland surrounding Cheadle was grass meadows with hawthorn separating each field. The meadows were used for grazing dairy cattle and haymaking, but corners, and on occasion whole fields, were neglected scrub. These neglected areas, where blackthorn and bramble flourished, were home to rabbits, fox, wren, robin, blackbird and finch. Down towards the slow-moving brook, the meadows became waterlogged, studded with yellow buttercups and the occasional purple marsh orchid and populated by green plovers picking their way through the marsh. The brook's meandering path was marked by twisted and scabby alders growing along its edge. On the brook's tightest corners, where the water ran deep, brownies would linger in the shade of an alder and kingfishers and sand martins would burrow.

Catching rats with ferrets and terriers, lamping rabbits with longdogs and poaching game were all popular pursuits in Cheadle. Aged fourteen I bought my first shotgun and hunted crows, pigeon, rabbits, pheasant, and squirrels. I left school in 1982, aged sixteen, by which time I was hunting with a passion. Gymnastics, Cheadle Health and Strength, all that was in the past. All I wanted in life was to become a gamekeeper.

WOODLANDS

My first position as gamekeeper was on Lord Lichfield's estate at Shugborough Hall in Staffordshire. This was a short-term placement on a government youth employment scheme, but six months later I was offered a full-time job as 'underkeeper' on an estate near Porthmadog in North Wales. This opportunity was thanks entirely to my parents. Unbeknownst to me, when I was fourteen and still at school, they applied on my behalf for a place on a new scheme run by the British Amateur Shooting and Conservation Society to place young people for a week with a gamekeeper. When I was selected they surprised me with the news and drove me to Wales. This first visit was a success and I returned several more times, taken to Wales in the school holidays and picked up again a week later.

A part of a gamekeeper's work is to control and protect. To hunt down. To kill. And my life as a sixteen-year-old gamekeeper was black and white. Birds and animals that ate pheasant eggs or threatened pheasants were considered vermin. Creatures were hunted down and then killed before being displayed on a gibbet for the bounty the estate owner paid. Crows, stoats, weasels, foxes, rats, squirrels, jays and magpies, all hanging in a stinking, rotting line.

Politics in Wales was black and white also. The head gamekeeper was a large, thickset Derbyshire man always dressed in a camouflaged jacket and Wellington boots. Brian was a staunch supporter of Margaret Thatcher and extremely right wing. He revelled in the way Mrs Thatcher bullied and dictated.

I lived in a static caravan at the end of a rough track on the side of a small mountain called Moel y Gest, between the North Wales coastal towns of Porthmadog and Criccieth. The caravan, a large cream torpedo, looked toward the cliffs of Tremadog. I would frequently watch the brightly coloured climbers draped across the cliffs. Years later I learnt the names and climbed some of the climbs on these cliffs: *Vector*, *Sexual Salami*, *Cream*, *Void*, *Vulture*, *Sultans of Swing*, *Bananas* and *Extraction*. But at the time, in 1982, the names, the cliff, the activity itself meant nothing to me.

I worked every day, living on the job, for the job, lugging huge sacks of wheat to the woods, cutting tracks through forest, raising, feeding and nursing birds. Climbing was something happening on another planet, far outside my orbit as a gamekeeper. I lived in another world, far removed from the momentous events of the early 1980s – industrial strife, social change, economic upheaval. On the rare occasion I watched television, it showed images of the dark green South Atlantic swallowing burning battleships, in a pyrotechnic dance of death.

I remember the science fiction film *Blade Runner*, a film noir adapted from Phillip K. Dick's book *Do Androids Dream of Electric Sheep?* The book's theme is the nature of life. Is the life of a person any less valuable than that of an android, or 'replicant' as they were called in the film. What, in fact, does it mean to be alive? What crucial factor defines humanity? I didn't identify with the film's stars, the anti-hero Harrison Ford and the replicant Rutger Hauer, but with a character called J. F. Sebastian, a loner stuck on a blighted Earth, too ill and broken to join other, successful humans in the 'off-world colonies'. Instead, he had created his own menagerie of fantastical replicants to keep him company. In the same way, I felt separated from all my friends. I felt alone.

I was brought up to believe life is not for pastimes or leisure. Life is supposed to be a struggle. Satisfaction is something achieved only through hard work. I'm not sure if I was ever told this, or it became an inbuilt mechanism after watching Mum and Dad work full time and bringing up kids. Years later I took the same philosophy into climbing, but that philosophy also made me sneer at people I considered had not earned their freedom or their position.

Often, I walked alone, a loaded shotgun cracked across my arm. I remember the tractor beams of sun piercing the swaying forest canopy and the fern spores released from unfurling fronds dancing in the beams of light. Above my head oak leaves whispered. A smell of mould rose from the ground as I walked through the leaf litter.

A loud screech brought me out of my reverie, masking the quieter insect drone. As I drew close, I saw the shocking blue of a jay's covert feathers, its speckled paunch of cinnamon down. The jay spotted me and stopped crying. The bird was trapped inside a wire netting dome designed to catch pheasants.

The head keeper and I had made many such traps, which we had placed around the woods to catch breeding stock. Once caught, we would collect and place the pheasants in a large pen. When the birds started to breed and lay, we would gather the eggs carefully and place them inside a giant incubator. Three weeks later, the young pheasant chicks would hatch.

The trap had a round mesh tunnel, a funnel, which led into the centre of the dome where wheat was piled as bait. Once a bird had pushed through, it could not reverse out. The trap attracted other birds, including this jay.

I pulled back a bamboo pole sealing the top of the dome. The jay flapped and bounced, struggling against the netting. Cinnamon down floated in the dappled light. I grabbed the bird, cradling it my hands. The bird struggled, and then settled. Splayed stick feet stretched into the sky. My fingers squeezed against its softness. I could feel the ribcage expanding as the bird inhaled and a small heart pulsing in the palms of my hands. The forest insect drone returned. Applying more pressure, I constricted the rise and fall of the bird's chest until the bird could no longer breathe. Two shining beads looked at me before two leathery eyelids shut. And opened. The black beak opened, unable to draw breath, and closed. My hand remained clenched, clenched tight, until at last, after a final struggle, the bird's eyes shut forever, its head dropped, and its breathing stopped. *Time to die.* Black and white. The forest was silent.

When I started full time in Wales there was an underkeeper called Colin on a youth employment scheme, the same scheme that had got me a job on Lord Lichfield's estate – a six-month contract with the government paying £25 a week. Twenty five pounds a week was, at the time, the same amount given to an unemployed person on unemployment benefit.

Colin was from Scotland and about twenty years old. He was tall and gangly and introverted. A mop of curly dark hair poked from beneath his tweed deerstalker. The head gamekeeper's wife called him creepy; she said he would sneak around the house not talking. My immature perspective could not see the real reason for Colin's introverted behaviour. Wanting to be accepted, I would agree with her. *Creepy Colin.* It was not until he left the estate and the head gamekeeper's wife turned on me – ignoring me, turning others against me, eating in the kitchen away from me so she didn't have to feed me, talking to anyone who would listen about my creepiness – that I understood what Colin had endured.

I remember the endless nightshifts, rain tearing into the dark forest canopy, heavy drops from ancient oaks plopping onto my jacket. One night I huddled in the darkness, in the lee of a stone wall on the side of a lane, which cut through the estate, heading towards Black Rock Sands. The winter wind was blowing the rain horizontally into my shelter. A stream gurgled through moss-covered boulders. Max, the estate's Alsatian, whimpered and pushed close. The smell of wet, matted dog hair overpowered that of the forest. It was well past midnight, but I couldn't return until two at the earliest.

"Nightwatch," Brian called it, patrolling the estate in the dead of night on the lookout for poachers. I was sixteen and weighed ten stone. The pick-axe handle I carried weighed about as much as I did. The chances of actually detaining anyone were nil, while the chances of being beaten to a pulp were high. The dog was soft and useless, so I huddled and hid, and dozed fitfully as the fat drops soaked the shoulders of my wax jacket.

I woke with a start. Headlight beams cut the heavy rain and lit the dark between the trees. Car tyres swishing across the ground. The car slowed and stopped. I withdrew further into my jacket. The window of the car opened and after what felt like an age, a hand flicked out a cigarette. The cigarette bounced, sparked and fizzled. The window closed. The car moved on. The cigarette dimmed and went out. Marching through my mind were the boots of soldiers yomping through the mud into battle on the Falkland Islands. *"It's too bad she won't live, but then again, who does?"*

Through the shooting season I would get out of bed at five, walk to the woods and feed the pheasants, then return to the house. By then the shooting party and beaters had arrived. 'Beating,' crashing through the forests to flush the pheasants for the guns, took the rest of the morning and into the middle of the afternoon. I would leave the shooting party mid-afternoon to feed the pheasants in the woods for a second time. I walked on my own, listening to the crack of gunshot echoing from the hills, and imagined my pheasants being killed. In the evening I would go back on nightwatch. Work on these winter days generally lasted for eighteen hours and I received £38 per week from which ten was given to the head gamekeeper's wife for food.

I didn't question the pay, the hours, or the work – not until the gamekeeper's wife started to make my life intolerable. Then I began to ring home and complain to my parents. After a year and a half, Mum and Dad turned up unannounced and told me to pack my stuff. On the drive back to Cheadle, I sat in the back of the car watching as the rain-lashed mountains and sodden moors faded into the distance. I never returned to gamekeeping and it took years to rebuild the confidence I had lost.

CHAINS

Coming home from Wales was a dark time. I argued frequently with Dad about everything and felt mentally fragile after the abuse I had suffered. In my head living back in Cheadle was a step backwards. I was unemployed. I had given up. I had failed.

At first I blamed my parents for taking the initiative and coming to rescue me, but now I know the favour they did me – and what a strain my phone calls and unhappiness must have been. I didn't have a social life in Wales; the head gamekeeper wouldn't allow me to mix with anyone for fear of giving away secrets about where the pheasant pens were situated and how often we patrolled. Suddenly I had friends all around me again and going to the pub most nights was normal. It was like returning from a long and isolated expedition.

Sport and training had fallen away with the start of work. Now I had a girlfriend, I was drinking and smoking, and grabbing whatever bits of manual work I could find, generally labouring on building sites with my mate and his Dad or on the farms where I had spent much of my teenage years. I started a day-release course in Stoke to become a bricklayer, but gave it up and became self-employed instead, working at a large dairy farm near Rocester. After six months the Tories brought in milk quotas, which cut the income of many dairy farms. Once again I was looking for work.

Fortunately, an old school friend, Steven Barber, or 'Bung' as he was known, had begun work in the merchandising warehouse at the theme park, Alton Towers, which led to seasonal work. But as the second winter since returning home drew in, and the Towers laid me off, I was unemployed again. I worked unofficially on Littley Farm with the owner Roy Harrison. Roy was a dour, dirty-purple-berry, boiler-suited, wellington-bootshod forty-a-day-Capstan-full-strength dairy-farmer, who, beneath his gruff exterior, had a heart of gold.

Inside the asbestos-roofed breeze-block shed, bleary-eyed, I oversaw early morning milking, steam pouring from chewing mouths, clouds billowing from hot black and white bodies, piss flowing down semi-circular gutters cut into concrete, the milking machine's methodical, rhythmic sucking "Schlurp, schlurp…" – and the rattle of chains wrapped around the necks of the cows. After the milking and the mucking-out were finished, my day was free until milking and mucking-out began again in the evening. And in between I would go to Huntley Woods with my ferrets to catch rabbits.

I had kept ferrets since I was twelve years old and I loved spending time with them, smoking and thinking and listening to the insect hum of the woodland. Thinking was a big part of ferreting for me. Catching rabbits involved covering every rabbit hole with a purse net pegged to the ground – 'Why am I unemployed?' – lifting the ferret from its box – 'What will I do with my life if I can't find work?' – popping the ferret at the edge of a hole, giving her a stroke – 'To be a success, a person needs to work.' – and waiting.

The ferret, thick creamy white fur, pink eyes and pink nose would smell the air and the earth, she would sense the space and freedom and shake her body like a dog coming out of water, her coat pointed and spiked. Then with one last sniff, she would scamper down the dark hole, her back arched and chattering like an otter. The quiet of the wood would grow heavy as though the trees and ferns sensed death. A nuthatch, powder blue and orange, walked down a peeling silver birch trunk. Thoughts of being a failure ran through my mind. A tractor in the field. Cars and a police siren in the distance.

'Grow up, get a job, meet a girl, buy a house, have kids…'

Bump, bump, bump…

Thumping underground. Thumping, then a brown explosion of fur and long feet and a white bob tail. A magpie shocked by the movement screeched. The rabbit was tangled inside the purse net, soft fur poked through net holes. Big brown paws scrabbled which tangled it more. Unwrapping the rabbit, taking it by the back legs, hanging it upside down, the rabbit automatically sticks out its head.

'What's wrong with me? Why couldn't I stick it in Wales?'

A karate chop, just one swift killing blow to the neck did the job.

'Failure.'

Huntley Wood was, like a lot of things around Cheadle, a rural and industrial mix. The middle of the wood was a mountainscape of sand peaks and mining metalwork, large trucks and conveyor belts. On the weekend, with my girlfriend Sheila, we would walk my dogs – Murphy, an aggressive Patterdale Terrier with a wispy beard, a barrel chest, thick front legs leading to feathered feet like those of a grouse and a loyal, intelligent

Golden Labrador called Dipper. Through the woods we'd go, into the massive hole quarried out of the heart of the wood, climbing over the sand and gravel moraines. I would kick steps. Large round pebbles would roll away. Dipper would paddle, his big golden paws marking sandy prints in the shallow salt-flat. Murphy would muscle aside the rhododendron looking to kill anything that moved.

Sheila was only seventeen, long red hair, slim, pale, she could have been from Wales or Ireland. She could have had a feisty, fiery streak but she didn't. She was caring, compassionate and loyal. It was obvious she wanted to settle down and have kids. Sheila didn't want much from life apart from a person to love her and a family. I knew this way of life was not for me, but it was difficult to accept. This is what people were supposed to do.

I knew our relationship was doomed and at some point I would end it, to let her find what she wanted. Or I would cheat on her so she'd dump me. But I was twenty and selfish and at that time I needed the love she gave me, even though I offered her little in return. Dipper bounded back to me, splashing water, thick wagging tail, big brown eyes, unquestioning, undemanding companionship.

I had been working in the warehouse at Alton Towers for three years. I was now full-time and managing the warehouse, but I didn't see it as a career or somewhere I wanted to be in another ten years. It was a great place for my social life, although perhaps not so good for the cars I owned.

Alton Towers merchandising department warehouse workers – L-R: Dave, Nick, Steve, Andy. Dave Critchlow on my right always did fancy himself! Bung my good mate is directly on my left.

Racing and then writing off a mini-van and an Alfa Sud hadn't slowed me. Dad encouraged me to buy a Skoda, which promptly blew up. In recompense and I'm sure feeling a little guilty he bought me a Renault 4, and that did slow me down. Evenings would generally start straight after work. I'd sit on the stone wall outside the Wild Duck in the middle of Alton with my mates, Dyche and Bung, smoking and drinking, flirting with the part time girls who worked the summer season and then were gone, laughing, joking, getting pissed.

The sun filtered flame-red between the sycamores. I turned my face toward the sky to watch the swifts, their haunting screams penetrating the still evening. The swifts were just returned from their challenging journey. They appeared happy and confident in their fitness and skill, wheeling around the darkening sky, threading stars, scooping flies, screaming, wheeling, screaming. Perhaps it was not being settled to one place that gave them this apparent joy?

"You should apply for the prison service. Job for life, pension, growth industry."

That was how Dad put it after reading an article in the *Express* about the prison service's drive to recruit seven thousand new prison officers. What he didn't see, or neglected to mention, was the effect it would have on my personality, the horror it would introduce to my life.

And yet, bored with life at Alton Towers and almost on a whim, I listened to Dad and filled out an application form for the prison service. A few months later, I drove to Stafford Prison for the entrance exam and a month after that, having passed the exam, I returned once more to Stafford Prison for an interview.

SOUL MINING

Approaching the oak doors of Stafford Prison, I tried to swallow. The doors soared above me like a cliff. People wrapped against the cold walked quickly to work along the leaf-blown pavement.

The leaves rustled a warning: "Turn around!"

My throat was dry.

Towering turrets, round and grand, made from huge, unclimbable sandstone blocks, supported the huge frames of the Victorian double doors.

I knocked on a smaller door inset into one of these giants, jigging, from one foot to the other. I wished I had been for a pee. All of the moisture in my body had obviously drained to my bladder.

I could hear footsteps drawing close on the other side of the doors – on cobblestones, metal segs heel-caps tapping out a remorseless rhythm. A flap covering the small, barred window in the small door shot open with a guillotine snick. A red cherub face pressed itself against the bars.

"What do you want?"

Nick Bullock, age 22, Gartree Prison.

15

"Ah…" my throat failed me for a moment. "I'm here for an interview."

A key was thrust into the lock, its long chain swung and rattled. The apparition the other side of the door made me think of Bumble from *Oliver Twist*. Then I stepped through the wooden hole and left behind the smells, sights and sounds of the normal world.

Wearing the suit Dad wore for his wedding twenty five years before, I looked like a teddy boy – black drainpipe trousers, pointed black suede shoes, scraggy hair and spots. Bumble led me through the grounds of Stafford Prison, along with several other would-be prison officers. Inmates were digging manure into raised flower beds of red roses. They looked up and laughed, pointing at my suit. Embarrassed, I ignored the jibes, but felt shocked that the inmates were allowed to talk and make fun of visitors. I had a lot to learn.

Several months after the successful interview, and at the age of twenty one, I was back at Stafford Prison, beginning my first two weeks of work in the prison service. It was both frightening and fascinating, and every day was an eye-opener.

Stafford Prison was a category 'C' jail, housing a wide variety of prisoners. Some had been long-term, high-security inmates nearing the end of their sentences. Some were convicted of domestic crimes and sex offences. Most were habitual criminals in for standard offences – drugs, robbery, ABH, GBH. Most of the inmates in category 'C' prisons were serving short to mid-length sentences, anything from two to ten years. The higher category prisons, cat 'B' and cat 'A', held lifers and long-term prisoners and inmates who were notorious or serving such long sentences they had nothing to lose.

There were many different prisons. Some were deemed acceptable by the inmates, some were not. Wandsworth in London and Winson Green in Birmingham fell into the despised category. They were prisons with a reputation for zero tolerance. I learned inmates hated these prisons and the prison officers who worked in them.

Stafford Prison was the old Victorian design of building, built from solid blocks of stone with large accommodation wings, hollow warehouses stacked high with the unwanted. I remember the solid three-inch wooden doors, the pipes along the corridors, the bars, grates and wire mesh. The environment was claustrophobic. It was dark, and smelled of sweat and human waste. The sound of the pipes, the rattle of key-chains, doors slamming and human voices merged in my head, a raucous chatter like the honking of geese.

Our nervous little group of entrant prison officers was led through one of the wings and I looked directly into the pasty face of a man in his mid-thirties with the words "Fuck off" tattooed across his forehead. Never had I been so close to someone who didn't care. I discovered Stafford Prison had a reputation for being austere with a strict regime, although not as strict as Birmingham or Wandsworth. The prison officers were supposedly dogs, doling out beatings in a regime of intolerance. This strict atmosphere, I found out, was usual for a category 'C' prison although at no time were beatings legal, even if at times they appeared justified.

After a two-week induction at Stafford, I was sent to prison officer training college. Ordinarily, this would have meant Newbold Revel in Warwickshire or Wakefield in Yorkshire, but with the extra recruiting taking place, a reorganisation euphemistically dubbed 'Fresh Start', the prison service had opened two temporary schools. So I was sent to Ripley at the Derbyshire police headquarters.

There were approximately eighty new-entrant prison officers at Ripley, mostly men, but also a few women. The new entrants came from all walks of life – ex-servicemen, coal miners, engineers, builders, firemen, reps – people that had started their working life as something else and, for whatever reason, had found themselves out of work and hunting something more stable. Virtually no one I knew grew up wanting to be a prison officer. At least, *almost* no one, and if they did I wondered what had gone wrong in their childhood to make them want to lock people up for a living.

During the three months' training we were taught the basics of prison routine, the sort of thing that would become second nature after a few years. We had lessons on control and restraint techniques, a bastardised version of the martial art aikido, team building, man management, psychology or, as it became known to us, inter-personal skills, and race relations.

These last two subjects interested me. I had never thought much about what makes people tick and the reasons some people might act in a certain way, or why a person from an ethnic minority might feel threatened or act differently to someone who is not. I'm not saying I suddenly became sympathetic and tolerant, because I didn't. I'd had a deeply ingrained right wing upbringing. But now for the first time in my life I was hearing another side.

Getting to know some of the other trainee prison officers also knocked over some of my deep-rooted attitudes. At the time of joining the prison service I had very strong views about coal miners. I'd been a young child during the strikes of the 1970s and the consequent power cuts. I don't remember much about them other than thinking it was quite exciting that instead of watching TV we played games as a family by candlelight. I do remember Dad being very critical about the miners and the unions and the Labour government.

When I was a teenager, Margret Thatcher was in power and the miners' strike dominated the news. Employment was difficult to find in the 1980s and Thatcher's uncompromising message which felt like a dictatorship was tearing the country apart, but my right wing upbringing was so ingrained that I supported her and even voted Conservative when I was eighteen. The miners in my mind were militant troublemakers, fighting the police and attempting to bring down the government and the nation. They were even killing people by throwing blocks of concrete off road bridges onto taxis carrying miners who were breaking the strike.

Joining the prison service I was suddenly working alongside ex-coal miners who had been involved in the strike and who were intelligent, articulate people, people I could relate to. This made me question my values. I began to appreciate there was always another side, another way, a different view.

Near the end of three months of training we were told to choose three prisons where we would like to be posted. It was well-known among the new entrants that some prisons were virtually impossible as a posting direct from training college. These were called 'dead man's shoes' postings – Shrewsbury, Ford, Werrington, Sudbury – small prisons, generally housing low category prisoners and in nice areas.

The prisons you were almost certain to get if you chose them were high-security category 'A' prisons. These were known as dispersal prisons, so called because they were where the authorities dispersed cat 'A' prisoners, the most dangerous and notorious. Also incarcerated in these six prisons was a larger percentage of cat 'B' prisoners, less dangerous long-termers or lifers, and some cat 'C' prisoners. The thinking behind dispersal was obvious; putting all the country's category 'A' prisoners in one place would be asking for trouble.

When it was time to select my three preferred postings, I chose Gartree in Leicestershire, Long Lartin near Evesham and Strangeways in Manchester. All three held category 'A' inmates and all had a reputation for trouble. Gartree had just been in the news; two inmates on exercise had escaped when a helicopter pilot had been forced at gunpoint to land on the football pitch and whisk them out. It seemed inevitable that when we received our postings a few days later I had been given my number one choice – Gartree. I knew I had thrown myself in at the deep end. This trait would become my hallmark, even though I didn't know it yet. And it would be what I would draw on most when I started climbing.

ECHOES

Joining the prison service at twenty one and being posted to Gartree was as exciting as learning to lead a rock climb with no experience at all. The nervous anticipation, the thrill of not knowing how it's going to end up, the uncertainty, one minute I'm a boy from the country, a novice climber stood beneath the mighty El Capitan in Yosemite, and the next I'm face to face with three hundred inmates. There were Hells Angels that had tied women to trees, raped and killed, super-grasses from Ireland, mafia drug-runners and some really evil bastards who just hated and intimidated everybody. There were even Devil-worshippers, who howled when the moon was full.

Gartree held the genuinely infamous – Reggie Kray, the Guildford Four, Charlie Bronson, the Birmingham Six, the Shepherd's Bush murderer, Harry Roberts, still one of Britain's longest-serving prisoners, the Chelsea Barracks nail-bombers and the two coal miners, Dean Hancock and Russell Shankland, who threw the lump of concrete from a road bridge, killing taxi-driver David Wilkie.

Gartree also had armed robbers like Rookie Lee who reminded me of Ray Winston in *Sexy Beast*, likeable and funny as long as you weren't a nonce or a bank cashier. And old lags like George who in his prime had been as mad and bad as anyone, but who was now in his seventies and just shuffled about the landings in his leather moccasin slippers, rolled his own cigarettes, and stitched together cuddly toys holding a needle with his tattooed fingers.

Approaching Gartree Prison gave me the same feeling I would experience later approaching a mountain in the Alps or the Himalaya. It was a feeling of excitement and dread. That indefinable sense of adventure. I was about to open a door and walk in on something that could take me anywhere, a parallel world so different from ordinary life, and one that would test me to the limit. My stomach fluttered as I showed my identity card and introduced myself.

Three officers sat behind the thick Perspex window looking bored senseless with routine. One of them lifted a weary hand and pushed a button. A steel door with an electric lock buzzed and I entered. The solid metal door swung shut with a clang and locked automatically. I was inside. Passing through a second electronically operated gate and then a door, unlocked and locked again but this time with a key, I finally arrived at an outside area between the perimeter wall and a twenty-foot mesh fence topped with razor wire. The wall ran the circumference of the prison and the fence ran all the way around the inside of the wall, enclosing an area few will ever see.

Through the sterile area, inside the fence, there was a large open space with flower beds and lawns and sparrows and a tarmac road. Officers with Alsatians patrolled and feral pigeons sat huffed and sleeping in the barred window alcoves. Even inside this fenced area, which was inside a wall, I could see no inmates, other than trusties. Trusties, or 'red bands' as they were also known, took various jobs from washing windows and shovelling coal to the most undesirable job of all – collecting shit parcels.

When I first began working at Gartree the cells lacked toilets and inmates needing the toilet in the night had to use a plastic bucket. Instead of leaving faeces in the bucket to stink, they would wrap it in an envelope of toilet paper and throw it out of the window. The shit-parcel collector's job was to gather up and dispose of these packages.

Sometimes the parcels would get caught on razor wire fixed along the edge of the several prison entrance roofs or end up draped like tinsel around drainpipes. Human waste soiled the ground under the cells and used loo paper was flapping in the wind from the razor wire like bedraggled flags of surrender. I soon learnt to look where I stepped when entering the prison in the morning.

The main building was in the shape of a capital 'H' with an accommodation wing at the end of each leg. As well as these four accommodation wings there was another accommodation wing which was totally separate, housing around twenty five vulnerable prisoners who were segregated from the general population on Rule 43 of prison service orders. More often than not these prisoners were sex offenders who would be attacked if housed with the general population. The most notorious of this type of prisoner held at Gartree was the moors murderer Ian Brady, but most of the segregated inmates had at one time been in the newspapers.

There was another smaller wing, which served as the punishment block. This was run independently from the main prison, as a prison within a prison, and only held twelve inmates at any one time. Apart from the accommodation and punishment blocks, there were workshops where inmates made flip-flops, socks and vests, as well as woodwork and engineering shops, and a weight-training gym.

My first week in prison was spent on induction, learning the geography of the prison and meeting officers and staff in every department. Gartree had an education department and a large psychology department and, like other high-security prisons, it had a unit of dog handlers. There was also a hospital, which was a small self-contained unit, and the works, where plumbers, carpenters and bricklayers worked maintaining the fabric of the prison building.

Procedures at each prison were slightly different and so couldn't be taught at training college, so the nuances for an individual prison had to be learnt on site. Shop movement was a typical difference, shop movement being the period when inmates assigned to workshops or the gardens moved from prison to work, or from work back to the prison.

I also observed the daily exercise period, which took place outside. Inmates would walk the oval cinder track around the football pitch or have a kickabout for an hour, every day. Since the helicopter escape, the football pitch now had long wires with orange plastic balls like fishing floats strung all the way over it and in the wind the cables whined and whistled and the orange balls rattled.

Mealtimes were a stressful time. Many inmates were unlocked allowing grievances with staff or other inmates to be settled. Each prisoner chose each meal for each day the week before, but often the inmate would want something else that looked better on the day or would have forgotten to make a choice and so be given what the senior officer had chosen for him. Inmates often threw food at officers who stood serving behind the hotplates.

Serving something that was popular like pudding or chips was gripping. Nearly every inmate wanted more than his allotted amount and inmates standing in line would watch to see who was receiving more than their fair share and which officer was buckling to intimidation.

During evening association inmates could prepare and cook their own food bought from the canteen with their prison earnings or from their private cash allowance. Prisoners pooled their food and had cooking groups, taking it in turn to prepare an evening meal on the two cookers. Some of the prisoners, mainly cat 'A's and the inmates with money and status, ate better than I did. Later on, working on the landings, I watched whole joints of sizzling meat and roast vegetables carried past me. The smell was mouth-watering. Once in a while, the inmates would offer us a chip or a roast potato from their plate. Many officers accepted, but I nearly always refused. More often than not you would be asked, at some point, to reciprocate, or glance the other way, or bend the rules. It was rare the offer of a chip was as innocent as it seemed; accepting was not worth the hassle or inner turmoil. I couldn't take something from an inmate I would have to refuse something later or, in the extreme, wrestle to the ground.

At training college we had lessons dealing with this sort of thing, which was termed 'conditioning'. Over a period of weeks and months an inmate would build a relationship with you until the time came when he would ask you to do something obviously against the rules or the law. Sometimes officers were suspected of, or caught, smuggling contraband. I'm not saying all inmates were this devious, some were just being friendly, but I found it difficult to let my guard down. Most of the time you knew something was not for nothing. Over the years this lack of trust had an effect on how we treated people both inside and outside the prison.

The cooking utensils – vegetable knifes, spatulas, tin openers and the like – were locked away on a shadow board in the ground-floor office. There were other implements also locked in cabinets: hobby tools, which included craft knives and general tools like screwdrivers, wood saws, hammers and chisels. No matter how often I gave out tools and cooking utensils, I never felt at ease. On occasion implements went missing and a missing vegetable knife or screwdriver would be the talk of the prison.

After my week-long induction, I was given my first position, a wing officer on B Wing. There were four main accommodation wings run independently of each other housing approximately seventy five inmates each. There were around thirty staff for each wing, but there would only be about half that number working a variety of day shifts. Wing officers would also work a night shift. We worked one set of nights four times a year and each set was seven consecutive nights.

At the start of each night duty, the officer taking control of the wing would have no keys and would be locked onto the wing. The officer would then check that all doors were locked and every inmate was in his cell. The check, or as it was known, the roll count, was done by opening a small spy-hole and looking into each cell to see the inmate.

Often, you could see only a blurred shape, and sometimes not even that because the inmate had blocked his spy-hole. Then it was a choice, bang on the door or flick the light on and off to prompt a response, which could be anything from "Yes, Boss!" to "Fuck off!" Occasionally, not wanting the aggression and hoping the day staff had done their job, I would continue without getting a response.

The main landing lights were switched off at night. Illumination came from small overhead lamps, like emergency lights when the power goes off.

The landings were also lit by the yellow glow from powerful high-level lights outside shining through the windows. At the end of each leg, spider plants and geraniums in pots, a propped broom or hanging clothes cast eerie orange shadows across the grey floor. Mice scuttled from one side of the narrow landing to the other, feet scratching on the lino. Pigeons roosting in the air vents shuffled around. In my imagination, there was evil in every alcove.

One night in particular stands out. It was New Year's Eve. Celebrations had been feisty. The inmates were fuelled on hooch, class 'A' drugs and dope. But as the clock ticked nearer to midnight, all of them were now safely locked behind their doors for the night. The day shift had scurried away from behind the walls, relieved another shift was done, one nearer retirement. The night shift took charge. And I was the night shift.

I walked each landing attempting to check every inmate. The three landings on the wings were in the shape of an 'L', the long leg the upright of the 'L'. I was sure the day staff, in their rush to leave, hadn't checked every door was locked or that each inmate was in his cell. Although I shared the wing with seventy five people, I felt alone. So alone I could have been high on a north face, soloing and battling with the voices, pushing on into the night.

I could see piss flowing out from under a cell door and settling in a large puddle in the centre of the long leg of the three's landing. Through the thick door, I could hear groaning and puking noises. Most of the other doors shook as the inmates behind them pounded the metal with their fists and feet. I crept along the landing. The floor resembled a suspension bridge in a storm. The whole building seemed to twist.

Infamous street-fighter, hard-man and hostage-taker Charles Bronson, aka Metal Mickey, shouted and smashed his door with more force than the other inmates. As each minute passed and the hands crept towards midnight, the crashing and pounding and shouting swelled to a crescendo. Someone was kicking a door – or was it loose rock ricocheting off a wall? Was that swish of displaced air a table-leg being swung, or a spinning rock falling from the mountain walls above?

I imagined at every moment all fifteen stone of Charlie Bronson, hooch-fuelled and high on drugs, bursting through his steel door, an avalanche of fury. I was so certain the doors were not going to withstand his assault, I picked up a stave, and carried it above my head ready to strike should all that pissed-up aggression burst free.

Next morning, on New Year's Day, when the day shift took over again, it felt like reaching a summit and standing in the sun, a complete release from fear. The door unlocked to peace.

BELLS

Nearing the end of my first week at Gartree, I stood watching 'shop movement' as the inmates returned from work one afternoon, wondering if I'd done the right thing joining the prison service. Men of all description walked towards me. Some hung their heads, some held their heads high, some were large, some small. There were old men and others who looked like boys.

Many carried flasks and wore long grey duffle coats, most wore blue jeans and plimsolls, but some were obviously better off. They wore designer jeans, branded sweat-tops and smart training shoes. These were generally the armed robbers or cat 'A's or drug dealers. Some inmates were totally the opposite, dirty and unkempt and generally of low intelligence. They were usually dysfunctional, undereducated and underprivileged category 'B' and category 'C' inmates, who came more often than not from rundown inner-city estates. They had worked their way through the legal and prison systems by repeat offending or assaulting other inmates and staff until at some point they reached what they genuinely believed was the pinnacle of their life – doing time in a high-security prison.

The bulk of the group was that mainstay of prison populations, the mad and the bad, the mental-health patients, the murderers, the rapists, Hells Angels, blackmailers, kidnappers and extortionists – although generally the extortionists were studying politics or maths in the education department. Finally, there was another sub-group – the normal. The person like you and me, the person who in a flash of anger, a moment of weakness, a blur of passion, lashes out and kills or maims.

I stood bewildered watching this flotsam of society heading my way. The Alsatians barked and pulled at their handlers' leads, their snarls and barks bouncing off the brick walls before escaping through the wire fence and over the wall into the open farmland beyond, as distant as another planet. An inmate who was shouting and threatening headed my way.

"What the fuck are you then?"

He was thin and small and his head was shaved to the bone. He reminded me of a pigeon squab, loose and fleshy with a big wobbly head attached to a weedy body. I remember Dad telling me he used to find pigeon nests with squabs and tie a string to their leg. The string was threaded through the nest and tied so when the chick grew it couldn't fly away. When it was big enough, he would kill it for food. This pigeon squab didn't talk, he shouted. And his shout was a deep Ian Paisley type of rant, Irish and Scots mixed into one.

"You a new screw then are ya? Har har. You'll soon be like the other dogs, all bitter and twisted. How long you got left? Fuckin' years by the look of ya, har har. Yoor as fucked as me, so you are. I'm IRA. You better watch me else I'll get ya. I'll fuckin have yer kneecapped, so I will."

He strutted away with his concave chest puffed out, but then bumped into another inmate. "HEY! FUCK … YOO!"

Ann Johnson, one of the small number of women officers employed at Gartree, walked over. She was laughing.

"Ignore Lightfoot. He's harmless. Mad as a bag of badgers, but harmless. He's from Kent or somewhere like that. In for arson."

I felt numb and wondered what had just happened. I felt like an avalanche had carried me down a couloir and spat me out in another valley.

Walking around the confined corridors of the prison I noticed buttons everywhere. If an officer pressed one of these buttons, the alarm bell rang. It sounded throughout the prison. The control room had a team of officers and one of them had shown me a large map with lights that showed the position in the prison of each button. It was something like one of those interactive displays at a science museum. If a button was pushed, control would inform everyone where the alarm was and a bunch of officers would run to assist.

Every morning, the final job for the night shift was testing that the buttons worked. Three rings was a test, and it always took place in the morning between seven and eight. Coming in at the beginning of the day, the prison sounded like a giant telephone until the tests were completed. At any other time of day, or night, a single bell demanded immediate attention.

A few years later, I was sprinting out of the prison vestibule, the same vestibule where I had encountered Lightfoot as a naive and intimidated new boy. My legs were finely tuned from months of circuit training and running, propelling me to Seven Shop, the furthest workshop from the prison centre. After four years in the prison service I was training for the Physical Education Officer's course so I was fit. But some of the other officers were also fit and competition to arrive first at the source of trouble was keen and always a talking point for analysis after the event. Bullshit was obligatory – and necessary. It dispelled the tension. It was a matter of bravado to be seen running hard towards potential aggro.

On this occasion, the bell rang loud and long, always a sign that this was no false alarm. Hurtling through the vestibule doors, I almost knocked over another officer who was already struggling with the distance, looking like he was about to collapse.

Two hundred metres, almost there, and I burst through the door of the workshop. A body flew across a table, the attacker himself was grabbed, spun round and punched. His nose shattered. Two more inmates tore at each other. Training-shoe rubber squealed as feet were braced against the shiny linoleum floor. The polished lino took on the form of a Jackson Pollock, blood and mucus dotted between the sewing machines and boxes of vests. I saw someone land a head-butt, mashing soft lips, spattering blood. An inmate fell and the boots went in, kick him in the ribs. I regretted being so quick. The workshop instructor pointed to an inmate stamping on someone's head.

"That's the one who started it."

Poking my head out of the door, I could see the cavalry was on the way, puffing hard and red in the face. Grabbing the nearest inmate so I didn't have to get involved in splitting up the brawl now reaching a savage crescendo, the inmate, who was also glad for an excuse to stay out of the fight, and I stood to one side. The sweating mob of officers had caught up and entered the workshop like shoppers at a January sale, grabbing inmates like bargains. I made a mental note to run slower in the future.

Cheadle had been full of bravado and so called hard men. For some, fighting and trouble were part of growing up. The pubs at a weekend were like the Wild West and the town gave the world the infamous Cheadle Cowboys, who would travel long distances for a fight. As a teenager, I would walk to or from town in my T-shirt, often in the rain or cold.

Dad came out of the house one day, looking annoyed. "Do you think you're a hard man?" He clipped me round the ear. "Put a jumper on. If you want to be hard, start with me."

When I first had a pair of Doc Marten boots Dad hated them.

"You a bovver boy, then? Do you want to kick people?"

I never felt hard, although at times I pretended I was, or thought it would be good not to care about consequences, to be the sort of person that other people find intimidating. But this feeling soon passed. It wasn't me. Beneath my confident façade I was quite sensitive and shy, but when you are young, and even when you're older, it's difficult to be who you really are.

The prison service took me back to that time, when I was growing up and trying to be someone who I wasn't. I was and still am conscientious. I don't like letting people down. More than this – I don't like letting myself down. Facing personal demons has always been my way. When faced with aggression or bullying I will stand up for myself, even though I'm scared or feel intimidated.

FERMENTATION

For the first two years or so, working on B Wing was exciting and the novelty of having decent money and a secure job was comforting. It was everything I had grown up believing I wanted from life. You find a job that pays well, buy a house, get married, have kids and work towards a comfortable retirement.

At first I lived on the prison officer's estate, right next to the prison. My overgrown garden butted up to the prison wall. Everyone knew everyone's business; there were stories of wife-swapping and wild parties. The focal point of the estate was the prison officer's social club, a place I frequented regularly in the first six months, often rolling out at one or two in the morning, many pints and several whiskys the worse for wear, and so drunk I fell over repeatedly. I would still be drunk the following morning when I walked to the prison.

Many prison officers had a drink problem; it was a way to relieve the tension or cope with the constant pressure of stress and aggression. Some officers regarded lunchtime drinking as normal, others saw it as unprofessional, but it was a fact of life for many prison officers. Some would drink three, four, even five pints over the one-hour lunch break.

At first I didn't understand why some officers shook in the morning but were steady in the afternoon. It soon became apparent.

The inmates at a maximum security jail were there for a long time, especially if they were reasonably well-behaved, and in that time prisoners got to know all of the officers, their idiosyncrasies, their faults, strengths and moods. The prisoners had and used the time to study their guards. They recognised the good and bad, who had a hangover and those in need of help. Above all, they recognised weakness. They could smell it on you.

Prisoners would work on certain officers, getting under their skin until the bloody flesh was revealed. Resisting them was like climbing a technically difficult route. One hard move followed another until you either reached the belay or buckled and let go. Even though the officer knew it was against the rules, it was easy to fall into the trap of taking the soft option, especially if the officer knew he was not going to be in work for several days afterwards. It was like grabbing a piece of protection for comfort, or traversing off to the side.

The consequences for an officer who stuck to the rules were very difficult. Through my whole fifteen years in the prison service I tried to be honest, to play it straight down the line. At times it was exceptionally difficult, but if I ever failed, it wasn't from lack of trying and the voice of self-castigation later in the evening always had the final word.

Most inmates, but certainly not all, are out for what they can get. Who could blame them? If I were in a similar situation, would I be any different? Forming relationships with officers and then using those officers to their advantage frequently happened and an officer had to be on their guard against that kind of manipulation. If you were the kind of person who preferred to give an inmate the benefit of the doubt, it was difficult coping with the repeated disappointment of being used.

It's similar with climbing. We all believe a mountain has been climbed when a fellow mountaineer tells us he's done it. Yet once in a while, it turns out they lied, they didn't do the route and hid at the bottom on the mountain. If your trust is eroded this way on a daily basis, then your perception of human nature – and how you deal with people – changes for the worse.

Searching cells was a daily, detailed task, which broke the monotony of normal routine. The security department gave you the name of five inmates whose cell you had to search. Hopefully it wasn't one of the Hells Angels whose cells resembled dustbins. We were hunting contraband: weapons, drugs, cash, mobile phones or hooch, homebrew inmates made by stealing yeast and sugar from the kitchen. They also collected fruit, raisins or rice

"I felt safe." My house, my village, my bolt-hole.

and would throw it all into a container, anything from a mop bucket, a dustbin or even a plastic bag, and wait for the mixture to ferment.

Inmates were exceptionally talented at hiding hooch and moving it around. Gallons and gallons were sometimes found hidden behind panels, in pillowcases or stored in the false bottoms of bins and boxes. Inmates searched the day before knew it was unlikely they would be searched again for a month or so, and thus became the hooch-keepers for a week before the brew was moved on. It was a game of cat and mouse, following the sweet smell of fermentation around the wing, knowing someone, somewhere was holding gallons of illicit alcohol. The build-up to Christmas and New Year was a good time to play the hunt-the-hooch game, but mostly the inmates won.

When I was twenty two and after six months in the prison service, I bought a small house in Burton Overy, a quiet village nine miles from the prison. The house, two-up, two-down, was a one hundred-year-old farm labourer's mid-terrace cottage made of red brick and roofed with slate. Behind the cottage was a paddock with apple, plum, damson and pear trees and among the blossoming fruit trees, farm machinery stood idle, grass growing through chain harrow, old tines, tedders for turning hay and a muck spreader. A large mountain of black polythene-wrapped circular bails rose at the end of a curving mud glacier.

In front of my house, the narrow lane was overlooked by mature horse chestnuts where Tawny Owls nested and hopped from branch to branch, or just stood in the dark, a large silhouette squeaking and looking down at me from among the branches. The village itself was small and secluded. There was a pub, a thatched post office, a red telephone box, an ironstone church and a wooden village hall. In the middle of the village, a small field bordered by pointed iron rails housed several thick-set pedigree sheep. Unlike the swallows roosting on the phone wires criss-crossing the village, no one had a reason to visit Burton Overy unless they lived there. Immediately, I fell in love with my house, the village and most of all the tranquillity. I felt safe, like a child does at home.

FOUNDATIONS

In my new home I was a long way from the social club to drink in the evening and when I was at work it was too far to travel home for lunch. At first I spent lunch breaks in the officers' mess, lounging in a big reclining chair, watching the TV, smoking, drinking tea, listening to the 'clack' of pool balls and sleeping. Then, one day, I found myself so out of breath I nearly collapsed after running for an alarm bell. As I returned to B Wing I felt ill and dizzy, as though I was suffering altitude sickness. A principal officer, who was a keen runner, saw me red-faced, out of breath and sweating and knew exactly what was going on. He told me I needed to sort myself out. Feeling nauseous and suffering palpitations, I locked myself in the toilet where I sat on the seat. The painted bricks and the grey lino were spinning round me. At that moment, I vowed to do something with my life before I joined the other burnt-out wrecks working towards alcoholism and their first heart attack.

The following day during lunch break, for the first time in a long time, I went into a gymnasium. Floating particles of chalk dust were caught in the shafts of light piercing the reinforced glass of the barred windows running around the top of the gym. Varnished wooden wall bars, clanking weights, a knurled steel pull-up bar, swishing leather skipping ropes, grunts, the smell of effort, fusty blue matting – it was all just as I remembered from my days working out in the old chapel at Cheadle Health and Strength Club. Officers encouraged each other: "Go on, go on! One more, you can do it." A badminton racquet cut the air, swishing like a rope falling to the ground when pulled through an abseil anchor. A radio played music.

It wasn't long before I was part of the hardcore lunchtime crew, playing badminton, five-a-side football, weight training and circuit training, but smoking and drinking, a poor diet and doing no exercise for seven years had taken its toll. Regularly after a gym session I would lie in the changing room and vomit, but over the weeks and months, I grew fitter and stronger, trained more and started to believe in myself. Finally, after many failed attempts, I quit smoking.

The gymnasium in every prison has a full time team of physical edu-cation officers and during one lunch break, two officers training to become PE instructors rolled out a large blue agility mat, the same mats I had used for gymnastics as a teenager. The officers were practising forward and backward rolls, handstands and cartwheels. I asked if I could join in. Expect-ing a laugh at my expense they readily agreed. Since finding climbing, I have come to the conclusion that to be really good at something, starting young is the best thing possible. Four years of gymnastics four times a week had etched pathways into my brain and muscles that will never be forgotten. I stood on the blue mat and easily performed forward and backward rolls, backward roll to handstand, handstand to forward roll, and then a handspring and a headspring. The trainee PE officers stood flabbergasted.

My first posting as a PE officer at HMP Hollesley Bay Colony. Mal Adams – Falkland's War vet, paratrooper and all-round good guy (but what an absolute nutter!) – kabooms me on the trampoline. It sounds sexual but all it means is that he bounces in time with my landing and the result is flight much higher than normal.

"You should apply to become a PEO," one of them told me. "They'll love you and wrap you in cotton wool." I brushed aside his suggestion and left the gym feeling chuffed.

As the weeks went by my fitness improved and I became friends with the PE officers and the officers who regularly used the gym and I inquired more about becoming a PE officer. After a year and a half of working on B Wing, I wasn't enjoying sitting for long periods and locking people up. Finally, I decided I would try to get accepted onto the training course and discovered that getting selected was very tough and required a high standard of fitness and skill in many sports. Even being considered for the course was a long and arduous procedure, but once I had made the decision to become a PE officer, I threw myself into the preparation totally.

I did everything I could: rugby, circuit training, running, gymnastics, weight training, football, basketball, volleyball and trampolining. On days off I would cycle, swim, circuit train, weight train and run. I had never been a good swimmer, but a prerequisite for the course was holding a lifeguard award so I began swimming for an hour at the local sports centre before two hours of weight training. When my swimming had improved, I joined an evening class and qualified as a lifeguard. On days off I began visiting Welford Road Prison and taking formal PE classes – refereeing football, basketball, taking minor games classes, the sort of games that children play, like tag and British bulldog and running races, instructing circuit and weight training rather than the passive supervising that happened for most classes at Gartree.

Welford Road was a local prison, taking inmates directly after arrest and before or just after sentence was passed. They were either on remand waiting to go to court or else they'd been to court and were waiting to be sent to a prison where they would serve the majority of their sentence. The population in a local prison was more diverse, short-term inmates, drug addicts, thieves, and repeat offenders, generally young men who came from rough estates, but also old lags and a number of people with mental health issues. There were also the career criminals, armed robbers, murderers, rapists and sex offenders I was used to at Gartree.

On one of my first visits to Welford Road, returning from the pub at lunch which was a regular occurrence for the gym staff, I was told I could referee TPs. I had no idea what TPs were, but after collecting the segregation unit's inmates, most of whom were sex offenders, it soon became apparent that TP stood for 'target practice' when Bob, one of the PE officers playing for the staff five-a-side football team, booted an inmate when neither of them were even close to the ball. It was carnage.

The regime at Welford Road felt very different to Gartree, more controlled and strict because of the large turnover of inmates. Every inmate wore prison clothes and all inmates ate prison food. The type of relationships built with the inmates at Gartree, some of whom were serving twenty five years, didn't really happen at Welford Road. The only inmates officers came to know were those who were arrested and released so often their faces became familiar.

Two and a half years after joining the prison service, I had had enough of working on B Wing. The evenings and weekends comprised two officers on each landing drinking tea, sitting, drinking tea, sitting and drinking tea. On occasion I took a walk down the long leg trying to ignore the smell of cannabis wafting from a door or the rowdy cell where the latest batch of hooch was being sampled. I followed this with a walk down the short leg, perhaps enjoying a bit of a gossip with one of the more friendly inmates, before I resumed sitting and drinking tea.

There was the constant locking up and opening up, the jangle of keys, the buzz of electric locks. The weekends were the most soul-destroying. Sometimes I would be assigned the whole day, from eight in the morning until eight in the evening, to sit on the landings unlocking at the beginning of the morning, afternoon, or evening association period, and locking up again afterwards.

Sometimes I would be detailed to supervise visits, allowed in the afternoon at the weekend. This involved taking inmates to and from the visits room and watching as inmates met their kids, or wives or lovers and caught a hint of the free world.

Visits were not as you see on American TV, behind a glass window and talking through a telephone. They took place in a large communal room with a canteen and the inmates would sit across a table from their visitors. The room would be filled with smoke and screaming children, with anything up to sixty people. On occasion the wife or girlfriend of the inmate, wearing a short skirt, would sit on his lap and they would have sex. This, of course, was not allowed, but as long as it wasn't completely obvious the officers rarely stopped it. Animal instinct took over to the extent that they could have intercourse in front of a room full of people, including kids. I soon decided that no matter what a person's crime, conjugal visits in a separate room should be allowed.

Crying wives, crying children, crying inmates, arguments, a girlfriend smuggling dope as she kissed an inmate, assault – it all happened on visits. Sometimes one of the inmates I knew from B Wing would introduce me to his mum and dad or his wife. I found it interesting to see how some of the inmates changed from what they were when dealing with officers and inmates to how they interacted with family, although some acted exactly the same.

There was no one for me to embrace. The very best thing about working on visits – for me – was the exercise I got taking inmates to and from the visits room and the briefest taste of fresh air.

THE BLOCK

Deemed fit and healthy and less prone to imminent heart attack, I was well on the way to gaining the fitness and experience required to apply for selection to become a trainee PE officer but I needed a change from B Wing. And so I decided to spice up my life by transferring to the Punishment Block. The three-day selection process for PE officer training was still six months away but one evening, while playing football in the gym, I kicked the wall bars and smashed my right foot. My application was put on hold for an extra twelve months and I settled in for a long stretch in the Block.

It was a dark place. The corridor's plan was L-shaped with grey-painted pipes running around the low ceiling, the guts of the building exposed just as they are in the engine room of a ship. Footsteps echoed. The sickly-sweet smell of sweat, shit and fear clung to clothing and soaked into pores, into the painted brickwork, into the minds of the officers and inmates alike. Twelve steel doors faced into the gloom of the corridor, the hatred and anger locked away behind them.

The only light came from fluorescent tubes. There were no windows through which you could look on this microcosm of misery, enclosed inside another microcosm of misery. The normal rules of life did not exist here, or even the rules of the prison – just rules of survival. It was utterly secluded, another planet in a different solar system, a life apart. Normal values were not to be entertained. Normal values were a sign of weakness. And weakness was something to be exploited.

Working on the landings in a high-security prison, nine officers are in control of seventy five inmates. It's guaranteed that at least once or twice a day, and perhaps more, you will face confrontation. Many inmates lie and manipulate and intimidate, many push you to the edge and then withdraw just before doing or saying something that gets them placed on report. Many inmates know you are working against time constraints and drag their heels. It's their sport. It passes the monotony of existing inside an institution.

After several days at work constantly at loggerheads with inmates, my frustration would start to build. Other officers didn't help either, the yes-men among the staff of B Wing, the ones who wanted an easy life or were nearing retirement, or who were scared or intimidated and gave in easily. It could be anything, from extra food at the hot plate, to letting inmates on or off the wing or into cells or out of cells, handing out cigarettes, bringing food from outside the prison, allowing an inmate who wasn't allowed exercise to use the gymnasium.

This inequality and inconsistency among staff made the job difficult for those officers who stuck to the rules and I found this inequality particularly difficult to stomach. If an individual received special treatment, in my mind, everyone should. Just because an inmate was physically large and intimidating, he would get his way. Yet a quiet inmate, one who did his time living by the rules, was, in a way, punished for his correct behaviour, simply because he asked for nothing and received nothing.

The unfairness, the back-to-front injustice of the system drove me to distraction. So after two and a half years of this inconsistency, the Block was some sort of salvation. At any given time there would only be one inmate allowed from his cell supervised by four members of staff. For the first time since I became a prison officer in total control, the rules were rigidly observed and if the inmate didn't agree, it was hard luck, not an opportunity to intimidate.

Inside the Block, two teams worked opposite shifts and both concentrated on being consistent. The team I joined took absolutely no shit. We were all fit and reasonably young and went to the gym. Even so, having this new power, after the pressure and inconsistency on the accommodation wings, felt addictive and could easily corrupt. And the strict regime we enforced also brought stresses of another type.

I was twenty four when I started in the Block, still an impressionable young man. I wanted to be accepted. I was yet to find my own path and still carried the scars of the emotional abuse I suffered from the gamekeeper's wife in North Wales. Most people go through life wanting to be liked and accepted, it's normal, but like any of us, I faced the problem of finding out where I really belonged, while trying to fit in and meet other people's expectations. Doing so can lead us further and further from our dreams – assuming we even know what it is we truly want.

Worry and stress caused by the daily confrontation and fights, which in a way we brought on ourselves by taking a stance of zero tolerance, made the night my intimate companion as the clock hands slowly turned. In the morning, sometimes after only two hours of sleep, I would drag myself from bed. Then, like some android performing a ritual, I'd dress in blue trousers, white shirt, tie and epaulettes, whistle and key-chain. I knew I would be dressing again as soon as I entered the gloomy medieval environment of the Block. Like some apocalyptic knight, I'd don my suit of armour: flame-retardant boiler suit, plastic shin guards, thick leather gloves, steel toecap boots and a helmet. My shield was a rectangle of clear Perspex.

There was no way to avoid the oncoming fight. I drove the ten miles to work with the radio playing music I didn't hear. At some point most mornings, I almost crashed into the rear of the car in front. I could feel my guts twisting. Tension gnawed at my bones. Arriving at the prison car park I hoped there would be no spaces, so I could just turn around and drive home, but of course there was always space. Entering the prison I inhaled the miasma of fear and bitterness swirling behind the walls. I would joke with other prison officers, give that hearty, brittle laugh, share in the bullshit and bravado, my face a mirror. Just before opening the Block's four-inch-thick wooden door, my guts would twist a little tighter, I would breathe deeply, savour the last few seconds – and step inside the aggression.

Like firefighters in the station on a slow afternoon, four of us would doze in the Block's office. We'd be prone, relaxed on the surface, but each of us felt that knot of fear in our stomachs. Sooner or later the alarm bell would ring and we'd be pounding down the corridor, the anxious monotony broken. In the Block any bad shit happening would be flushed our way. We were the human U-bend between pan and sewer, sitting dozing, waiting, worrying, then suddenly jumping into battle at the sound of that alarm. It makes sitting out a mountain storm, waiting for the climbing to start again, almost a pleasure.

Saturday evening in the prison was generally a quiet time, but the bell brought us out of our slumber. It went on for a long time – never a good sign. The red phone immediately rang and the senior officer held it close to his ear. There was a red phone on every wing used only in an emergency. On the line was the officer in the control room, telling us where the trouble was.

This time it was on C Wing, where an officer, a gentle man who was well-liked and respected by staff and inmates alike, had handed a vegetable knife to an inmate who promptly stabbed him in the neck. He had scraped the outer tissue of the officer's jugular, who narrowly escaped death. The four of us opened the wooden door of the Block and waited. A few minutes passed and then the inmate, who threw down the knife immediately after the attack and held his hands up, came towards us surrounded by officers.

If an inmate offered no threat to himself or anyone else and was not fighting, it didn't matter what he had done. He was allowed to walk. Retribution could not be dished out for the sake of it. But after stabbing an officer this felt wrong. The four of us waited – tense, angry, resentful.

The inmate walked into the Block. Once inside we closed the door, locking out the world outside. The gloom was oppressive.

"Strip," the senior officer said. He was a short and stocky former ship-builder from Glasgow and he knew his business. On arriving at the Block the standard procedure was to strip-search all inmates who might have concealed weapons.

"I want a drink." The inmate, also from Scotland, made his own his demand, eye-to-eye with the senior officer, right in his face.

"You want a drink? Aye, well, the officer you stabbed has a wife who wants her husband tonight. But he's in the hospital where you put him."

The inmate quickly drew his head back and butted the officer. The sound of bone mashing skin and gristle sounded like a piece of rotten fruit hitting a concrete floor. The senior officer reeled from the blow, his head jerking backwards and a tooth falling from his mouth. But he quickly recovered, grabbing the inmate's head.

The rest of the team jumped on the inmate and dragged him to the floor. We wanted this. We fell in a whirl of flailing limbs and fists. We wanted the inmate to keep fighting. We wanted to hurt him. But after a few minutes of struggling, he burnt out and we applied arm locks, dragging him to the strong box, a special cell, like a padded cell, but not as comfortable and without furniture or windows, which deadened the sound of shouting and screaming. Here he was stripped and placed in a body belt.

At the time, this retribution felt right; prison morale would rise when they heard the inmate had been given the treatment. But years down the line I feel ashamed that I was involved in this sort of thing. The inmate was obviously troubled. Something that night had pushed him over the edge, but instead of trying to understand him, we dished out violence. He would have been expecting this. Maybe our violence was something he felt he deserved. Yet aggression just breeds aggression. I doubt our victim had questioned his own wrongdoings. Instead he simply felt things were now even.

I remember another day when the red phone rang. Kev, one of the long-standing Block officers picked it up and a wry smile crossed his face. Kev was one of the weight-training regulars, not massive, medium height and solid rather like a rugby centre. But he was tough. I was never sure about him. I liked Kev, but his bravado had to be a cover. I couldn't believe anyone liked bother that much.

Putting down the phone and rubbing his hands together, he danced out of the office, his ginger moustache twitching with pleasure.

"Oh, we're going to be having fun soon." Kev could hardly contain himself. "They're bringing Houston down."

His words filled me with dread. Houston was a giant, at least six foot eight with the frame of a Russian shot-putter. He was in prison for holding his parents captive inside their own house after shooting his father with a crossbow bolt – and for the attempted murder of a police officer with the same weapon. He had arrived at Gartree with a terrible reputation for fighting other inmates and intimidating staff, especially female staff, and it was certain that at some point he would be visiting us in the Block.

We stood waiting and bullshitted. Kev and Tim and I laughed, but all the time we waited I was terrified. The prison was banged up after breakfast. This was usual procedure, when prisoners were being taken to the Block. If they caused trouble, there were no other inmates to join in or witness the proceedings.

A figure appeared suddenly, filling the Block's open door frame. Ten officers, maybe more, surrounded a Shrek-like giant, struggling to fit alongside him. The four Block staff took control and escorted him to a cell where the command was given to strip. He refused and, of course, we jumped on him.

Expecting a savage fight, we went in hard and crawled over him like ants, but instead of being swatted, we watched as Houston crumbled. We walked him to the strong box in arm locks, applied extra tight, and the man that had been intimidating C Wing staff for nearly two weeks began crying.

"Don't hurt me."

He spoke in a childish way, a little like Gollum from *The Lord of the Rings*. All four of us were shocked. Here was the terror of the prison crying and begging. We placed him in the Box, but for once we chose not to place him in a body belt. After a few hours we returned, telling him off like a naughty child before re-housing him in one of the regular Block cells.

Two months later Houston was removed from our care and transferred to another prison. The Block staff received a commendation for looking after him, but he had been no trouble, we simply treated him like a naughty child and he responded. He did present some unique problems, like the morning we opened his cell and he stood with his back to us, having a conversation with what we discovered was an erect, carefully modelled, foot-long turd, which he had stood on his window-shelf. We told him off while attempting not to laugh. Houston could see we found it funny so he started to laugh as well, and our tough approach ended with us all laughing together, while staring at the erect shit.

I still feel quite upset at the failure of the system to deal properly with people like Houston. He was a child in an intimidating body and got short shrift because of it. Inmates like Houston deserved more than to be locked in a prison where the staff, overworked, undertrained and unrewarded didn't have the necessary skills or time to deal with his problems in a way that would help him or society.

It also angered me, and still does, that when something did break down or go terribly wrong, the blame more often than not ended up resting solely with the prison officer directly involved. The newspapers might scream for blood, but most mistakes were due to lack of support, training and appropriate resources.

I regret that I was involved in so many violent incidents. I regret that I was drawn along just like a football hooligan, and never actually stopped to think or ask myself what exactly was going on. I rarely questioned why people became so aggressive and why we were all acting in the way we did. Later in life I began to see things more clearly and I feel now that in most cases it is a failing of our society that produces such hate-filled inmates.

Despite having many regrets about my conduct, I must make it clear that I don't regret every encounter, involving what could sometimes be severe physical violence as restraint. There were some incidents about which I feel no shame or remorse, incidents that were so horrible and so dangerous that there could be only one response – sudden, determined, highly aggressive physical force. Being a prison officer is not just practically difficult, it is morally and ethically difficult. How does one decide when it is appropriate to use violence, and decide how much violence? Sometimes the decision is simply one of self-preservation.

GUILT

The Punishment Block performed another function apart from keeping a prisoner confined and separated. It served as a courtroom. Anyone who broke the laws of the prison, offences ranging from swearing at an officer, stealing, fighting and causing disruption, to intimidating behaviour or being somewhere they shouldn't, was placed on report, or, as it was more commonly known by officers and inmates alike, nicked.

After a nicking, a brief report detailing the charge was written and handed to the inmate at seven-thirty the following morning, and an hour later they were escorted to the Block for adjudication. The hour allowed the inmate time to prepare his defence. Adjudications were like court proceedings. The Governor was the judge and the Block's senior officer acted as court bailiff, reading out the charges.

The officer who had reported the incident stood facing the inmate on the left of the Governor at the head of a table. The inmate would stand at the opposite end of the table facing the Governor. Two officers would stand either side of the inmate with their backs to the Governor but facing the inmate. Sometimes a witness was called but this didn't happen often.

Adjudications were a catalyst for trouble, especially if the hearing went against the inmate and almost always when the Governor doled out his 'award'. The most usual punishment was a loss of privileges or private cash allowance for a period of time, or a fine. He might also dole out a period of solitary confinement in the Block, anything from a few days to a week or even longer.

Burleigh, a six foot three black guy with dreadlocks, muscles and an attitude, stood facing the Governor shouting the odds. Charlie Bushell, the Governor, was also a big man, although more around the waist, and wore a large beard. He also had attitude and shouted back in his booming voice.

Standing inches from an agitated Burleigh, I began to get light on my toes.

"Get him out of here!"

"I'm not fucking leaving until you change your decision."

"Officers, take him away."

At once, I grabbed an arm and Tim, the second officer, a feisty, terrier-like ex-military man, took the other. Burleigh shoved us both away. I rebounded immediately and grabbed handfuls of dreadlocks in an attempt to get him on the floor. At that time I weighed thirteen stone. I could bench-press one hundred and twenty five kilos and run a mile in six and a half minutes. But Burleigh also worked out and must have weighed at least a stone more.

He stood up with me still hanging onto his dreadlocked head and charged. We crashed through the adjudication room door with me hanging on like a hyena, but Burleigh drove me into the opposite wall. Tim followed us out of the room and grabbed an arm. Attempting to bring him to the floor, I wrapped my arm around Burleigh's head and lifted my legs but once again Burleigh just picked me up and sprinted before slamming me into another wall. Mark, the third Block officer, eventually caught up and together we overpowered Burleigh and took him to the Box.

Another adjudication episode with Tim and Charlie Bushell was even more physical. Charlie bellowed "Get him out of my sight," but instead of arguing, the inmate, a fit young boxer called Brown sprinted from the room and into the long leg of the Block. He ran to the dead end of the wing while pulling off his t-shirt and wrapping it around his right hand to give his knuckles some protection, expecting to throw some punches.

He hadn't planned on Tim and I sprinting just after him. When he reached the wall at the end of the long leg and spun round, we were only a few feet behind. Tim body-checked him and Brown bounced into the wall. As he rebounded, I hit him hard, taking him to the ground. Tim followed up and dropped onto him, grasping his other arm. Mark, who had once again been supervising from outside the adjudication room, grabbed Brown's head. Dragging him into the Box wasn't a problem since he was so light but Brown, who loathed authority, fought all the way, screaming obscenities, spitting and biting, struggling and kicking.

Price was a cat 'A', and infamous throughout the whole prison service. He strutted and swaggered, wearing the cat 'A' uniform of blue jeans and long grey duffle coat with arrogant pride. Price might have postured and talked big, but he was the real deal when it came to being bad. He liked to make people think he was some kind of London gangster, which he probably would have been if he had been out of prison long enough. In truth, he was just a dangerous thug brought up in a rough area of London. Price had been in and out of prison all of his young life until at the age of twenty one he was sentenced to three-and-a-half years and taken to an adult prison.

When I first met Price he was thirty two, fit and healthy and still in prison from the original three-and-a-half years stretch. He was now serving several different sentences, all handed down from outside courts for offences in prison, which came to a total of twenty eight years.

Price had been nicked and was walking to the Block, swaggering and posturing in his usual style. The three of us, Rob, Tim and myself, waited in a cell. Strip-searches were a part of prison life and a full strip was a part of the normal procedure for entering the Block, but it was not popular with either inmates or staff. On many searches, the inmate was allowed to keep his underpants on.

This failure in the system arose from staff being lazy or intimidated. Inmates would call you gay or ask if you enjoyed looking at men's genitals, to put pressure on the officer not to make an inmate strip properly. It may not appear a serious flaw in security but inmates were masters of concealing items and one of the usual places to hide bank notes, drugs and weapons was inside a tube, often an empty underarm deodorant container, up their back passage. One inmate was known to cut a pouch into the fleshy skin on the inside of his cheek or into his gums where he could hide a razor blade. Another was known to hide blades in a pouch of skin cut into his heel.

Strip-searching was done only on certain occasions: after a visit, on entering the Block, before being transferred to another prison, or before a routine cell search. It was inevitably an issue of control. An inmate refusing to strip could be nicked and forcing them into fully stripping left the officer in a position of superiority. But an officer who could be intimidated into not forcing the inmate to strip completely was marked out as someone to be intimidated and manipulated.

Rob, a large ex-policeman who enjoyed trouble and didn't give an inch to anyone, told Price to strip, which he did – down to his boxer shorts.

"Take down your boxers."

"I'm not taking my boxers off. If you want them off, you take them off."

Rob moved toward Price and told him if he wanted trouble, he could have it in the Box.

"You think that bothers me? You think I care? Let's go."

Price walked from the cell, strutting like Vinny Jones in a Guy Ritchie movie. The long corridor was quiet. The usual Block senior officer was off duty and his replacement was in the office doing paperwork. Price swaggered the length of the Block's long leg, before turning into the short corridor leading to the Box. Rob, with Tim and I following, turned after him.

The corridor was dark and narrow, requiring us to walk in single file. Ahead of me, Rob's broad shoulders filled the tight space but as soon as Price reached the cell area, he spun round and punched Rob in the face. He fell to the floor like a bag of cement, his face split and bleeding. A single punch was all it took. The two of us jumped over Rob and pounced on

Price before he could draw back his arm for a second shot.

Price was strong and fit and he didn't go down. I grabbed an arm as it swung towards me and held on like it was the ends of an abseil rope being blown out of reach. Tim hung off his other arm, but was driven repeatedly into the wall. We had to get him on the floor, where our combined weight would pin him down.

Price had other ideas. Thrashing wildly, he drove us repeatedly into the walls in turn, trying to head-butt us and spitting in our faces. Eventually, he slipped and we all crashed onto the painted concrete floor, but the fight continued. We became a writhing bundle of limbs. While wrestling with an arm, I saw Rob, who was now conscious, crawling along the corridor away from the Box. I was sweating, breathing hard, fighting for my life, and still there was only two of us, separated completely from the rest of the prison.

Tim was fastened to an arm and being waved around like a flag by a gale. I attempted to twist the other arm but Price was too strong. The senior officer, alerted by Rob, stumbled into the Box to be confronted with a bloody tangle. We screamed at him together.

"Hit the fucking bell!"

The officer ran out, hit the bell and returned.

"Grab his fucking head. Grab it, for fuck's sake."

Three of us had a better chance, and within seconds of the bell sounding a bunch of bodies poured into the cell.

A year later Price was in court charged with grievous bodily harm. The solicitor acting for Price argued that Rob had propositioned Price and as we walked into the Box Rob had touched him up. Rob was married with two children, and had no record of any sexual offence. Price had been convicted for all kinds of things, but none of that could be mentioned.

Price also had a good solicitor, whereas Rob had a junior brief provided by the prison service. Price was acquitted. He stood in the defendant's box laughing out loud as the verdict was read out. I couldn't believe how gullible the jury had been, but most of all I couldn't believe how the solicitor, a well-educated person, could manipulate what had happened to create such doubt in the jury's mind, to treat something as serious as this as a game.

The solicitor knew Price's background and must have known he was guilty, but he stood and argued the case anyway. Everyone deserves the right to a legal defence, and I'm very aware of miscarriages of justice, having known some victims. But for an intelligent and privileged person to be paid to argue a lie, with the consequence that a violent criminal was free to bully, assault and maim, disgusted me. I know it's naive, but I could never prostitute myself to defend the guilty.

FLOW

———

Sometimes I think of the mountains as a brutal place and I can't be the only one who feels that way. Yet mountains are not brutal. Death and injury, trauma and distress do occur there. Being in the wrong place at the wrong time can cost you. Sometimes it's because of a mistake, a wrong decision, or just bad luck. Sometimes ego and ambition get in the way. Accidents happen. But a mountain has no soul. It's never the fault of the mountains.

People, on the other hand, can be brutal and by that I mean all of us. Some people seem to be brought up to be brutal, others are just born that way. The worst brutality is that driven along by a collective feeling of righteousness. Working in prison, I saw a lot of that.

Aged twenty one, when I joined the prison service, I discovered aggression and violence, loathing, prejudice and hate, and by the time I turned twenty five, my cynicism about human nature was deep rooted. At twenty one the doors had closed, leaving me transported to a parallel society of people the mainstream world would rather forget. The shadows clinging to this other world, the shadows behind the prison walls changed me.

I learned that if you add sugar to red-hot cooking oil, the mixture would stick to your victim's skin. I learned that a PP9 battery slipped inside a sock makes a superb cosh to smash a skull. A table leg can be wielded like a baseball bat. If you're handy, you can melt a Bic razorblade into the head of a tooth brush, the perfect weapon for slashing at your enemy's throat. I even discovered that in the hands of IRA terrorists, a tube of steel could be adapted to fire a single round.

I had charged into cells blacked out and on fire, smashed to bits and barricaded, or with every surface smeared with swirls of shit. My everyday routine included not stepping on parcels of shit thrown from cell windows. Every single day came with the promise of violence, even if it never materialized. All this was part of my life in the late 1980s. I found myself becoming lost in a miasma of prejudice, paranoia, bitterness and loneliness.

It was not only the prison changing me. It was the realisation people could be untruthful and manipulative, lacking in soul and compassion.

I witnessed an inmate take a teacher hostage and hold a craft-knife to their face. The inmate, still holding the teacher, walked to the vestibule and demanded to be allowed through. The officer on duty refused to open the door, so the inmate stabbed the teacher in the eye. The inmate was overpowered and taken to the Block. The incident was reported in the newspapers as a near-escape. But the inmate was still in the prison building locked behind several doors, behind a fence, behind a wall. I stopped buying and believing newspapers after that.

I had recently split from Sheila, my long-standing girlfriend, and for a period I saw several women. Sometimes the relationships coincided. I didn't really care that much about other people or even myself. I didn't know what I wanted. I was confused with life and where it was taking me. I found committing and opening up and being comfortable in the company of other people increasingly difficult. Because of this, I chose to be on my own for a lot of the time.

I no longer had my dogs. Living by myself in a small house with a shared backyard was not conducive to keeping a Terrier who, like a climber that needs to climb, or a writer that needs to write, needed to kill. It was what Murphy my Patterdale was born to do. Since buying my house I had tried keeping Murphy in the backyard but he barked and snapped at the neighbours, two old ladies who were terrified of his aggressive nature. I tried keeping him in the house, but every night returned home to find it a wreck.

I couldn't walk him unless he was on a lead. He would run off and return several hours later covered in chicken shit and blood. When I walked him around the village at night, he would pounce on any dark shape that moved, growling and snarling, slathering, chomping, barking and snapping.

Murphy, my Patterdale Terrier, had as much attitude as many of the inmates. It moved and he killed it.

One time I grabbed him, but his lips and gums were pouring blood, punctured by the spines of a mortally injured hedgehog.

Finally I could take no more, but couldn't inflict Murphy on anyone else. I didn't know what to do with him. At my wit's end, I drove to my parents' house one night, pulling up an hour into the journey in a gate entrance in the middle of nowhere. I took Murphy from the car, and grabbed my loaded shotgun. On the other side of the gate, he sniffed the earth of a field of stubble and pulled on the lead, wanting to work the hedgerow.

Dipper, my Golden Labrador, sat patiently in the back of the car, brown eyes transfixed, watching us walk in the field through the steamed-up windows. His sad eyes suggested he knew what was about to happen. I sat Murphy down. He stood and pulled. I sat him down again. He stood and pulled.

"Sit down, won't you? Make it easy on me." But he pulled and barked, wanting to work the hedge and kill something. I lifted the twelve bore and sighted the bead. His eyes blinked. I fingered the trigger. He shook his head, his small feathery ears flapping against the side of his square head. His black button nose shone in the moonlight. I fingered the trigger, looking into Murphy's eyes, my own deepset pools of black emotion. But I couldn't fire. I couldn't pull the bloody trigger.

I had shot hundreds of animals and birds in the past but it wasn't the terrier's fault he was the way he was. He was just doing what he was born to do, and what I had raised him to do. I walked him back to the car, the tubes of shorn barley crunching underfoot. Opening the door, Murphy jumped inside. Dipper's large solid head nuzzled him, as if knowing how close his friend had come. In return, Murphy snarled and latched onto his soft jowl.

Reaching my parents' house I told them what I had driven up to do. Mum and Dad loved Murphy but Dad was particularly attached to my troublesome terrier. Dad looked on him as one of life's underdogs, a misfit toughing it out, standing up for himself, battling even in the face of certain defeat. Dad said he and Mum would look after Murphy from now on.

I returned home with Dipper, the perfect dog and companion. He welcomed me home no matter how long I had left him. I could turn him out in the morning or at night and he would amble around the village causing no trouble. When he had seen enough, he would return to the front door and headbutt it to let me know he wanted in. Dipper didn't have the slightest bit of malice. Even the old ladies next door loved him. Yet the nearer I got to taking my entrance exams for the physical education course, the more concerned I became. I could leave him with my parents, but it would be like giving up on a friend.

Returning from the prison one night, Dipper was waiting for me. I opened the front door where he pushed past, keen to get out and walk around the village. I walked inside but almost at once a scream made me spin round. Dipper had collapsed and was lying on the pavement and quivering with pain. I drove him to the vet's, where I laid him in a metal cage and stroked his broad head. I walked away with his big sad brown eyes watching me leave. I imagine he thought he had let me down. I never saw him again. The vet said he had a growth on his spine, which had paralysed him. The best thing was to put him out of his misery. I returned home to an empty house, sat on my old sofa and wept.

At last the time came for my three-day physical education selection exam, which I passed. Several months later, I left normal prison routine behind to begin a transient life training to become a PE officer. I had no qualms about leaving the Block. The thought of ignoring news and society, locking myself into twelve months of exams and high-intensity training while moving around the country was exciting, something I relished. But nothing was certain, and even though I had been selected for the course there was still no guarantee I would be successful. If a trainee didn't perform to the high physical and educational standard required they would be sent back to normal prison duties.

The first five weeks were spent at a training college near Blackpool. The gymnasium was a huge converted aircraft hangar. Every day we did circuit training and class teaching practice, taking control of the group – and we all took part in games like five-a-side football or basketball. We took turns to organise, coach, encourage and referee these games to gain experience in class structure, control and teaching. At the end of each session, an instructor de-briefed us and gave us a mark. At the end of five weeks we were interviewed and told whether we would be allowed to continue.

Even though this stage in our training was critical, most nights we would hit the pubs of Blackpool, usually ending up in Yates's Wine Bar drinking several pints of strong lager and visiting the kebab house before collapsing into bed and starting again next day the worse for wear.

Lining up on the gym floor at eight in the morning, in regulation white T-shirt, white shorts, white socks and white training shoes, the officers knew most of us were hungover. The day would start with sprints and shuttle runs and a circuit. Phil, one of the training officers, loved sending people who made a mistake or said something stupid to the wall-bars. The class continued as normal while the unfortunate who had messed up hung from their arms, high on the bars with their feet off the ground, their grip progressively weakening. It was like hanging on a hold, high on a climb, fingers slowly unfurling.

"Bend!" Phil shouted, taking a second from teaching to turn and yell instructions to his current victim, his command echoing off the panelled wall. The victim bent his legs and lifted them to his chest and held them there for what felt like forever.

"Stretch!" Phil finally shouted, the merciful command to lower the legs.

"Straight legs lift!" With knees locked, the victim raised his legs into a half-lever position and held them there, body trembling more and more violently, legs drifting lower and lower.

"LIFT THOSE LEGS!"

The wall-bar treatment hurt but I couldn't help laugh and find the whole procedure funny. I actually liked the banter. Another of Phil's specialties saw us finishing the day with a seal-walk race. We would all stand in line ready to be dismissed and Phil would give the dreaded command: "Take off your trainers." Everyone knew what was coming.

In our stocking feet we lay side by side on our fronts, propped up on straight arms like we were about to start press-ups. Our legs and pointed feet remained on the varnished floor. Mentally and physically drained from twelve hours of exercise and education we waited for the command.

"GO!" Phil shouted, and we raced. Dragging our legs behind us along the polished wooden floor, we pulled ourselves forward using only the strength in our arms and shoulders, looking like seals on the beach. The old aircraft

Trainee PE officers on the final day of a three-day expedition near Plas y Brenin, North Wales. I'm leaning on the shoulder of Lee Dobson, an ex-South Wales coal miner. I completed both my original prison officer training with Lee and then my PE officer training. He was a good friend and one of the people who helped change my opinion of coal miners.

hangar was vast but after dragging my body its full length and back again, it felt the size of a continent. I must have done something right, because at the end of the five weeks in Blackpool, I qualified for the rest of the year.

Some stages of the twelve-month course were long, up to two months, while others were just three weeks. Some took place at national training centres. One early component was a three-week period at Holme Pierrepont, the national water-sports centre in Nottingham. As with most sections of the PE course, we were given intense training, mainly in kayaking, but also in sailing, gaining star awards, teaching qualifications and the canoe lifeguard award. Most of the course members were beginners, but after the first week we were tackling the world-class white-water slalom course.

The River Trent flowed brown and slow beneath the bridge at the beginning of the course. Looking back upriver, power station chimneys, like the smoking tentacles of colossal sea anemones, marched along the banks of the polluted river into the distance. I dropped my kayak into the turbulent current, slamming into stopper waves, skittering across white water, surging through before my yellow plastic boat slammed into a wall of water recirculating uphill, which walloped my face.

The river's brown sticky stinking froth felt like an angry inmate shouting the odds, the yellow boat twisted and bucked. A high brace, twist the hips, a low brace – and I was through the first constriction racing down the roaring water. I dabbed the paddle and eased past a boil of aerated bubbles, swinging into an eddy flowing gently upstream. Here I could pause, so I breathed deeply, exhilarated, but knowing the biggest challenge waited just below.

The 'washing machine' was a fierce brown bubbling hole referred to as a sticky or a keeper hole, meaning it tended to trap buoyant objects that entered it. A sticky could be difficult to punch through, but great fun if you dropped into them from side on, and ridden like a bucking horse. I swung the kayak back into the torrent and dropped sideways into the hole, instantly bracing with a high paddle rested on the top of the growling reverse wave curling above my head. Instructors stood on a bridge crossing the washing machine, shouting encouragement, whooping and laughing.

"Okay, now get out," one of them shouted. But I couldn't. Every time I attempted to punch through I was smacked in return – and pulled back into the trough.

"You'll have to capsize!"

I bumped and jostled with the current for a few more seconds then gave in and lifted the bracing paddle. The water grabbed my boat and spun me round. Immediately the world flipped from brightness and noise to quiet and the bubbling brown murk. Swept beneath the sticky, I opened my eyes to see blurred bubbles and brown water, and felt a roar in my ears, like blood pumping through my head. I also felt at peace, in a world away from violence and hate. And then I was out of the boat, pulling for the surface. The roar of the water resumed and from the side of the river one of the instructors threw me a rope and dragged me to the side.

The bulk of the course after Holme Pierrepont was spent in the prison service's college attached to Lilleshall National Sports Centre in Shropshire. Lilleshall at the time was the Football Association's rehabilitation centre and the home for the British Gymnastics Squad. While at Lilleshall, trainee and qualified PE officers doing further training would happily mix with the likes of John Barnes and Terry Butcher, and other football stars receiving treatment for injuries.

A two-week section of the course was dedicated to becoming an instructor in control and restraint, so we were able to teach other prison officers the approved method of restraining violent inmates. The instructors were PE officers who had specialised in riot control, hostage situations and unarmed combat. One of them was a gigantic hairy bear of a man from the southwest who called people 'my lovely' before he mauled them.

One evening, after a day learning control and restraint techniques, some of the officers returning from the bar met a Premier League and Scottish international football player receiving treatment for an injury at the rehab centre. Walking past, he began mouthing off, calling them screws and being aggressive. Hidden behind his back, he held a golf club. He didn't know 'the bear' was also returning from the bar and quietly stalking his prey and in one deft move he grabbed and took away the golf club. The footballer, who was tall but quite skinny, spun round to be confronted with a monster quietly calling him 'my lovely'. He had a quick rethink and decided prison officers were not as bad as he had originally thought and ran away to become a presenter on the TV.

As each stage passed, the next would be more intense and specialised. After several months I was a swimming teacher, a weight-training instructor, a gymnastics, basketball and volleyball coach, a football referee and a kayak instructor and lifeguard. In between each course, I was required to return to prison for normal duties and with each trip back I knew I wanted to become a PE officer more than anything. The thought of failing the course and returning to normal duties scared me into working and studying harder when the course resumed.

After successfully completing most of the training year and surprising myself at being near the top or top in most of the written exams, the moment came for the segment I looked forward to the most – a three-week stay at Plas y Brenin, the National Mountain Centre of England and Wales. I didn't know why this part of the course attracted me so much. Maybe because it was near the end of the course and the instructors had spoken of it as a jolly. Maybe it was the three weeks I had spent on the canoeing and sailing course at Holme Pierrepont, where I discovered that the outdoors and adventure appealed to me a lot more than pumping iron or team games. I stepped out of the prison gate, and headed to Wales.

ROADS

Rain splashed off the car windscreen as I drove to Plas y Brenin. I pictured myself ten years before, sat in my parents' car, watching the sodden hills disappear, the torment of my days as a gamekeeper near Tremadog disappearing with them. This time I sensed everything would be different.

For three weeks, images of mountains and climbers inching their way up sheer cliffs surrounded me. Our days were spent in the hills trying to fathom how a compass worked and completing classic scrambles like the steep and airy Bristly Ridge on Glyder Fach and Tryfan's exposed North Buttress in the Ogwen Valley. Evenings were spent eating massive meals washed down with bullshit and beer, and then a slideshow for pudding. Most of the seventeen trainee PE instructors found these evening lectures a distraction from the more important activity of drinking and revelling in the disco at The Swallow Falls Hotel.

Not for me. I felt I had finally found my calling. I experienced a mixture of relief and excitement rolled into one. Those around me looked on in horror at pictures of ice-encrusted climbers clinging to freezing rock, or squeezed onto a tiny ledge with legs dangling over a precipice. I, on the other hand, felt I'd come home. This was so obviously what I was born to do. I could feel the truth and simple honesty of that fact.

Nick Banks had given the most memorable slideshow. At the time, Nick was director of Plas y Brenin and a Kiwi who had climbed Everest and much more besides, although like most novices, the 'Big E' was all our ignorant ears heard. Even the nightclubbing, city-dwelling ones amongst our motley crew knew Nick was different. Banks showed a collection of slides he called 'North Faces'. I watched in awe. I was unable to tear my eyes from the images. I started to dream.

For the final week in North Wales course members were given the option to take the training week of the nationally recognised summer mountain leaders' award with Plas y Brenin staff or going out on the hill with our own instructors to tackle more classic walks and scrambles: the Snowdon Horseshoe, the Glyders, the Devil's Kitchen and then an afternoon's rock-climbing session. I opted for the second option and for the first time my feet felt the now familiar pain of my toes squeezed into rock boots.

My fingertips buzzed as the rough rhyolite wore at my skin. My forearms ached and hardened with lactic acid. My brain was utterly absorbed in fathoming the puzzle of a rock face and the sequence of moves that would bring me to its top. I was enthralled. In that final week I made a pact with myself – climbing would become my life.

I began to read avidly about mountains and climbing, and quickly developed a ferocious ambition to emulate the climbers I read about, those uncompromising personalities I placed high above the dull valleys on lofty pedestals. I devoured climbing literature like Chris Bonington's *I Chose to Climb* and *Everest the Hard Way*. Joe Tasker, Martin Boysen, Alan Rouse, Julie Tullis, Mick Burke, Dougal Haston, Doug Scott, Nick Estcourt and Alex MacIntyre all became familiar names. The more I read the more I wanted to climb. When the last day of the year-long physical education course eventually arrived, I was unleashed into the world not just as a new PE officer, but as a brand new shiny climber. The problem was,

Left: A weekend in North Wales. An escape from Suffolk with Mal Adams and Dave Boyle, both ex-paratroopers, both as hard as nails, both salt of the earth. Unlike Mal, Dave was more controlled and sensible, thank God. *Right:* The same weekend with the fourth member of the weekend and the third ex-para, Dave Bowman. Dave, like Mal, was a PE officer at Hollesley Bay and one of the fittest people I have known. Regularly we would race and compete in circuits – Dave had the ability to absolutely beast himself and then go some more. I got my own back a year or so later when I led *Cenotaph Corner* with Dave seconding. Dave had no climbing fitness. He managed to jam his body repeatedly into the corner while being pumped stupid, forcing me into hysterics while belaying him from above. *Photo: Mal Adams*

I wanted to be a climber with some wear and tear – and I knew only too well that I had a great deal of catching up to do.

And at first my plans went somewhat adrift.

"Where would you like to be posted Mr Bullock?" I looked at the suited civil servant sitting across the desk. Was he serious?

"I would really like to be posted somewhere near Manchester or Sheffield," I said. Then as an afterthought I added: "Anywhere near rocks or mountains, really."

The suit looked at me as though I had just asked to use his toothbrush after spending the evening with his daughter. "Near rocks or mountains? Are you taking this interview seriously, Mr Bullock?"

"Oh, I think you misunderstand me. You see, I want to be a climber."

"A climber?!" He was actually spitting on himself. Soon the suit's suit would need cleaning. Then he stood up, driving his chair backwards across the floor, strode to the door and opened it. Clearly, the interview was over.

A week later I received my posting to Hollesley Bay Colony in Suffolk, the most easterly prison in the country, overlooking the North Sea. It was about as far from a rock or hill as you could get in Britain.

At first I refused to go. There was a place vacant for a PE officer at Gartree, and the PE principal officer at Hollesley Bay told me he had been instructed to cut two of his officers within a year. It was obviously daft to send me away, and a waste of thousands of pounds of taxpayer's money. But after digging in my heels I was warned that if I didn't transfer to Hollesley Bay, I would be returned to normal duties and transferred anyway. Even worse, the PE officer course costs, getting on for thirty thousand pounds, would be clawed back from my wages.

I felt like some of the inmates I'd known, those who'd tried to deal rationally and politely with certain officers and civil servants, only to find their heads being smashed against brick walls, mostly metaphorically but sometimes literally.

During my time at Gartree, I came across several inmates using their intelligence and patience to battle the cumbersome machinery of the criminal justice system. One high-profile case related to those convicted of the Carl Bridgewater murder. Bridgewater was shot dead at Yew Tree Farm in Staffordshire when he disturbed burglars while delivering a newspaper to the house. The elderly couple who lived there were away and Bridgewater, seeing an open door, decided to look around. He was taken into the living room, sat on the sofa and shot point-blank in the head.

Pat Malloy was arrested following a similar robbery at a farmhouse in Romsley, ten miles from the scene of the Bridgewater murder, on the other side of Stourbridge. During questioning, Molloy told police that he had been in an upstairs bedroom while burgling the house when he heard a gunshot downstairs. Shortly afterwards, Jimmy Robertson, Vincent Hickey and his cousin Michael Hickey were also arrested.

All denied committing murder, but three of them were convicted. The fourth, Molloy, was found guilty of manslaughter. In February 1997, after nearly twenty years inside, the last in a number of appeals finally saw the men's convictions overturned after the Court of Appeal ruled the trial had been unfair. Police, it transpired from a new technique called electro-static document analysis, had fabricated evidence to persuade Molloy to make a confession. Molloy died in prison in 1981. The case exposed widespread corruption in the West Midlands police. No one else was ever charged for the murder.

Tim Caines, an inmate I knew well, was also battling the system. Tim was jailed for life for the killing of his work partner, Coventry solicitor Colin Hickman in 1994. Tim has always protested his innocence, saying that he was taken to Hickman's house under duress by a third party who then attacked the lawyer, stabbing him sixteen times. It has now come to light that Hickman was connected to the Brinks-Mat gold robbery and also to Kenneth Noye who is serving a life sentence for a road-rage stabbing on the M25.

Tim, well-educated, intelligent and articulate, refused to be intimidated by inmates who didn't like him for what he was and what he believed. He was also one of those inmates who certain less intelligent officers found threatening. I met Tim when I worked in the gym at Gartree. He had recently been sentenced and transferred to Gartree from Winson Green in Birmingham. Tim thought he was fit until he joined one of my circuit sessions. By the end he realised he was fit, but not fit enough. He was hooked and became one of the regulars.

He also remained determined to prove his innocence, but was always polite and articulate in going about it. Unfortunately, on occasions he became depressed as he overcame one brick wall only to find another just behind it. I didn't really know if he was innocent or guilty. I suspected innocent, but that was irrelevant at the time. What I saw was one unfair obstacle after another being carefully positioned to block the progress of Tim's appeal. And I strongly suspect that the only reason for this was to slow down the procedure just in case it turned out that Tim actually was innocent.

In my time at Gartree there were several cases that got national attention, including the Birmingham Six, the Guildford Four, Winston Silcott and the Bridgewater Four. Silcott was charged and convicted of killing a policeman called Keith Blakelock who was hacked to death in 1985 with a machete during riots at Broadwater Farm in Tottenham, along with two others. Their convictions were also quashed after evidence that statements were fabricated was proved, again with electrostatic document analysis.

It is too easy to make judgments about someone by bringing in personal opinion or prejudice, or by focusing on past history, or by the media persuading us one way or another. Nor could I get over the fact that many of these unsafe convictions were overturned through a technicality, rather than outright proof of innocence. I suppose that's a consequence of an adversarial system of justice, but I couldn't, and still can't, help thinking that the innocent person in the dock could quite easily be you or me.

All it takes is for you to be in the wrong place at the wrong time and for some laws to be 'bent', and for some 'evidence' to be fabricated, and any one of us could end up convicted of something we didn't do. And the only way to escape that horror would be by maintaining the will to continue and receiving a hefty dose of luck. I wonder how many burned-out innocents languish in our jails?

Dogged determination is a trait I have in abundance. Some may call it a pigheaded refusal to accept the inevitable. However, I can't really be sure that my prodigious stubbornness would have been enough if I had found myself in Tim Caines's position, convicted but, as he claimed, innocent, and even now still in prison. But I do know that my determination stood me in good stead during the ten months I was forced to spend in Suffolk. Working extra shifts gave me the opportunity to string together several days off, which were spent driving to the Peak District or North Wales to climb. I cheered every time I crossed the border leaving Suffolk and cheered even louder when the rolling countryside of the Peak came into view.

I had a dabble in the Churnet Valley, grovelling, slipping and pulling pebbles from lumps of sandy rock. I was soon convinced that cleaner, more solid rock was necessary for an innocent young climber with no one to tie into. So I ran from my parents' home to The Roaches, one of Britain's premier gritstone crags in the north of Staffordshire, just a few miles from Cheadle.

This first experience at The Roaches was everything I craved. The rock's sandpapery texture felt like heaven. Wind roared through chimneys, blowing water seeping from the crag, scouring runnels in the rock. Grouse whirred across the open moor, wings skimming the purple heather. On this clean solid rock my climbing grade shot up. Wearing rubber-soled walking boots, I carefully picked my way up most of the easy climbs on an area called the Great Slab, part of the crag's Upper Tier: *Right Route*, *Pedestal Route*, *Black Velvet*, *Jeffcoat's Chimney*. Each time I pulled over the lip at the top of the crag the wind blasted my face, and for a moment I felt like a kite, threatening to billow into the air. Turning away from the moors I gazed at the Cheshire Plain spread out wide below me. Life seemed suddenly vast and full of half-seen possibilities. The road, so long and straight since my first day of starting the job, began to meander.

My standard improved with each escape I made from Suffolk. Buying rock shoes, learning new techniques and developing finger strength helped. Unfortunately, buying a harness and a rope did not. I had become so used to soloing, when the opportunity came to climb roped with a partner, my lack of experience meant I tackled harder climbs with absolutely no idea how to place protection. If it was easy, why bother placing any gear? If the climbing became difficult, I'd protect it then. Not once did I think: "Looks steep ahead so better place something now where it's less strenuous." I took big falls, some of them painful. Luckily, I survived. And with each fall I dusted myself down and vowed to improve.

Coming from a non-climbing background, the technical aspects of how to go about protecting myself by top-roping or shunting routes didn't occur to me early in my climbing career. I really did start to climb in blissful ignorance. I had a guidebook, a pair of sticky shoes, and a chalk bag. Combine this with determination and a large library, and I convinced myself the climbing world had no idea what force of nature was about to be unleashed.

A climbing day on one of my escapes would generally involve running to the crag. I'd give a quick read of the route description – and climb. If I was lucky I got to the top. On many occasions I didn't; I was forced into a terrifying climb down, reaching the ground a quivering wreck. Yet the buzz was amazing. It took me outside my everyday prison existence. These lovely, innocent and ethically pure years were wonderfully fresh and exciting. I felt I had escaped an infected planet.

Ten months passed at Hollesley Bay working in a department of ten PE officers, most of them keen paddlers, and most a law unto themselves, especially Dave and Mal, two ex-paratroopers. This improved my canoeing, and certainly improved my canoe lifeguard skills, but it did nothing for my climbing.

The canoeing classes followed a format conforming to no procedures or safety manual. The other PE officers, a wild and reckless bunch of mavericks, stood on top of a shingle bank putting the class, several youths aged eighteen to twenty one, into their canoes. They were then launched down the steep shingle bank to enter the deep, fast-flowing river estuary like a gannet after a fish. Already in my canoe, bobbing out in the North Sea, I would wait. It was a laugh, watching these hardened London teenagers scream as they flew toward the water, only to hit the choppy brown river-mouth and immediately capsize. It was my job to paddle over and rescue them before they were swept to Belgium.

During my time at Hollesley Bay, Michael Howard, then Home Secretary for John Major's Conservative government, made sweeping changes, not only to the outdoor pursuits element delivered within the prison service, but to anything that involved taking inmates out of prison. This decision, ill-thought-out and rushed through, was a knee-jerk reaction to a *Daily Mail* crusade against Mark Hook, a boy in custody who had been taken to Egypt, Kenya, Zimbabwe and Zambia at the taxpayer's expense, earning him the moniker 'Safari Boy'. It made me wonder who was running the country, the government or newspaper editors.

I couldn't believe how such a reactionary, even ignorant, judgment could be waved through without the slightest regard to the consequences. Overnight, all social interaction inmates had with people outside the prison service stopped. The group of inmates we took to help a local mentally disabled swimming class was axed. The gym orderly who spent a day a week on work experience, the group of inmates at Glen Parva who were training to become pool lifeguards and have a chance of employment – they lost their chance too. The lack of vision and double standards of politicians never fails to amaze me. Years later Howard was discovered to have charged the taxpayer £17,000 for the upkeep of his garden at his second home.

I know there is a strong right wing element that believes prisoners should be locked away without any help or training or interaction with people not drug users, criminals or prison officers. I certainly met a few inmates whose key I would happily have thrown away. But inmates are individuals and should be treated on an individual basis. In the long run, to lock someone away does not help society. All it does is remove a problem for a certain amount of time, and on the inmate's release, society then has a bigger problem. Outdoor pursuits with prisoners is possibly the most powerful tool I ever saw in the battle against re-offending. Giving an offender a different outlook on life is something that should feature strongly in any rehabilitation.

Even though it was a great place to work, I hated being in Suffolk. I was desperate to return to somewhere nearer rock-climbing and winter mountaineering. I had not yet climbed in winter but knew it was only a matter of time. Nick Banks's images of frozen cliffs and north faces were burned in my memory.

Eventually, the opportunity to return to Gartree Prison arrived, as everyone knew it would. I returned to Leicestershire several thousand pounds to the good, having received expenses courtesy of the taxpayer for a move that served no purpose other than justifying a civil servant's self-importance.

The night I left Hollesley Bay was as wild as some of my inexperienced on-sight soloing. After a night's drinking, no taxi was willing to take a team of wrecked PE officers home. So one of our group, a noisy ex-paratrooper who had fought in the Falklands, decided he would drive a group of us several miles back to our house near the prison. He was steaming like the rest of us, and discovered he'd left his house keys in the pub. Nothing as insignificant as a locked door would stop him though. He returned to his house, followed by the four of us, and kicked in the door.

His wife and children who were in bed at the time must have thought someone was breaking in and laid low. Or else they were used to it. He found his spare keys and the five of us jumped into his Nissan. Most people driving over the limit would at least attempt to be cautious. Not our Falklands' vet. He drove like he was in a grand prix, weaving down forest roads at ninety miles an hour.

Just before reaching the prison and the turning for our house, he approached a crossroads with priority for cars on the other road. We had to give way. Instead, imagining himself to be Michael Schumacher, he dropped a gear and accelerated. What he hadn't taken into consideration was the road on the opposite side of the junction was slightly offset.

Gripping the wheel, leaning forward, his eyes glazed and laughing maniacally, he booted the throttle. The car flew across the junction in a dead straight line and we hit the verge. The car flipped onto two wheels. Like a scene from a James Bond film, we slid back onto the road, still doing ninety and still on two wheels.

Failing to correct, the car flipped onto its roof and we continued screeching along the tarmac upside down in a shower of sparks until we jolted to a halt in a ditch. Groaning and bent double on the ceiling of the car, I spun around, kicked out the rear screen and crawled out. One by one the others followed. We pushed the car further into the ditch and ran off. Next day I walked to the prison to say my goodbyes and left Suffolk for the final time.

DREAMS

Returning to Gartree was a double-edged sword. While I was now where I wanted to be, living in my own home tucked away in a secluded village, the prison was still an extremely stressful place in which to work. I became solitary when not climbing, preferring to sit in the peace and quiet of my house, or drinking a beer at the village pub.

Sometimes I'd stay over at my girlfriend's house. Samantha lived in a rough neighbourhood in southwest Leicester. Many of the people living on the Braunston Estate had done time, so leaving Sam's house in the mornings, dressed in my PE officer's tracksuit, was a little worrying. Sam had a son whose father was black, and hanging out with him made me more aware of people's prejudices and assumptions, including my own.

It's easy to have an opinion, and it's easy to feel superior when you are not the one saying something wrong. But if you remain quiet and say nothing, what does that reveal about you? I couldn't swallow my anger and be silent. When racist comments were thrown around at work, and even out of work, it didn't take long before I started to contradict them, no matter whom that upset. I also tried to cut anyone I considered to be a racist or a bigot out of my life. Unfortunately, this was almost impossible at Gartree.

During this period, the Conservative government and the right wing press were on a campaign against single-parent families. I knew how hard it was for Sam, and how hard she worked to bring up her son. This tabloid witch-hunt made me wonder about politicians who were spending more and more taxpayer's money on their second and even third homes. Their annual 'allowances' were as much as any single mum would take in a decade. I found myself enraged about such inequality and double standards.

I'm not sure why or what it is in my character that caused me to become so enraged by double standards and people not being truthful. People who were intelligent and in a position of power who then used this position to stamp on the people they deemed lower than them, people who had trusted them by voting them into power appeared arrogant to me. Maybe this was a trait passed down from Mum who was fiercely loyal to

Dad and her friends. But if that loyalty was, in Mum's mind, betrayed, she would cut that person from her life without looking back.

At work, my whole day was now spent in a gymnasium but there was still an underlying current of threat and aggression. In a prison there is always tension, whether it's something simple like having to finish the PE class on time or refereeing a game of basketball between teams of very volatile players.

The type of person I dealt with was usually on the hunt for something out of the ordinary, something to pass the monotony of the day. My attitude didn't help. I still played things straight down the line and working in the gym had, if anything, more grey areas than life on the landings. Inmates were supposed to be in the gym for a set period of time but harangued me to be let out early or let in late. If they were let out, officers on the wings had to deal with inmates who should have been somewhere else.

The officers would call or visit the gym to complain and it was the same the other way around when inmates appeared and banged on the gym windows demanding entry. At times arguments between officers would flare up. In a prison, dealing with another officer's inability to stand up to an inmate was a big problem.

In Gartree's gym, we had four basic grade PE officers, including me, a senior gym officer and a principal gym officer and the six of us couldn't work together closely enough to remain consistent. It was always a battle with inmates because they never knew what the line was and would consequently try it on.

Even though a year had passed since finishing the PE officer training course –and deciding I wanted to be a climber – I had still done very little and had a great deal to learn. Sam, my girlfriend, worked at a local leisure centre and was serious about training. She also loved the outdoors but knew even less than me about climbing. When we went out together she blindly trusted my very limited experience. Looking back, she was quite fortunate I didn't kill her and very fortunate she didn't have to scrape me off the ground at the bottom of a climb.

Soon after returning to Gartree I travelled on my own to Las Vegas, for the wedding of an old friend from Alton Towers. After three days' celebrating, I hired a car and drove through Death Valley to Bishop, Tuolumne Meadows and my final destination, Yosemite Valley.

I had read about Yosemite in Julie Tullis's book and the pictures of massive granite cliffs captivated me. Reaching the Valley I did what I'm sure everyone does when turning the corner and seeing El Capitan for the first time. I swung the car over to the verge and stood looking up at it, gazing and dreaming. The cliffs were bigger and steeper than I could ever have imagined. As I had only started to climb properly since returning to Gartree, and was still doing my on-sight soloing, the thought of climbing one of these skyscrapers was so far beyond my imagination it might have been a spacewalk.

I drove around the one-way ring road looking up slack-jawed, often swerving and almost crashing, until I pulled into the car park at Camp 4, the fabled climber's campsite. There were three other tents on my pitch and later that day the owners returned. John and Grant were Kiwis while Ian Berry was from Warrington in England. John was very experienced in the Valley having done several big walls over several seasons. Grant was an experienced rock-climber in New Zealand and Ian was an experienced summer and winter climber having climbed in Scotland and the Alps.

We congregated that evening round our communal wooden picnic table and Ian asked me if I wanted to climb with him tomorrow. I accepted, of course, but lay in my tent later that night worrying that I didn't know how to climb with two ropes and that I would make a fool of myself. I needn't have worried. It was obvious to Ian I had very little experience with rope-work and my climbing technique was clearly non-existent. Yet what I lacked in experience I made up for with strength, stamina, flexibility and my relentless determination.

I spent three weeks at Yosemite and climbed every day – on Cookie Cliff, Knobby Wall, Glacier Point Apron and Middle Cathedral. By the end of my holiday I was climbing the same grade as Ian, albeit with a lot less style and a nasty case of tendonitis. My climbing learning curve was as steep as El Cap but the biggest impression was on my outlook. For the first time I got to know people for whom climbing had become not a hobby but a way of life.

At the grand old age of twenty eight, I was exposed for the first time to a culture that didn't seem to live only to pay the mortgage or buy a new car and a bigger TV. Settling down to a profession, marriage, children and a dog were totally off the radar for many people in Camp 4, although quite a few of them did have dogs. It was the next trip, the next campsite and the next climb that were the most regular topics of conversation. I was thrilled by the idea that someone could live this way and on the flight back from America I made the decision to pursue this dream, even though I didn't have a clue how to go about making it reality – or if it was even possible.

INNOCENCE

My continued reading of Chris Bonington's Alpine exploits made me determined to climb snow and ice. I gleaned that the way to advance towards climbing in the Alps and the Greater Ranges, my ultimate ambition, was to serve an apprenticeship of British winter mountaineering. So I bought a pair of axes, stiff boots and crampons and drove to North Wales at the first opportunity.

It was the week between Christmas and New Year. Snow lay heavy, covering the fields, lapping against the boulders where sheep huddled for shelter. The wind had left frozen wispy waves alongside the road approaching Pen y Pass and across the deserted car park. The youth hostel, buzzing with people in summer, was dark and silent. Burdened with a borrowed rucksack stuffed to overflowing, I strode off towards Snowdon heading up the Pen y Gwryd track, skirting frozen puddles and kicking steps into fresh snow. Wearing a newly purchased breathable jacket, I felt ready for anything the weather could throw at me. Head down, sheltering my face from the driving snow, I nearly bumped into folk being blown the other way.

"My, that's a big rucksack," said one chap, wrapped from head to foot in the best Gore-Tex money could buy.

"Aye, it is. I'm out for a few days," I said proudly.

Mr Gore-Tex looked me over carefully. "Take care!" he concluded.

Setting off once again into the white I was sure I had just met Joe Brown. It certainly looked like him from pictures in my well-thumbed books. Buoyed from my chance meeting with a man I had read so much about, I scrambled into the maelstrom, pulling on ice-covered holds with gloved fingers and clearing snow from encrusted cracks, until I stood on the summit of Crib Goch.

The awkward knife-edge ridge leading from Crib Goch to the Pinnacles at the end of the difficulties was either coated in verglas or polished smooth by a million boots. Every now and again, gusts of wind grabbed and shook me as if I were a naughty child. The rucksack threw my balance, and my feet skittered on the greasy surface. With so much brushing of wet snow from the holds, my woollen gloves grew sodden and my fingers numb. Wet, wind-driven snow splattered heavily against my jacket. I was on my own, with my fate in my own hands, and it felt liberating.

Later, driving the heels of my boots into firm snow – was this névé? – I crunched downhill until I stood in the base of a cwm behind Snowdon's summit. Then I worked my way beneath the dark cliff of Clogwyn Du'r Arddu

Me soloing *Cascade*, grade V, on Craig y Rhaeadr – the wet crag above Ynys Ettws and the Climbers' Club hut in the Llanberis Pass in North Wales which was to become my unofficial summer residence later on in life. Having left Scotland in poor conditions I heard Wales was 'in' and drove over to find this. A teacher/climber staying in the CC hut took this picture – thanks!

in the gloom of late afternoon. Pitching my tent, I climbed into my sleeping bag and wrapped myself in dreams.

Next morning, there was heavy snow on the wind, and more snow hissing over the folds of Clogwyn Du'r Arddu's dark face. I had read about Cloggy in Julie Tullis's book *Clouds on Both Sides*. Clouds were now swirling across Snowdon, an ominous turmoil that parted occasionally to reveal tantalising glimpses of the 'Black Cliff'. I wanted to see the climbs Tullis had written about so poetically. Grabbing my axes, I set off towards the crag, aiming for its snow and ice-covered tiers.

Five hours went by, five hours spent climbing up, climbing down, traversing and breathing in the atmosphere of this extraordinary place. The wind blasted powder into my face. My ears, nose, fingers and feet became numb. The cold burned. Exhausted, soaked and satisfied, I returned to my tent nestling among the boulders beside the dark waters of Llyn Arddu, with only the wind and the night and Tullis's words for company.

The final day of my mini-expedition was the high point, quite literally when I crossed the summit of Snowdon, crawling on all fours like some kind of snow-snail, with my belongings on my back. At any moment I thought the wind, like a thrush, would get hold of me and smash me against a rock. Staggering down the rock-strewn slopes, the wind roared at me as I crossed through the gap of Bwlch y Saethau, the pass of the arrows. Then, taking the ridge opposite, I climbed to the summit of Lliwedd. A break in the clouds offered a flashed view of the Glyders' spiky white cockatoo's crest.

The wind finally relented as I dropped towards Llyn Llydaw and the vegetated cliff of Lliwedd sheltered me. The temperature increased and the ice covering the Miner's Track turned to slush beneath my feet. Suddenly my three days camping and surviving in the hills had come to an end. I was back at my starting point, Pen y Pass. As I unlocked the car, I was already wondering – what next?

That night, I camped in the Llanberis Pass, in the corner of a field beneath a deserted farmhouse. My solitary tent, pitched behind a stone wall, looked forlorn. During the night the temperature plunged, and I woke shivering, despite being wrapped inside my cosy borrowed sleeping bag. It made no difference. I was too excited to care about being cold. Squeezing out of the tent, the air seemed to crackle.

I gazed up at the mountains and immediately spotted a snow-filled chimney-line. That's it, I decided. I'm ready for a more technical challenge. I wolfed down breakfast with as little chewing as possible, and in what seemed like minutes was scraping and wading through deep powder snow, sometimes buried up to my chest. Struggling in the snowy depths of the deep chimney that I'd spied from my tent below, I found myself grappling with chockstones, fighting my way past constrictions, sweating, swearing – it was everything I had imagined it would be.

Emerging from the chimney, I traversed into Cwm Glas. The small tarn beneath the steep cliffs was frozen solid. Silver streaks ran down the steep rock leading to the ridge above. I climbed into Parsley Fern Gully, and for the first time my crampon points bit perfect névé. Forget the hard snow from a few days before; this stuff seemed like polystyrene, squeaking every time I kicked my feet or placed an axe.

Breaking through a cornice and out onto the wind-blown ridge of Crib y Ddysgl, I caught sight of a magnificent triangular face, rising like the Eiger before me. My eyes scanned the obvious gullies that ended abruptly right at the summit of Snowdon. Ripping the mitts from my hands, I flipped through the guidebook, numb fingers struggling with the pages.

Eventually I discovered I was looking at Clogwyn y Garnedd and the lines I'd spotted were called the Trinity Gullies. The names of the cliff's features set my heart racing – the Spider and the Fly, names from Bonington's Eiger epics. For me, at that moment, tracing the cliff's white lines with innocent eyes, I could have been in Switzerland. I promised myself I would be back next morning.

That night sleep was difficult, but for once it wasn't the cold that kept me awake. As soon as light started to filter through the tent walls I could stand the delay no longer. The Miner's Track, now frozen and crunchy, passed in a blur, and I soon stood beneath the triangular face I had seen the day before. I could now pick out the fine detail of ice gullies and overhangs. My crampons snapped into place, and in no time I was kicking into névé.

I soon reached the Spider, a large snowfield with several 'legs' extending from its bulk. Thick ice curling over rock barricaded an easy exit at its top left-hand corner. Here, the walls closed in, forming a dark corridor that dripped with icicles. Taking a rest before climbing the crux, I turned to take in the view below. Llyn Llydaw was frozen solid with a wind-blown dusting of snow swirling over the ripples of the lake's ice-skin. The Miner's Track, crossing on its causeway, slashed a black line across the toe of the lake, the isolated corner shaped like a frozen tear, weeping from its far side.

The low temperature had locked up all the water, and conditions were perfect. The teeth of my axe-pick bit into thick ice. The front-points of my crampons penetrated with a single kick. The gully walls closed in to thicken the atmosphere, but they couldn't imprison me. Soon I was romping up the final snow-slope and in an explosion of polystyrene bricks, I broke out, smashing my way through a cornice near the summit.

My sudden appearance startled some early-morning walkers.

"Hello! Sorreeee!" I sing-songed.

Standing under the face for a second time, and without stopping, I started up *Left-Hand Trinity*. The guidebook suggested this climb was more serious than *Central Trinity*, but the conditions were good and as I was soloing the warning about poor belays didn't concern me. Once again I reached the Spider, but this time traversed further left into the middle of the face and climbed directly up the Fly, a smaller snowfield. The repetitive blows with my ice tools into the easier-angled névé made my knuckles swell and ache.

Pulling once again through the summit cornice I met the walkers I had previously startled, now huddling behind the ice-smeared trig point at the summit.

"Hello again!" I yelled happily, sweating on the freezing summit, steam billowing from me.

They stared with wide eyes at this apparition of glee. "How did you get up here again?" they asked in unison.

"I've just climbed the second of the Trinity Gullies." I kept my reply as nonchalant as I could.

"Wow! You must be really good. It looks very steep. And you have no rope."

Pleased to get the praise I was after, I walked merrily down once again from the summit. Despite the icy wind that sliced into me, I decided to complete the trilogy and climb the hardest of the Trinity Gullies – *Trinity Right-Hand*, Grade III.

That evening, I burst into the living room of my parents' house in Cheadle, still dressed in my climbing gear having driven straight from Pen y Pass. They turned to look at me, startled at my wild appearance and damp smell. We looked at each other.

"You're going to read about my climbing in a few years," I said.

Dad turned back to the TV. "Aye, okay Nick. Just get a drink and shut up, will you? I'm trying to watch *Only Fools and Horses*."

GERMINATION

Buoyed by my Yosemite trip and a few winter routes in Wales, I caught the bus from Victoria Station in London and travelled on my own to Chamonix. It was April and I was nervous. I hardly spoke a word of French, but my desire to see Chamonix overtook my anxiety at not speaking the lingo. Stepping off the bus in the middle of Chamonix with a large army duffle slung over a shoulder, I walked to the tourist information office and hit them with one of the few phrases I knew.

"Parlez-vous anglais?"

Fortunately they did, and I was soon slogging up the steep hill to the gîte next to the Brévent Ski Lift.

I spent ten days in and around Chamonix, and much like my experience in Yosemite, the spectacular snow-covered peaks looked way beyond the realms of my experience, yet it was the people I met and the lifestyle they had chosen which made the biggest impression.

I met Roger Sarrasin, a young Canadian who had taken a year out after school. Roger arrived at the gîte fresh from Nepal and we immediately clicked. He was from native North American stock, short and wiry, quiet and thoughtful, his shiny black hair hidden beneath a striped woollen hat. We rock-climbed together around the valley and dreamed of climbing Mont Blanc, just like all the others with no idea who come to Chamonix. When I returned to Leicestershire, I spent a week at work before Roger arrived from France and we set off to climb.

With bloated forearms and weakening fingers, I pressed on. I still had little understanding of grades, protection, technique, rock types or routes to avoid. Feeling indestructible, I had left Roger secured to several pieces of gear, perched on a large airy ledge with a deep crevasse at its back, twenty metres above the ground. The shafts of afternoon sun didn't reach far enough to warm this dark corner on The Roaches' Lower Tier.

Wedged beneath a huge chockstone that bulged and overhung, I knew the fun was about to begin. A fist-sized crack split the roof. It was clear that the technique needed to surmount this monstrosity was the much-read-about hand jam. Bring it on, I thought. I wanted desperately to simulate the exploits and experiences of the 1950s gritstone gurus.

Matinee HVS 5b. First ascensionists: Joe Brown and Don Whillans, 1951. A jamming testpiece.

The name was enough to strike terror into the heart of many a seasoned climber. Not me though. I was complacently ignorant. Having just climbed *Elegy*, a higher-graded climb to the right, this route would be easy. The shiny new gear hanging from my harness was redundant, since I still had little idea how to use it. But then I wouldn't need to, since this climb was so much easier graded than the last.

I make a fist in the crack and twist until it hurts. Leaning back on the jammed hand, I stretch to peer above the bulging chock inches from my nose. Reaching above I drop my other arm into the flared off-width. Camming elbow and wrist, I make an arm-bar. It holds. Pushing knees, thighs, feet, ankles, anything into the damp depths of unseen fissure below, I attempt to lighten the load on my upper body. I manage to free the lower hand.

All of my weight now comes onto the upper arm. Suddenly, the arm-bar holding me in position begins to creep. I try to find a hold above by ramming the free arm into the crack above, which is even wider. Where have all the holds gone? Turning the palm of my left hand and bunching my knuckles does nothing to improve my situation. I turn the hand in the opposite direction; still it does nothing. I can't do this. I don't know how to do this.

A mad last-ditch effort and I'm twisting the right arm even tighter into the crack. Blood oozes from my wrist and traces a snail track to my elbow. Squirming, thrutching, trying to keep my knees sprigged, I'm like a caterpillar, knees to chest. No, *no*, the bloody arm is slipping. My legs shoot out from beneath me. My arm-bar and hand-jam fail. I'm spat out like an olive pip, arms flying out from my side.

The massive chockstone I had only just surmounted disappears into the distance. Roger dives for cover taking in as much rope as he can. Missing his head by inches, I hurtle on past him and my feet hit the ledge on which he is now sprawled. Flipped upside down, my full bodyweight comes onto the rope. There's a resounding thud. My back takes most of the impact, but my un-helmeted head quickly follows and is whiplashed into the rock.

Unconscious for a few seconds, stars and bright lights explode inside my head. I come round upside down and I'm unceremoniously lowered into the arms of several off-duty policemen. They have witnessed the whole debacle, and suitably impressed by the length of fall, especially as I've climbed past so many gear placements, they insist on driving us to hospital in Stoke.

Seven head X-rays later, and a few stitches, I'm discharged with the instruction not to climb for a week. A good weather forecast and my mad-for-it attitude push that advice to one side. Next day we are weaving down country roads on our way to North Wales, our target the *Cenotaph Corner* of Dinas Cromlech.

Comes the Dervish in the Llanberis slate quarries. I don't really know when this was taken – I've climbed the *Dervish* loads of times, but it certainly isn't from the first time I climbed it which was followed two days later by my fall from *Extraction* at Tremadog resulting in 'bed rest' at Ysbyty Gwynedd, followed by several weeks in plaster, vegetarianism and a new, more determined, outlook.

My girlfriend Sam and I had split by this time and my appetite for climbing and living the life of a climber was ferocious. At least working in prison gave me plenty of opportunity to travel to the Peak District and solo routes. I met a likeminded PE officer, Clive Taylor, who worked in the young offenders centre Glen Parva, near Wigston in Leicestershire. It wasn't long before we were regularly travelling and climbing together, the blind leading the blind. But we were keen and fit and hungry for adventure. It soon became apparent that I was the better climber and so I would generally be the one leading and Clive would second.

During the summer I took and passed my mountain leader's award, closely followed by a basic rock-climbing qualification. I began to think of gaining more qualifications in outdoor education, which might eventually give me enough expertise to leave the prison service and start work instructing people in the hills. Yet I soon realised that much like my life as a PE instructor, I would have little interest in teaching people. I just wanted to go climbing for my own personal satisfaction and enjoyment.

While being assessed for my single-pitch supervisor's award, one of the questions in a written test was: 'Who made the first ascent of the route called *The Bells! The Bells!*'?' I had never heard of it and so couldn't answer the question. But afterwards, while going through the answers, my instructor Fran made a comment that grabbed my attention. She said she wouldn't expect people taking such a basic climbing award to know who the author of a 'chop route' like *The Bells!* was. When I heard the term 'chop route' I didn't know what she meant and so I asked. Fran described a type of route where the climber is prepared to take themself into a serious situation that could, in the extreme, end in death.

This fascinated me. To step off the ground not knowing where the climb would take you but knowing you might die was a million miles from what I understood about climbing. I could only guess at the strength of mind required or the confidence in one's abilities. Yet I read more about the route *The Bells!* and its brilliant creator John Redhead. The seed was sown.

Camping at Tremadog behind Eric Jones's cafe, I was bouncing with enthusiasm. The previous day I had led my first rock climb graded E3, *Comes the Dervish*, a precarious climb on tiny edges of sharp slate in Vivian Quarry above the mountain village of Llanberis. I'd soloed gritstone slabs at this grade before, but somehow that didn't count. I felt I'd made a breakthrough. Flushed with success, I now needed to push even harder.

My partner for the day, Stu Lorrie, was experienced, middle-aged and safe. Stu was a PE officer at Deerbolt, a prison near Barnard Castle.

Being one of the most experienced climbers and mountaineers in the prison service, he instructed outdoor pursuits on the PE officer training course at Plas y Brenin. Most of the trainees thought Stu strange; he walked the hills playing the bagpipes while wearing a kilt and swam in the lake. I thought Stu was quirky and good fun, an individual not afraid to be himself.

He suggested starting on an HVS. An HVS! Silly old sod. This was way beneath a man of my calibre. Hadn't I just led E3? Four grades higher? Even so, to keep our climbing relationship harmonious, I reluctantly agreed.

Having slipped around in the mud walking up the steep path to the crag, we eventually arrived at our climb. *The Fang*, HVS 5a. I didn't want to waste time on a climb without an 'E' for extreme in its grade, so I volunteered for the first pitch.

No sooner has the silly old sod tied on I'm away. The description for the first pitch mentioned a crack. So when a crack appears directly in front of my face I follow it. I place a large nut, and although it rattles and shifts around in the crack, it's no problem. I'll soon be high enough to make it redundant. Higher still, I place two more nuts into the crack.

Not used to standing around messing with gear, my arms burn with fatigue. Climbing beneath an overhang I press on, pulling myself above the lip sure in the knowledge a jug is waiting. But there is no jug. If anything the holds are even smaller. Hanging around trying to make sense of the moves to come, I can't believe how hard I'm finding it. Yet defeat isn't an option. The art of giving in gracefully is one I haven't learnt yet – and still haven't.

Adopting my well-practiced down-climbing technique, I push with the soles of my shoes against the sharp sides of the wet crack below. This relieves some weight from my arms. Grunting and panting, I lower myself to the refuge below the overhang. My fingers, squeezing the life from the bigger holds, turn pale. Once I am wedged beneath with my whole body jammed in, I frantically shake the lactic acid from my forearms.

The silly old sod then suggests giving in. He doesn't seem to know I don't do that.

"No, I'll have another look."

This is HVS. I'm an E3 leader! SILLY OLD SOD!

Setting off again, the pressure from my partner to back off causes me to speed up. I pull once more over the roof, and find nothing new. Crimping my fingers onto tiny holds, my eyes dart left and right, up and down. Sweat runs down the ridge of my nose to free-fall onto the gnarled tree roots far below. The damp scent of forest mildew rises, I suck in the loamy smell overwhelming my senses.

Forced to retreat again, the fruitless search for holds has drained my forearms. Feet skitter. Water seeping from the crack is running over the footholds. I lower myself shifting all of my weight to my feet. They stick for a second then skid. My numb fingers snap open and I fall. On the way down my forehead whacks a sharp edge and I'm knocked out instantly. My unconscious body wheels down the face, snagging on rock, then hitting and twisting. All the wires unzip, except the first. I hit earthy root-covered ground then slide headfirst down the steep muddy rock-strewn gully below, bouncing off rocks and roots before stopping thirty feet below Stu.

The silly old sod slithers after my broken body. He quickly fishes my tongue from the back of my throat. I am bleeding all over from where the ropes have skinned me. Other climbers rush over to help. They carry me down to the road where I am promptly bundled into a car and whisked off to hospital in Bangor, an hour away.

Three days later, I emerged from my comfortably numb existence. The drip was removed and I lay in bed trying to make sense of what happened. The climb I mistakenly thought was *The Fang*, was in fact a climb called *Extraction*, a fierce E2 with a reputation for spitting people off and unzipping their protection. Perhaps the silly old sod hadn't been so silly after all.

The injuries I sustained in the fall were serious. I had dislocated my shoulder, smashed my right foot, which had been operated on and wired, skinned half of my body with rope burn and hit my head so hard I needed stitches and regular checks to make sure there was no internal damage. The consequences were no less profound. Dad picked me up from Bangor Hospital in Wales and drove me back to their house in Cheadle where I stayed for three weeks.

For the first week or so I was exhausted. My body needed rest. But towards the end of the second week the pain in my shoulder subsided – especially with the aid of strong anti-inflammatory tablets – and I began to train again. My right foot was still wired and in plaster, so I borrowed some weight-training equipment and worked my upper body, doing lots of reps with light weights.

After six years of weight and fitness training and playing rugby, I had reached just over thirteen stone when I began to climb. Now I decided I had too much heavy muscle, so I stopped eating meat apart from fish, cut down on alcohol, cut salt and sugar from my diet and vowed to get better and fitter and lighter. Not for a moment did I consider giving up climbing, which some people thought the correct and sensible course of action.

Instead, I decided to concentrate more on training for climbing and at the end of the third week at my parents' house they drove me back to my cottage in Burton Overy. Getting around was difficult with my foot in plaster until I decided to try and drive, which turned out to be relatively easy. Driving in a plaster cast is a skill I've now perfected.

LOYALTY

Still in plaster, dozing on the sofa, a knock on the door made me stir. Sue Westwood, one of the psychologists from the prison, had come to visit. Gartree has a large psychology department and Sue, along with some of the other psychologists, came by the gym at lunchtime for staff aerobics or circuit classes. Now she wanted to know how I was getting on.

This was the first time Sue and I had spoken out of work and about subjects other than exercise and music. It was interesting to get a different view on life and on people, inmates, politics, religion and anything else that popped into our conversation. Over time Sue would become a close friend and sounding block, someone I trusted, although we would often argue. Sue is feisty and holds nothing back. But in the future as now we always parted company as good friends. Despite my injuries, I felt better for talking about subjects I knew I couldn't with colleagues.

At the time of my fall at Tremadog, I had worked in the prison service for seven years. Apart from a few PE officers, one or two other officers, and a very few old friends, I had few people in my life I would call close. Working in prison was having an effect on the way I thought about people. Trusting others became difficult. Instead of running the risk of someone letting me down, as I saw it, I just didn't allow anyone into my life. I became fiercely private.

There was a saying I heard most days in prison. "There are only two things in life you can be sure about. One is you'll die and the other is people will always let you down." I can't think of a more cynical thing to think, but at that time I believed this maxim to be correct, until one evening when Sue corrected me in her usual direct manner.

It was also around this time that I began to look at myself and question my beliefs. I began to at least attempt to understand more about what makes people act in the way they do. I tried to be more open-minded and sympathetic, although there were still aspects of my life I could not and would not change: tolerating people who I considered to be racist or sexist, or people who lacked consideration for others. Prisons are full of this type of person and on both sides of the bars. Sick to the stomach of living with a lack of consideration and cynicism, I began to plan my escape from prison life.

Many officers talk about leaving, although resigning from the prison service was virtually unknown. Security is a way of life for many of us and not only did the prison service pay well enough, it gave me plenty of time off and offered one of the best pension schemes in the country. Leaving would be a big risk. Yet time was becoming more important to me and the more I became interested in climbing and travelling for climbing, the more I realised that time is the most precious commodity and something no one gets back.

Since buying my house, I had struggled with the concept of owing the bank, of being held hostage by politicians and their views on interest rates. Owning my house and paying a mortgage kept me in a job I hated. In the early days of my mortgage I almost despaired, as John Major's government pushed interest rates up time and again, until I began to struggle. I felt that some politicians, although not all, lived a gilded existence feeding off the back of workers, giving themselves wage increases and bonuses while telling the rest of the country to tighten their belts. I don't know the alternative, but I do know politicians have been proved corrupt and this surely breeds the attitude that if they can do it, why shouldn't the rest of the population?

It had been a long time since I had voted Conservative and I now considered myself a Labour supporter. I visited my parents' house in Cheadle frequently so I could be near The Roaches or Dovedale and would get into savage arguments with Dad about politics and the unions, or topics like racism. Dad really struggled to understand me and couldn't grasp the reason I didn't eat meat anymore. He took my vegetarianism as a personal slight on his own diet and would make jibes about how I thought I was better than him.

I don't think he ever grasped that we argued because I wanted to understand views apart from my own, even if I didn't hold those views, and it didn't bother me at all that he smoked or ate meat. What I was angry about was watching my once intelligent and articulate father choose to become an alcoholic. He had absolutely no consideration for those around him.

"It's my life," he'd say, "and I'll do what I want with it."

Working in the gym, we were usually left alone as a department. As long as we turned up for work and didn't give the principal officer, who was nearing retirement, a hard time, we were allowed to train as often as we wanted. I particularly enjoyed the fitness side of the job, specialising in circuit training – bodyweight circuits, circuits with weights, shuttle runs and interval training – aerobics, running and weight training. I gave up all contact sport for fear of an injury, which would put me out of climbing.

Two of the other PE officers in the department, Mick Greenslade and Rich Sawbridge, became close friends who were mad keen on training and sport. Mick was older than Rich and me with more time in the job. He was tall and gangly but with thin arms because he didn't do weights. Mick's passion was team sports – football, basketball and rugby. Ordinarily he was placid, but get him onto a sports field or a basketball court and he became competitive and very aggressive. Most games ended with Mick arguing or fighting.

Rich was a year older than me, an ex-coal miner from Coalville in Leicestershire. Given his powerful, stocky frame, it was no surprise he was an excellent rugby player and runner but Rich also excelled at golf. His handicap was freakishly low. He was also a gifted trumpet player. I had known Rich since he joined the prison service a few years after me and he worked on B Wing. Rich was laidback and friendly, but if he thought you a fool he would let you know very quickly. He frequently came into work with a broken nose or a swollen fist after the weekend's rugby.

The inmates at Gartree only respected someone they considered fitter than themselves. It was similar to growing up in Cheadle. If you could prove yourself, you were respected and left alone, and so when it came to fitness, I went all out to be the best I could. Competition between the inmates and myself was intense and since returning to Gartree I had built a hardcore bunch that trained with me twice a day.

I grew to like and respect this motley crew and if we had met in other circumstances I think we would have been friends. Mike and Harry were brothers, as cockney as the Thames and as likeable as Michael Caine. They were serving a life sentence for the murder of a policeman and the attempted robbery of a post office with a third man. Mike and Harry attempted to run off when a police sergeant arrived at the scene, alerted by a phone call from the wife of the post office's manager. But the third man had a knife and savagely stabbed and killed the policeman. All three men were given the same sentence. I didn't trust another regular, Barry. He was cunning and, I suspect, would rob his granny if he thought he could get away with it. But I liked him. He was bright and articulate, and I spent many evenings with him deep in conversation. We would sit next to each other while I supervised the weights class, chatting for an hour or two about camper vans and travelling the world.

In all my time as a PE officer, Barry was the only inmate who finished some circuits before I could. He was certainly a better runner. So when competition was fierce or I was feeling tired, I would include some weight-training exercises in the circuit which gave me the edge and guaranteed that I finished before him.

I suppose I have always been competitive, although more so with myself. But in prison, where everything you did was watched and assessed, it was impossible for me not to be drawn along. I have always believed that to live is to compete in some way or other, but at times some people take it too far. I've never really strived to beat other people, and I'm genuinely not that bothered about losing to others.

Competition for me is about having to struggle, and I'm often disappointed if others are not a little bit better than me or at least as good, only because I need the challenge of others' strengths and brilliance to test myself. And if someone is much better than me, then I'm frustrated by not being able to get near him so I can experience the thrill of struggle. The only person I want to beat is myself. Although as someone once pointed out to me, the word 'beat' has a double meaning.

The inmate whose company I most enjoyed and who I did class as a friend was Gary. He was funny, although he didn't try to be. He was just naturally amusing and his take on life made me laugh. He told stories with gusto in a whining Potteries accent while swinging his arms and thumping your shoulder. The thing I most liked about Gary was his open and honest attitude. He called a spade a spade, and I felt he was straight down the line.

Gary was a couple of years older than me, slim and about six foot with a shaved head and always clean shaven, apart from a pencil thin moustache. He lived up to his Italian roots by being feisty and loyal. I imagined him dressed in a tailored suit and starring in a Martin Scorsese film. We connected because we both originated from Stoke-on-Trent. Gary had been a coal miner in Newcastle-under-Lyme, a place I had regularly gone night clubbing when I was with Sheila and working at Alton Towers. Gary and I had drunk in the same bars and often we sat and talked about them.

When he was first transferred to Gartree, serving a fixed sentence of fifteen years, he started exercising by running around the cinders track while on daily exercise. Then he had become a cleaner on the wing and began to attend gym on a regular basis. Gary was now as hooked as the others in the group but would also come to the gym for a chat.

Gary had been married to his long-term girlfriend and they had a daughter. I'm sure it wasn't always a bed of roses but, as Gary put it one day, he worked long hours and overtime to buy a nice house and give his family a good standard of living. I could see how it was a matter of pride for him to look after his family. Yet being away and working long hours took its toll. His wife began having an affair with another miner.

Gary suspected what was going on and confronted his wife who denied the affair, but still continued cheating on him. Rumours spread at work and Gary took a lot of stick. Eventually his wife left him, but instead of walking away, he chose retribution. He went to the door of the house where he knew his wife was living and knocked. When his wife opened the door, he hit her in the centre of the forehead with the ball end of a hammer he had brought with him. Although she survived the attack, she was left permanently blinded.

There are so many men in prison who are violent and many who have directed their violence toward women, often women they love. Being surrounded for so long by this atmosphere of aggression, the cloyingly thick cloud of testosterone, does have an effect. For some it softens the horror, it almost normalises the brutal animal instinct but for me it did the opposite – it made me more aware of the horrors and the consequences.

At times I found myself wondering if I lacked some 'normal' animal emotion. I could never see myself so utterly out of control that I'd kill or attempt to kill but the fact that I have questioned myself for not being aggressive in this way is also frightening.

I could never condone Gary's actions; his violence toward his wife was truly appalling. But having worked in a prison, an almost all-male environment like the pit where Gary worked, I understand the constant mockery he got from workmates, of not being a good enough man, not man enough to keep his woman, and how that would have ground him down.

Of course, he should have been stronger and ignored it but others in that position eventually crack. Gary was far from being the worst person in Gartree. I took each inmate as I found them, and I found Gary's honest approach to be refreshing – even if his black and white views were also a little scary.

TUNNELS

Fully recovered after my fall from *Extraction*, I continued training – circuits, running, weights, cycling, aerobics, swimming – partly for the sake of keeping fit and getting involved with the inmates, but now also for climbing. I grew my hair, no longer keeping it the regulation short back and sides, no longer just another gym screw but someone unafraid to be different. It was hardly a rebellion but regular comments inside the prison made me feel I was breaking free from a stereotype, becoming someone like a climber. I had started to climb late in life so every day became important and I became very focused.

At work I grew more intolerant with anything that took me from my fitness classes or anything I thought would improve my climbing. I became even more isolated from people other than climbers, prison officers and inmates. I knew what could happen when out on the town. I knew the type of people I'd meet there and I preferred not to mix with them.

At the time, Leicester didn't have the kind of indoor climbing walls that have become so popular and revolutionised training. But I discovered an old railway bridge twenty minutes from the prison in Northamptonshire. I drove or cycled to Slawston Bridge regularly after work or in my dinner break. The bridge was made from blue brick, ironstone and gritstone and being plumb vertical, the climbing, all on small edges and pockets, was sustained.

Occasionally, school groups used the bridge for top-roping and I learnt that the brilliant rock-climber Johnny Dawes had climbed on Slawston Bridge when he was a pupil at Uppingham School. The bridge became a haven, somewhere to escape. One dinnertime I drove to the bridge with Nige Masters, the gym's senior officer.

I had first known Nige at Welford Road when I practised class teaching before qualifying as a PE officer. Nige was a big guy who played football and drank beer to a high standard. He laughed and joked and played the fool. We pulled up at the bridge and immediately, like most PE officers would, Nige threw himself at the rock.

Lesley, my sister, and my ferrets. Chalk and cheese, that's my sister and me, not the name of the ferrets. Although since becoming a nomadic full-time climber we get on really well and it's not just because I store all of my mountaineering gear at her house.

Me and Murphy, my Patterdale Terrier. Both skinny and both with attitude but only one is a natural born killer. *Photo: Sheila Salt*

Passing out (I mean successfully completing the PE officer training course, although I'm sure I did later on) as a newly qualified PE officer with long suffering girlfriend Sheila Salt. *Photo: Richard Pratt*

PE officer training at Holme Pierrepont, the national water-sports centre, Nottinghamshire. Many of us grew to know the fish by their first names during our time in Nottingham.

Trainees and trainers, on the PE officer course. Lilleshall National Sports Centre, Shropshire. Can you spot me?

The Hollesley Bay Colony PE Department. L–R: Mal Adams, Tony Brammer, me, Dave Bowman, Rich Carter. Although I hated being in Suffolk, working with these guys was always a hoot.

Michael Tweedley celebrating having successfully surfed the Hard Very Far Skyline buttress at The Roaches.

Jules Cartwright, Jamie Fisher, Owain Jones and me posing before the Shark's Fin expedition in my garden in Burton Overy to try and get some money from a sponsor, promo hand-out. Coloured trousers de rigueur.

Owain Jones who showed me the ropes on my first 'proper' Alpine climbing trip.

Breaking my kneecap resulted in a slightly honed body. Recovery took the form of two hour weighted pull-up sessions, interspersed with a thousand sit-ups and an hour of straight leg aerobics. This picture is actually me taking the piss as Michael Tweedley and I had climbed Tess of the d'Urbevilles in the morning, an E6, but were struggling to climb anything else. This picture is taken on the top of a climb in the Llanberis slate quarries called German Schoolgirl, an E2 (easy), on which we had both struggled. We gave up for the day after this.   **Photo:** Michael Tweedley

Bruce French, ex-Nottingham and England wicketkeeper but more than this a great friend. If I was ever getting up myself I could always rely on Bruce to let me know about it.

Early days in Scotland. Continuing to the top of Carn Dearg via Ledge Route after climbing The Curtain.

Me and Jules Cartwright after pushing it out in bad weather on Teng Kangpoche, Nepal. One of us looks decidedly more knackered than the other.

Owain Jones, Jamie Fisher and Jules Cartwright sampling the expedition cheap booze at Tapovan base camp while on the Shark's Fin expedition.

Owain Jones on the Mer de Glace above Chamonix before we climbed the Swiss Route on Les Courtes, which was my first 'proper' Alpine route.

Owain Jones in the middle of washing his nether regions at Tapovan, India, during the Shark's Fin Expedition.

Meru Shark's Fin, India. Simon Yates, while guiding Shivling, suggested we have advance base camp on the ridge between where this picture was taken and the start of the climb, which led to much more work carrying gear. Live and learn, and on this trip I learnt a great deal.

The Shark's Fin. Owain Jones and me fixing ropes before returning to the bivvy. The following day it dumped with snow (I know this because it dumped with snow every day!) and we retreated. **Photo:** *Jules Cartwright*

Owain Jones on the approach slopes of the Shark's Fin. On our second attempt Owain chose not to repeat these slopes thinking they were avalanche-prone, which truth be told they probably were but the three of us were pushy and driven and stupid and young…

The Right-Hand Pillar of Frêney above Courmayeur, Italy. This climb, climbed with Jules Cartwright, was enchained with a new link-up on the Grand Pilier and included my first and only summit of Mont Blanc. This experience is close to being my most enjoyable climb ever in the mountains. I can still taste the beer we drank sitting in the sun while waiting for the tram to take us back to the valley.

Jules Cartwright forcing the issue and failing on what was to become a new route on the Aiguille Sans Nom called *Borderline*. Eventually we traversed out right from beneath this corner and spent another two days on the face until abseiling to the La Charpoua hut and bum-sliding all the way to the Mer de Glace and the pub.

Jules Cartwright high on the new link up, *Lost in the Dark*, on the Grand Pilier d'Angle.

"Staying alive matters, but staying alive right at the very edge of where you are capable matters more." Starting out on *The Bells! The Bells!* A serious climb where strength of mind is as important as finger strength.   **Photo:** *Tim Neill*

Not satisfied with traversing he began going up, and up, and up. The bridge is about seven metres high with sloping, overhanging coping-stones at the top and, for the untrained, forearm fatigue is only a matter of minutes away. Just below the coping-stone finish, Nige, all fourteen stone of him, began shaking and frantically fishing for a hold, sweeping the top of the coping-stones with his hands. He found nothing and laughed. Shaking more, sweeping and hunting, he laughed again, but now the sound was high pitched, demented. I quickly climbed below him to try and hold his foot to the rock but he laughed, then screamed and let go. On his way down he took me with him.

I hit the grass at the base of the bridge and Nige landed on me. We both lay in a crumpled groaning pile at the side of the road laughing and hurting. I was back at the bridge a day later with one of the other PE officers and he also fell from the coping stone top-out. But I had learnt my lesson and stood clear this time. After that our boss Alex banned me from taking anyone else to the bridge.

The greatest advancement in my rock-climbing ability came from travel-ling to the recently opened climbing wall in Nottingham. I felt the benefits of training indoors and climbing on overhanging plastic immediately. I also enjoyed the company of the people who climbed and worked there. They weren't inmates or officers. They weren't aggressive. They were just climbers with a laidback climber attitude.

By the winter of 1994, I was hungry to become a proper winter climber and after my first route on Ben Nevis, climbed with fellow PE officer Clive Taylor, I felt I had succeeded. Our ascent of *Glover's Chimney* turned into an eighteen-hour epic after we got stuck behind a slow-moving party in front of us. Reaching the summit plateau of Ben Nevis at night and in thick cloud, we were met by gales reaching one hundred miles an hour.

Slawston Railway Bridge on the border of Leicestershire and Northamptonshire. *"The best climbing in Leicestershire and the only climbing in Northamptonshire."* SALVATION!

We crawled among snow-covered boulders still roped together, following a compass bearing and nothing more, utterly isolated from the lights I imagined glowing orange along Fort William's high street. Clive was a triathlete and so used as his base-layer an all-in-one Lycra suit. This kept him warm but was not very practical and as we crawled in the storm, Clive admitted to me that he'd wet himself to save undressing.

The following day, after crawling from the summit slopes of Ben Nevis, I wallowed in a comfy chair in front of the coal fire at the MacIntyre Hut in Onich. The strain and battle the previous day had taken a toll but I felt mentally cleansed. I thought back to huddling in the lee of a boulder with Clive and saying, 'Right this is not the time to panic, we will carefully make our way from here and we will get down safe and alive.'

And as we worked together battling the weather and conditions not once did I feel aggressive or violent. I felt an inner calm as though this was where I should be. The situation was stressful but it was certainly not the same stress I had faced on a daily basis from the time I worked in the Block. This was honest, it was me against elements, me against me. There was terror but unlike in the Block, horror did not follow – just deeper understanding.

Later that winter I hooked up with Stu Lorrie, my partner on *Extraction*, and a few other PE officers who were into winter climbing, to do some easy routes and walking but after they left I was surprised to find I could actually climb harder and quicker by myself. I soloed *Green Gully* and *Comb Gully* on Ben Nevis and my first Grade V on Craig Meagaidh, a climb called *The Pumpkin*. My success over the winter made me feel at peace and finally in control of my own destiny. Climbing was not something governed by rules and regulation, by keys, locks, bars, gates, Home Secretaries and interest rates. I revelled in the freedom and adventure.

Bouldering by myself in the spring of 1995 at Stanage Edge in the Peak District, a climber called Adam Cooper, also bouldering, came and stood beneath me to offer advice. We climbed together and although Adam was obviously more experienced than me, he did not appear to climb any harder. Secretly I felt pleased, although his technique made my laboured efforts look agricultural. Adam was unemployed, had lost his driving licence through drink-driving, and had a large, gothic tattoo on one shoulder. His buggy, hash-smoking eyes reminded me of some of the people I met at work.

But with my new, more liberal outlook and short of a regular climbing partner, we swapped phone numbers. Not that I had a telephone at the time. I usually gave out the prison gym number. He called me there one day and we soon became regular climbing partners. During that summer we racked up over one hundred and twenty routes, mostly between the grades of E2 and E4. More importantly, I was climbing at crags I had so far only dreamed about: Froggatt, Millstone, Burbage and Chee Dale in the Peak District, the less accessible slate quarries in Llanberis and further afield on mountain crags in the Lake District, the sea cliffs of Pembrokeshire, and Clogwyn Du'r Arddu – Cloggy – where a few years before I had camped in winter.

One warm evening, we walked up to Cloggy, a golden light reflected in the polished railway tracks, marsh grass glittered and shone, swaying in the breeze. Bivvying near the lake we drank a bottle of Bulgarian red before settling down to the sound of lapping water, the breeze blowing through the boulders keeping the midges away. Next morning we climbed the crag's great classics, *Troach*, *Silhouette*, *Curving Arête*, *Great Wall* and finally, in the crimson evening light, Joe Brown's classic *November*. Returning to our boulders at midnight we drank a second bottle of Bulgarian red and bullshitted about the climbs.

I led my first E5s with Adam that summer, a tenuous line of thin holds first climbed by John Redhead called *Poetry Pink* on the Rainbow Slab in the quarry above Llanberis and *Right Wall* on Dinas Cromlech. Now the memory of Fran explaining to me what a chop route was, and who had climbed *The Bells! The Bells!* wormed into my subconscious. So one day we visited the route's location, the North Stack Wall at Gogarth, on the very fringe of Anglesey's Holy Island, not to try *The Bells!*, but to look for a route that just scraped an E6 grade called *The Cad*.

Dew-glistening spiders' web hung from shrubs growing alongside the worn coastal path like a celebration. But arriving at North Stack's cliff-top, I felt a stab of disappointment at finding a mossy, lichenous wall. I lay on my stomach, head and shoulders over the edge of the cliff. Arms straight and palms pressed against the rock to support my upper body. A salty wind blasted directly up the crag, stinging my face. Flakes of rock crumbled under my hands and spun away in the wind.

I was desperate to find something resembling a route, something in the green swathe of lichen that looked climbable. I leant out further, Adam gripping my ankles to stop me joining the boulders below. The sea ran white-flecked-green along the length of the cliff. Gogarth is a bulwark against the swell of the Irish Sea. Seagulls wheel and scream. The sky is overcast, like a Turner painting. Didn't the guidebook promise *The Cad* to be the best wall climb in Wales?

I couldn't know that this wind-battered place, this haunt of seal and seagull, would get so deep into me and make my soul a part of its seascape.

And I hadn't a clue that the struggles and triumphs of the wall's two greatest creators, John Redhead and Andy Pollitt, would be burnt into my psyche until I became intimate with how they moved, how they thought. But that was for a life to come.

Disgusted and a little scared we ran away, vowing never to return to North Stack.

Instead, we walked over to Yellow Wall at South Stack in search of a classic climb called *The Moon*. Adam and I abseiled to the foot of the intimidating wall and stood on a large ridge of grass-covered rock pushing against the sea. We looked up, mystified.

We soon decided we had abseiled in the wrong place but could see, way above us, the final pitch of our planned climb – or that's what we thought the crazy overhanging crossword of grooves above us may have been.

Still uncertain, we decided the easiest way to escape this crazy wall of grooves and sand was going to be the way we'd spotted – no matter if it was a route or not. The yellow-orange rock was like nothing either of us had seen before; it was sand and clay and mud and pockets of talc and feta cheese and fins of quartz and dirt and spiders.

"Okay, I'll get us out."

By this time in our climbing partnership, I knew I was the bravest, or at least the one who would beat himself up if I didn't at least have a go. Asking Adam to climb a sand-filled corner would have been a waste of time and he was already looking a tad peaky at the prospect. We had no idea what climb the corner was, but it looked the easiest way up the wall. An hour or so later, wide-eyed, limbs wrecked, utterly shocked, covered in sand and dirt and nearly vomiting, I pulled from the top of the groove looking like a builder and feeling pleased to still be alive. Later we discovered the climb was called *The Sind*, a Joe Brown route graded E3, and if we needed any more evidence that Gogarth was not rock-climbing but some sort of punishment, this was it.

Never again.

Soon I was back in Leicestershire, working, existing, the summer cut short. It frustrated me, wasting days off work, travelling only for the day to be washed out with rain, sitting in a car and not training. So at the end of August, I gave up rock-climbing and focused on the coming winter season. I had already taken chunks of leave for Scotland and I knew that my experiences the previous winter meant my ability was going to see some major advances.

HONESTY

Earlier that week on Ben Nevis, after reaching the top of a fantastic icy cleft called *Vanishing Gully*, I had stood balancing on the snow crest of Tower Ridge. The wind blew fat flakes of snow around me as I looked through swirling cloud. In between the flurries, coming in and out of focus, was the imposing wall of the Orion Face dominating everything around it.

Feeling small and vulnerable, I stared across at Orion for a long time. I could see two specks slowly inching their way up. The climbers were dwarfed by the face, lost to the world of white, lost on a sheer 1,200-foot wall. I envied their position, their solitude – their escape. And I vowed to emulate them later in the week.

I took the decision so seriously because almost three winters had passed since I'd started winter climbing, and I was discovering why it is among the most frustrating pastimes known to mankind. I had finished a great summer of rock-climbing with Adam, and then, every day since the beginning of winter, I had craved to get to grips with Jimmy Marshall and Robin Smith's great classic – *The Orion Direct*.

The grandeur of the Orion Face draws anyone's eyes. In me, it caused pangs of longing. *Cold Climbs*, a coffee-table book full of images and stories of British winter climbs, had intravenously supplied me with an armchair-fix. It wasn't enough: so here I was, three years in, yet devoid of the route that would hopefully lead to bigger, greater, grander things across the Channel. But, the frustrating uncertainty of a Scottish winter, the drip, drip, drip of Highland water-torture, started long before I could even set foot on the boggy path that approaches the mountain.

After another day of bad weather I could stand it no more. My trip to Ben Nevis was almost over. This was my last opportunity of the winter to climb *The Orion Direct*. I couldn't let it slip from my grasp. How could I even contemplate the long drive south without this route in the bag?

After dragging myself from the warm hut into the dead night, driving through the Fort, racing along the golf course, slithering up the steep muddy bank, squelching through the bog and battling the moon-like surface of the wind-blown, rock-strewn plateau beneath the hut, I finally stopped alone in the dark to consider my position. Rivulets of sweat ran cold down my back. I cowered behind the stone walls of the hut, built in 1928 as a memorial to Charles Inglis Clark, who died of his wounds fighting in Mesopotamia in 1918. I began fighting with the wind to let me add more layers of fleece and Gore-Tex. Throughout the whole of this battle, fingers had to be warmed and re-warmed, arms had to be swung, toes curled.

An hour later I was beneath it, the huge Orion Face bursting steeply from its snow cone. A track zigzagged its way down the slope to finish at my feet. Thick steamy breaths billowed from my heaving chest. Snow that had fallen over previous days had hidden all trace of those who had climbed the face earlier in the week. Thus another plan turned to folly. I had hoped for an easy passage following the steps of others. Knowing others have gone before you eases the mind of the solo climber. Any intricate and

Playing up to the camera. A self-portrait from one of my many solo missions somewhere in Scotland.

complex route finding could be arrogantly dismissed. But the steps of those climbers I had watched from Tower Ridge were long gone. My sleep-deprived red-prickled eyes struggled to pick the line. I hoped the fresh layer of snow had had time to consolidate.

Stepping from the snow cone, I left behind me normal thoughts and feelings. The door opened. It opened to let me enter an ice-encrusted, white world of the vertical. Each kicked step I made was one of enlightenment. New. Clean. True. I had no harness, and no rope for escape. I had no thought of confrontation with aggressive inmates, or the ignorance of politicians – or the manifest unfairness of the world and the lives of the less fortunate.

One of the finest climbs in Scotland, with all the atmosphere of a major Alpine face. Start left of Zero Gully where a broad ledge leads to the foot of a prominent chimney line leading up towards The Basin. Climb the chimney for two long pitches.

Patches of ice were good and the occasional placement solid. These offered some respite from the steep and insecure climbing that appeared, shockingly, to be the norm. I hunted for pick-placements beneath the fresh layer of powder and for dribbles of ice in the corners. My front-points scrabbled on black rock when they broke through the fragile skin of ice stuck to it. But bridging across the chimney with my legs tensed gave my crampons purchase. Night finally lost its battle with the rising winter sun and the early morning, cloud-filtered-light showed my position. I savoured the situation of white space.

I could see occasional shallow steps where the chimney I now followed was at its steepest. Weaving from left-to-right across rib and buttress, I found cracked and rusty pitons, glimpses of the past driven into dirty, turf-encrusted cracks. Pieces of frayed and rotten tat threaded through the eyes of the odd blade or angle piton. The way above always looked difficult but once committed to a sequence of moves I found there was usually a hidden corner or a patch of solid snow. Like a speck in the centre of a giant hand, I crawled upwards, clinging to my newly discovered lifeline.

Route finding was the key – and eventually I reached The Basin, a large patch of snow clearly visible from far away. Plunging axe, arm, foot and thigh deep into fresh powder I crossed this, moving from left-to-right hundreds of feet above the snowfields at the foot of the face.

The hut was a little model far below. I could see the gusts of wind sending twisting clouds of snow into the air and lashing against the hut's grey walls. Miniature red gas cylinders lay – a vibrant heap behind the hut. The scene was one of desolation, of abandonment, as if after some horrible battle.

There was not a soul in sight. I imagined I could hear the blades of the wind-turbine fixed to the roof of the hut buzzing like an aircraft's propeller, threatening to rip from its fixings. Then the hut disappeared, momentarily lost to cloud sweeping down from Coire Leis.

Kicking a ledge big enough to stand on without the worry of over-balancing and toppling backwards, I took the guidebook from the pocket of my jacket.

Move up and right across snow to the foot of the second slab rib. Descend a little, move around the right side of the rib, then climb up to and across a steep icy wall on the right (crux).

I moved down a little, repeatedly plunging my leather boots into the soft snow until I stood beneath the steep slab. The only line of weakness was a thin corner-crack on its right. There appeared to be no footholds. This was definitely a steep icy wall but it looked harder than the grade suggested. I started to climb, my situation precarious, my nerves jangling. I balanced my front-points tentatively on small edges of rock. This was no good. I'd only just begun the slab but I couldn't commit to the moves. Feet scraping the rock, I reversed. I questioned my drive. Unable to accept failure without at least another go, I started to climb once more, but I could only manage a couple of moves more before reversing again. There had to be another way? Re-reading the description I started to wonder if I had descended and moved right far enough.

Hugging the base of the rock-rib, I eased around to the right-hand side that had been hidden from view. Relief. A steep, ice-blobbed wall joined a snow patch beneath the final tower. Climbing this wall, moving from the relative safety of a solid pick-placement through moments of danger, made me feel wholly alive – reminded me of what I imagined a life could be.

Since finding climbing I had already changed from a homemaker looking for comfort and stability to a migrating bird that leaves behind the known and flies to the new and challenging. People mostly like to know what's around the corner, the next day, the next week, month or year. We hatch and look from the comfort of the nest and we see space and a big sky and adventure but before you know what's happened you are surroun-ded by the familiar, back in your safe territory and scared to take flight for fear of the unknown.

Long moves from one good ledge onto a patch of névé, then onto a smear of ice, completely absorbed me. I seemed to be in a new, brighter reality. Occasionally tired from a difficult move, I found a place to relax, until I forced myself on to meet the next challenge. And at last the wall was climbed, and I moved easily to the foot of the final tower.

This looked down on me, dark and mean – and steeper than anything I'd encountered before on the face. Nestled just beneath the summit ridge, the snow and ice was less than below. The wall to the right of my position looked to be too steep. Leaning into the snow I consulted the book.

Follow left-trending snow-ice grooves to the snow slope beneath the final tower. This can either be climbed directly on steep ice or turned by following a groove and chimney line on the left to reach the plateau at the top of Northeast Buttress.

I climbed the snow slope front-pointing and stabbing the picks of both axes into the fresh skin, before stopping beneath the tower. Leaning back to study my options strained my neck. I tried to read the deep chimneys, runnels and corners for a possible exit. The face looked like a sculpted and furrowed desert plain with wind-blown snow snaking over its surface. Soft like flour, the powder clung to all it touched. The weakness I looked for was masked. The tower showed me a strong and impenetrable front. But I hoped this front was like that of some of the inmates from the prison. I hoped there was a way past it.

Yet search as I might, I couldn't decide the best way. The usual exit was hidden and having no rope would leave me stuck should the chimney turn out to be too difficult. Often when soloing, the described route is not always the easiest. Sometimes it is better to choose a more difficult but obvious line. At least you will know what is to come and can prepare mentally. This was one of those occasions.

Above me I could see a deep chimney, blocked by an overhanging chockstone, leading to a near-vertical open-book corner. I moved up, still undecided if this was the line I should take. A faint trail of steps leading into the bowels of the dark fault and disappearing above the overhang convinced me this must be right.

The walls closed around me. Steep. Suffocating. If this was life it would be easy to give in, decide I had done enough now to justify my existence. The weight on my shoulders became heavy. Leaning over me, blocking the way, a runnel of ice dribbled from above the large boulder blocking the chimney, thin and delicate. Wedging into the cramped cave beneath the boulder, I gained a purchase on the right wall. I heaved. Back-and-footing-bridging-pressing-straining-fighting I made progress until level with the top of the boulder. Although still in the confines of the chimney, the space and emptiness beneath was sickening.

'Come on, for Christ's sake. Concentrate on what is ahead not what is below.'

The voice in my head was screaming at my flagging arms and legs that everything was under control. Heaving myself up from a placement in the corner above the chockstone, scratching-scraping-sweating-gasping, wedged into a tight, dark corner, I knew there was now just one direction. Retreat was impossible.

Taking a breather on top of the boulder gave me the first opportunity to look ahead. A runnel of snow leading to the open-book corner had a slither of ice, thin and shallow, running like a trickle of dirty brook water. No good. I needed a river. Tufts of moss, green islands in the brook of ice, frozen and covered in a fine white mist of frost, grew as sporadic and weak clumps, clinging to existence in this bleak nowhere.

I could see steps leading to a spike beneath the corner. The sling draped around the spike had a new-shiny screwgate karabiner hanging from it. My boat had sprung a leak.

"BASTARDS!"

I couldn't believe it? The climber's footsteps had lured me onto this icy island, and then, having the necessary equipment for escape, sailed away into a shimmering sunset. If I couldn't climb the corner I would be marooned without a shore to shelter on.

Two, three, four moves into the corner, and I knew I was fully committed. The whole of the Orion Face dropped away beneath my insecure position. Waves of shimmering, turbulent ice ran over crest and fold, rib and corner, all the way down the face until pounding into the beach of snow hundreds of feet below. This was more than my mind could accept or wanted to acknowledge. Now the exposure and the effort of pushing myself was almost making me wretch. I knew I had made a mistake.

The walls either side of the corner were smooth with only the smallest of nicks on which to place my crampon front-points. It was like a small *Cenotaph Corner*, that soaring book-corner in the middle of Dinas Cromlech in the Llanberis Pass, but without the crack where the walls met. Unfortunately though, it was not vertical like *Cenotaph Corner*, if it had been I would have opted for the long wait for rescue, huddled at its base. As it was, its just off vertical angle tricked me into believing I could balance and rest. I longed for an opening in which to slide a pick and layback from, but there were none. The only purchase was from millimetre-thick pick placements in the tufts of frozen moss.

Inch, by slow, careful, tenuous inch, I made some progress. Time became irrelevant. Above, I aimed at small edges to stand on and thicker patches of moss in which I could gently stab my pick. Between these oases, I made insecure moves while all the time expecting my feet to shoot from the smooth wall. Reaching each small haven of safety offered some relief, a time to breathe, a time to reflect, to relieve the tension before studying the next section and working out a sequence.

I really did feel sick. A hand held my intestines and clenched. My head was in turmoil. Voices screamed. Time stood still.

My life depended on frozen moss.

Halfway, a ledge and a clump of moss deep enough for the whole blade of one axe offered security for a time. Although I needed the rest, the fear of becoming attached to my haven was too frightening, so I quickly decided to continue. The move to begin this second half was as difficult as any below, and I had made the mistake of looking down. Petrified, the whole process of psyching up and moving had to be endured again.

Trembling, I pushed the front-points of my left boot onto a sloping edge at hip height and hooked one tooth of my right tool into moss high up in the corner. Slowly, so slowly, weighting the left foot and laybacking from the right placement, straining, terrified, I lifted the right foot an inch... testing... foot and pick placements... they held. I moved up.

There was no time for contemplation now. I kept climbing in recurrent spasms of movement, like twitches of delirium. Finally the end was in reach. I pulled from the top of the corner relieved to be free, glad to be on my own. I would have scared anyone had they been nearby. With my thousand-mile stare I must have resembled myself after a fight in the Box.

A yell of release, a shout of life, a scream for the living.

Embarrassed, I turned right and began kicking a trail of footsteps to the summit of Ben Nevis.

TRACKS

Climbing had taken over my life completely by 1996. While at work, if I wasn't weight training, circuit training or running alongside the inmates, I would read about climbing and dream. I had exhausted most of the books written by the older generation, so I now started on more up-to-date accounts. A few names seemed popular, but three in particular struck a chord with me – Paul Pritchard, Mick Fowler and Ron Fawcett.

Each in his way was very different but all three appeared to have thrown everything they had into climbing and adventure. I especially liked the writing of Pritchard and the adventurous nature of his new climbs in North Wales and the Greater Ranges. Fowler appeared to be a sensible taxman who turned into an understated and extremely talented mountaineer for a few weeks of the year. Ron Fawcett, although of an older generation, was obviously the master of hard traditional rock-climbing.

I suppose the thing about them that really appealed to me was this – even though they all appeared to get so much out of the physical side of climbing, they appeared to love the whole package, the people, the places, the freedom, the liberation. Climbing was not a conventional sport, a place on the podium, something to do to lose weight instead of yoga or aerobics. These were people who needed to climb to survive. They were in it for the long haul and not just to be the best.

Leicester now had a new climbing wall called The Tower and I soon became a member. I still climbed at Slawston Bridge but The Tower gave me overhanging climbs that were dry. More important, it put me in contact with other climbers. I met Michael Tweedley and Iain McKenzie at The Tower, two students and both very keen climbers. Michael spoke with a strong London accent even though he had lived for a long time on the island of Mull in Scotland. It was funny when he put in the odd "wee" this and an "awright cock" that into the same sentence. Iain had so much enthusiasm he reminded me of Tigger from Winnie the Pooh.

Climbing at the wall with Michael and Iain brought me on as a climber. Both were obviously better than me, so I couldn't understand how neither had led climbs outdoors at a similar grade as me. When we climbed, as a three, outdoors, it was generally me on the sharp end. Having more experience now, it's easy to see how important the psychological element of climbing is and it's that aspect of the activity that compelled me to lead some of the bolder climbs.

Now I realise this attitude has been with me for most of my life, but it was only through climbing I began to understand that part of me needs to take challenges head on. It was this attitude that as a child resulted in me spending a great deal of time in the local hospital's A&E – and in Dad driving, "by accident," he said, over my pushbike leaving me without one for most of my childhood. Dad refused to buy me another after social workers turned up making enquiries about why I had so many accidents.

Once again I took time off through the summer and went rock-climbing, mainly with Michael but sometimes with Michael and Iain together. We had some hairy times and I took some mighty falls. They both studied at Leicester University and sometimes couldn't get out of lectures, so I would drive to The Roaches by myself and boulder. Or, using new-found skills, set up a top-rope to work climbs before soloing them: *Thin Air*, *Entropy's Jaw*, *Track of the Cat*, *Ascent of Man*, *Ascent of Woman*, *Willow Farm* and my first E6, *Piece of Mind*, were all climbed this way.

If I wanted a less scary day or wanted to climb a lot of rock, I started by walking to a buttress called Far Skyline with a book and a small piece of mat. Here I bouldered, climbing short problems I could safely jump off. The gritstone was coarse Herringbone waves of crisp ancient rock imprisoning the odd pebble. The grass landing was flat and the sun took the edge off the chilly breeze. Grouse strutted among the purple heather, chuckling and dancing with fat Christmas pudding bodies.

It was peaceful sat up there but occasionally a lone walker or a small group passed. They could see me sitting there reading my book between problems but they continued to talk as if I wasn't there, or else it didn't matter that I overheard. Most of the conversations were of work and home, children, holidays, plans for the following weekend, stresses and strains, problems and arguments with the boss. It made me wonder why in such a beautiful, peaceful place people needed to talk continuously of routine, of problems. Why did people continue organising and planning? Why couldn't they just engage with the open country and the space?

A few days after working and then soloing *Track of the Cat* on the Hard Very Far Skyline buttress, a steep undercut slab hidden beneath the path surrounded by spindly larch trees like an audience, I returned with Michael to climb *Nature Trail*, done first by Simon Nadin, a brilliant local who climbed many of the crag's best hard routes. After that, and with lots of daylight left, I soloed *Track of the Cat* for the second time that week. Michael watched me and as I sat on top looking down, he began to follow. Michael knew I had worked the climb, but watching the ease with which I moved must have convinced himself that it was easy. And now, here he was, quite a way from the ground, nearing the top of the buttress.

I sat fascinated knowing how Michael, certainly a better climber than me, but not very good at coping with being on lead, let alone climbing unroped, would get on. He made another move up, and another, but now, only a couple of moves from the top of the buttress, about forty feet above the ground and higher than the top of the trees, he faced a move which had taken me a few goes on a rope earlier in the week.

The secret was to take a hold to his left but with his right hand. This balanced the body enough to allow a step up. He would then be able to reach a good hold near the top with his free left hand. I looked into Michael's face, which was now sweating and flushed. His prematurely thinning hair revealed his large forehead, which was now deeply furrowed. I could see him fighting with thoughts of impending failure. I half-expected to see steam billowing from his ears.

"Michael. Listen… LISTEN… grab that hold with your right hand, then step up using the outside edge of your right foot. DO NOT grab that hold with the left hand."

Michael's eyes were glazed and squeezed into the centre of his face. He looked like a constipated baby sucking a sherbet pip.

"MICHAEL! DO NOT GRAB THE HOLD WITH YOUR LEFT HAND."

Left: Me soloing *Track of the Cat* (E5) on the Hard Very Far Skyline buttress at The Roaches, Staffordshire, for the second time in a week. *Photo: Michael Tweedley* *Right:* Michael Tweedley soloing *Track of the Cat* just before he decided to surf off into the distance and dive for the trees. *"Do not grab the hold with your left hand Michael. Nooooo!"*

It was no good. Reaching up, he grabbed the crucial hold with his left hand.

"No!" Immediately Michael's body, now out of balance, swung away from the rock like a barn door. He twisted and peeled from the rock and then was falling. The slab is almost vertical and Michael skidded down it, his screwed-up baby face becoming smaller and smaller the further he fell, except for his eyes, which grew wider. Nearly at the overlap, skidding and falling, he kicked at the rock, which spun his body so he faced outwards. Totally desparate, he dived for a tree, hitting the top of a thin larch, he wrapped his arms around the trunk and carried on down – crashing, snapping, crashing, snapping – before he hit the ground with a loud thud.

"Michael! Michael, speak to me…"

But Michael lay completely still, saying nothing. I ran and skidded down the steep slope at the side of the buttress and was soon beside Michael's prone form.

"Michael! MICHAEL!"

Nothing. Fearing the worse, I knelt over him preparing to resuscitate him, but not really wanting to start. Kissing Michael was not on the top of my list of things to do. I shook his shoulders instead.

"Michael."

Then without any sound or warning, one eye cracked opened and a grin spread across his face.

"Ha, ha! Got you!"

At the last minute one weekend, I drove to the Llanberis Pass with Michael and dossed behind the wall near the Cromlech Boulders. In the morning, after a short sleep, we walked up the steep hillside to Dinas Cromlech and after a warm-up I led *Lord of the Flies*, a famous Ron Fawcett E6. The following day, I climbed *King Wad*, a Paul Pritchard E6 on Scimitar Ridge, I thought I was invincible.

Earlier that summer I had taken a big wall climbing course run by Plas y Brenin. I wanted to learn the skills that would help me climb some of the big walls I had stared at open-mouthed while in Yosemite. One of the instructors on the course was called Owain Jones and afterwards we remained friends and planned to go to Yosemite together. Unfortunately the trip didn't happen, but Owain suggested we should climb together in the Alps.

To begin my Alpine climbing with someone who had already climbed the Walker Spur on the Grandes Jorasses and the Central Pillar of Frêney on Mont Blanc was too good an opportunity to miss.

Owain and I stood in the middle of the Leschaux Icefall, tiny flecks on a giant sheet of ice-sandpaper, lost among the frozen grains towering above us. This was the first time I had stood beneath the North Face of the Grandes Jorasses, and it was everything I had envisaged. I was looking up at a cold monolith of stark beauty, which seemed to challenge me. "Do you think you're hard? I'll show you hard." Ice streaks, runnels, ribs, loose stones and pale rock-scars – my future was uncertain, an empty echo from the vast walls.

Lifting my rucksack from the snow, I threw it across the mouth of the crevasse in front of me and stood in awe of the man who caught it on the opposite side. My torch beam pierced the dark, reflecting off the snow-crystals and his slight figure. His features were like a piece of furniture, angular and polished beneath his crop of sandy hair. Determination and confidence billowed from him like the condensation on his breath.

Valery Babanov, my age but already a mountaineering star, had set off before us, hoping to solo a hard, modern line, the Colton-MacIntyre. Owain and I hoped to climb the Croz Spur, the original route up this inspiring north face, but neither Babanov or Jones and I will make it through the complicated icefall.

Two days later Jones and I returned, following the wavering trail of Jamie Fisher and Jules Cartwright's footprints. I had talked them into going for the same route after our first unsuccessful attempt. Owain and I had met Jules and Jamie on the sloping campsite in Argentière, run by Bernard Ravanel of the famous Chamonix family. This was my second time to the Alps but my first with a partner and we were having a good trip. I had climbed my first proper Alpine routes, including the Swiss Route on Les Courtes with a full traverse of the ridge to the east before dropping down onto the glacier beneath the Triolet and the North Spur of the Aiguille du Chardonnet.

Jones and I were in the campsite planning our next climb, the Croz Spur, when two bedraggled climbers turned up. Cartwright and Fisher had just returned from the North Face of the Eiger having sat beneath the face, in the rain, for three days before giving up. They laughed about their failure. Cartwright, tall and gangly, looked and moved like Shaggy from Scooby Doo. Fisher, with his red hair and freckles, reminded me of a sweet innocent child who, when no one was watching, would swing cats by their tails and pull legs from spiders. They argued and took the piss out of each other, and cracked opened a blindness-inducing five-litre plastic demijohn of the cheapest red wine available. I was in awe of their tenacity and courage, and their experience for two so young, but in the morning, when I saw the empty demijohn, I was most in awe of their drinking prowess. Bernard Ravanel arrived and started shouting. Jules had done a runner the previous summer and Bernard remembered. But eventually they hit on a compromise and moved their tent in front of the site office.

Climbing through the night on the Croz, the stars in the black night lost their edge as the sky paled to slate grey and eventually the morning's murky-river brown, revealing a thousand innocent mountains locked together in a chain. I belayed and shivered. Looking across the face, I watch a solitary dot lost in an arena so gigantic it seemed an optical illusion. The dot was abseiling. Babanov had once again hit an impasse in his quest for the Colton-Macintyre. Once again I struggled to comprehend the Russian's tenacity, or that one person could have so much drive and confidence. I sat belaying, watching and shivering.

"Okay! Safe." Owain above me was attached to solid granite. Time to move.

Two days later we walked the narrow road to Courmayeur having successfully climbed the Croz. In the hedgerows, small birds jumped from branch to branch, their call piercing my weary brain. The pure water of a tumbling mountain stream sparkled in in the sunlight. I scooped handfuls, guzzling and guzzling again and again, guzzling my surroundings too and the contented feeling of weariness after a battle well fought. A small, three-wheel vehicle trundled towards us, a mongrel of motorbike pick-up truck. Two creased and suntanned workmen sat in the front. They wore fedoras and their boiler suits were impossibly smart, like they were dressed for a party. When they saw us, they stopped, looked at us more closely and then pointed toward the Jorasses. Owain and I nodded in unison and with that they laughed and pointed at the back of the truck. Throwing our rucksacks into the truck we climbed aboard and shoved their gardening tools to the side. Then the truck wobbled into gear and we were away, laughing and buzzing all the way to Courmayeur.

THE WORM

Returning to the prison after a climbing trip was always a shock. One moment my world was crisp mountain air, skin-of-the-teeth adventure and laidback friends, the next it was walls and gates and locks – and cynicism, hate, depression and a profound lack of motivation. A few of the inmates, particularly the group I regularly trained with, knew I climbed and asked me about what I had been doing. I told them tales and they loved them, telling me I was crazy or brave. But most didn't care.

Everything at work, like life, ticked along, much the same as it would for some people until they retired. The new senior officer was keen to kick the PE department into the twentieth century, but he didn't have much influence as the principal officer, with years in the job, was counting down the days to retirement. All of the basic grade PE officers loved training and doing their own thing, including me, and we didn't want change. The inmates, who could get as much gym as possible as long as they were not supposed to be anywhere else, were also content.

The amount of physical training I did took on epic proportions. Most days I would train alongside the inmates, twice in the morning, an aerobics class or a running class followed immediately by a forty five minute circuit. At dinner time I would climb at Slawston Bridge, or run along the canal near the prison or train with the staff, generally doing a circuit or aerobics. In the afternoon I would weight-train by myself alongside the inmates for an hour and a half.

Sometimes I would cycle the nine miles to work and train as normal before cycling home in the evening. The local cycling club used a stretch of road for time trials. Always competitive, if I saw a Lycra-clad low-profile cyclist in the distance pedaling a sleek carbon bike, I'd attempt to catch them. The shock in their faces as a punter dressed in trainers and tracksuit carrying a rucksack flew past was worth the meltdown I always experienced in the final two miles before my village.

I was totally addicted to training. It passed the time, gave me credibility with the inmates and made me feel good about myself. It also gave me chronic overuse injuries in my Achilles, knees, lower back and most of all my elbows. I popped Voltarol like Smarties, and when the Votarol failed I arranged appointments with a specialist and had cortisone injections.

I returned from Slawston Bridge one afternoon intent on a weighted pull-up session, which involved sets of pull-ups of a different style – full chins, half chins, lock-offs, lowers, half locks – all with extra weight strapped to my waist. In between each set I completed one hundred sit-ups. I would always ask the inmates if they wanted to join me, but only Gary was daft enough.

It was a great laugh for me and the other inmates when Gary moaned and screamed and begged to stop and then, after I bullied him, he would go on even longer until he turned paler than his already pasty white. All the time I worked in the gym at Gartree, Gary was the only inmate who ever joined me in these sessions and he didn't care if he looked a fool. He just enjoyed the training and the banter and the camaraderie – and so did I.

One afternoon, the gym was packed. At least thirty inmates were pumping iron, working themselves into sweaty oblivion. Condensation ran down the reinforced windows, windows that were too high to look through. The air was pungent and oppressive. Our excellent sound system was turned up and the walls vibrated to the heavy bass line of The Prodigy's *Smack My Bitch Up*. Weights crashed, biceps curled, pumped up with blood and decorated with elaborate tattoos. The inmates in their small prison vests soaked with sweat would shout encouragement at each other.

"Go on! Go ON! Yes, yes, yes! You can do it, push, one more, one more."

The speakers boomed, weights crashed, cables creaked, sweat ran and the walls shook. Then the gym door opened, and the number one governor, the boss of the entire prison, took a grey-suited step into the gym. The sweaty, smack-my-bitch-up-high-intensity-fervour reached a crescendo as he stood there, the thick sweaty mist settling on the wool of his tailored suit, the bass vibrating through him. Then he turned, stepped out, locked the door and walked away.

I continued with my chins but ten minutes later the principal officer came down the stairs to tell me the governor had rung him with the order that he never wanted to hear music like that played again.

Throughout that winter, I continued my Scottish soloing mission, climbing many more hard classics, sometimes linking up to five routes in a day on Ben Nevis. I made friends with new climbers, and I began sharing adventures with some of them. My life became compartmented. I had climbing friends and I had prison. I had time off to climb and I had prison. There was no crossover. It made for lonely times when I was in Leicestershire.

I hadn't been in a relationship for some time. Earlier liaisons hadn't worked out and I preferred to keep my life uncluttered and simple. Things always appeared to turn complicated, and the fallout left me feeling sad and disappointed – and a failure. A girl from my school days, with whom I was besotted, suddenly got in touch and came to visit. But after the weekend I drove her back to Cheadle realising I had moved on and she hadn't; we were now so very different from the teenagers we had once been.

Increasingly I questioned the pressure I felt to conform, to fit in with the aspirations of those around me. Of course, this was nothing like the pressure that many others face. In comparison my life was easy, especially when compared to many of those living in the developing world. But I couldn't accept what had been doled out to me. I should have felt lucky to have what I had. I actually did feel lucky and privileged even though I was unhappy for a lot of time. That feeling of being like Oliver and asking for more when others in the world had so little made me feel guilty.

Jules Cartwright and a big bag full of metal on Meru Shark's Fin, India. *"I do not believe in any god, but unable to tear my eyes from the worn rope, I did pray."*

I have always had these feelings. When I was growing up, aged around nine or ten, money was short and I remember Dad rifling through bills and complaining or Mum being concerned and upset. I felt like a burden and asked Mum if there was anything I could do to help the situation or if she wished that she hadn't had children. I hated school but I think being less of a burden on my parents was as much a reason for leaving home and starting work at sixteen as anything.

I became fiercely independent, not afraid to be classed as different because I was unattached. I didn't sit down one night and decide relationships wouldn't happen, I just didn't actively seek them. If a woman showed an interest, she needed to fit completely into my idea of what was right or what was going to work so both parties were happy. I don't mean she needed to be perfect or stunning looking and I wasn't looking for a lifelong partner with every conversation, but I had witnessed so many relationships fail because the people involved appeared to rush in for fear of being on their own and not because they were right for one another.

Knowing what is best and works for me but also what is best and works for the woman involved had to be a more considerate way? It wasn't worth the turmoil and the feeling of being a failure as another relationship imploded and both of us were left feeling like we'd been shipwrecked. I didn't mind being on my own. Dealing with the everyday stresses, which came from working in a prison, took a heavy toll. Being alone in the evenings was the best way to recover.

While climbing with Owain Jones in the Alps, we had discussed going on an expedition and eventually decided on India the following September, more specifically the Gangotri Region and the Shark's Fin on Meru, one of the most holy – and beautiful – mountains in the Himalaya. Determined to make the most of my rock-climbing before losing fitness on expedition, I continued to train hard through the winter and in the spring emerged fitter than I had ever been.

In the slate quarries above Llanberis, the sun caught the crisp, square-hewn edges of the Colossus Wall. Shadows sliced across the sloe-coloured rock and streaks of water sliced the shadows. Michael Tweedley laid his hand on the rock; it was warm and glittering in the sunlight. Confident after several hard routes the day before on Colossus Wall, I suggested going back there, just around the corner from Colossus, to climb *Cystitis by Proxy*, another John Redhead route with a very technical but well-protected crux.

"Why am I still falling?" I thought, after slipping from the hard move near the top of the slab. I'd clipped the bolt right by it, so shouldn't have gone anywhere. Now, facing out and surfing a wave of velvet slate with my knees, I looked down to the base of the slab rushing towards me. Michael had been sat a little way out from the slab and was now waterskiing toward the rock, with his hands on the taut rope in front of him.

I hit the thick ripple in the Rainbow Slab that gives this cliff its name some thirty feet below the bolt. My right knee took the full impact, hitting a gargoyle of rock poking proud from its ebony sheen. Stars exploded and the pain was intense, but after a few minutes I pulled back up the rope to the bolt and finished the route.

Belaying Michael as he followed me, I knew something was wrong. Everytime I attempted to straighten my leg, it went into spasm and locked. Michael reached me and I told him we needed to leave. Walking back from the quarries was uncomfortable, especially carrying a rucksack full of gear and after spending the evening at the campsite icing my leg with two bags of frozen peas, which had no impact on the swelling, Michael drove us back to Leicester.

A week later, I had finally reduced the swelling and was climbing again indoors. I had seen my physiotherapist and considering everything I was able to do, she thought that in a few days all would be well. Then again, having private health insurance, I booked an appointment for an X-ray just in case.

Mike Allen was a big man with a head of tight curls and a boisterous manner. He was also one of the leading and most knowledgeable surgeons in the country when it came to sports injuries, working closely with the top rugby union club Leicester Tigers. After seeing Mike regularly with various ailments, particularly my overworked elbows, we knew each other well. But this time he really couldn't believe what he was hearing.

"You've been doing what?"

He held the X-ray of my right kneecap to the light. The patella was split neatly in half.

"You did this when?"

He shook his head repeatedly, tight curls bouncing, and then laughed. Putting a bearish arm around my shoulders, he marched through the hospital with me hopping behind and introduced me to a group of nurses.

"Meet the madman. He's crazy. He's got a broken kneecap and he's been climbing on it. Full leg plaster for seven weeks."

I drove home from the hospital very carefully, half-sitting, half-standing. Braking wasn't easy with a straight leg. Six weeks later, after convincing Mike the kneecap would be mended so wouldn't need the extra week, freshly cut free from the plaster, the kneecap had knitted together well. While still off sick a few weeks later, I made my ascent of *Tess of the D'Urbervilles* on Dinas Cromlech where the injury this time happened to someone else – and I found myself staring down at Michael, desperate for his attention as the victim bled from an arm wound on the ground beside him.

Only weeks after coming out of plaster I was packing for Meru. Mum and Dad took me to Heathrow to meet the other climbers, my friends from the Alps: Jamie Fisher, Jules Cartwright and Owain Jones. This would be my first expedition, and my first time in Asia. Stepping from the airport, Delhi's poverty was obvious and immediate.

Landing late at night in the stagnant heat, and the stench of humanity was everywhere. Like the inside of a prison on a summer night, I sensed bodies all around me. A taxi took us to the hotel. We rattled along rutted roads. A thin man wearing a loincloth straddled an elephant. People were lying on the pavement, on stretched sisal hammocks, beneath straw shacks, on top of buildings, even on islands in the middle of the road.

Jamie and Jules had both been to India before and appeared relaxed, emanating confidence. Perhaps their privileged upbringing prepared them for this kind of thing? Owen, from a good middle-class background, looked a little uncomfortable – whereas I was struggling. We reached the hotel and ran for the air conditioning.

Delhi raised emotions in me that I hadn't known existed. It turned my black and white into shades of orange and red and green. My black and white upbringing was suddenly and finally finished with. The day after we arrived, we walked the streets. Crippled beggars, legs pointing at odd angles, dragged themselves through the dust. The lucky ones had a small cart, just like the kind I would fill with wooden blocks as a child. Instead of giving them a present at birth, their parents had mutilated them to give them a job for life. Mothers carried milk bottles for starving babies and waved them under my nose. Brown-eyed children, skinny and dirty, tugged at my trouser leg, held my fingers, fingers that crimped rock and dipped in chalk. Inequality hit me hard. All I could do was pull my fingers away and head to the mountains.

On Meru Central we 'struggled', struggled with the heavy snowfall, the altitude, the exposure and our lack of experience. The rack was too big and our objective too difficult, 6,500 metres of unclimbed, uncompromising vertiginous granite. An avalanche-prone slope at its base led to a mixed ridge of geometrical blocks plated together like armadillo armour. Touch one, I felt, and they'd all be off.

The ridge itself was a worm, which curved right and then left. A kink in the worm's body, as though someone had stuck it with a pin and it had writhed, gave steep and overhanging climbing. Above that, the vast shield of rock was like a crow looking for a meal, so the worm veered left to escape. We knew this worm of loose ancient rock was different to anything we had ever seen or climbed before, and we also knew, like the worm, that we were scared. The shield of rock was the fin itself, a smooth and overhanging monolith four hundred metres high.

The Himalayan snow was clean and white, yet in my mind it plastered the rough granite like shit smeared on cell walls, as though I was locked inside with someone on 'dirty protest' in the Block, all that shit pushed into their ears, eyes, and hair. I felt anxious and trapped with little experience of how to deal with all the intensity going on around me.

Huddled all night, wrapped in a Gore-Tex bivvy bag at 5,500 metres on a crest of snow, the wind buffeted me towards the void dropping sickeningly on each side. The bag's fabric pushed into my face, damp and claustrophobic, like the gloom of the Block, like life's expectations. Seven years after I had worked there, the expedition brought back deep memories and dark times.

The rime-encrusted granite rock-wall above wore me down. It whispered to me, daring me into the unknown and my character would not let me back down from the challenge. There was no escape, no way around the confrontation. The wall was like a murderer holding out his meal tray, waiting for more food at the hot plate. Wooden fingers fumbling to tie the laces of frozen boots were like the delaying tactics before opening a cell door, with an unavoidable confrontation waiting for me on the other side. The ice-coated metal hardware was racked, and the frozen-solid ropes uncoiled.

Fisher, Cartwright and I reached a high-point four hundred metres below the summit. It doesn't sound far, but the summit may as well have been in outer space. The Shark's Fin, the mountain's final rampart of overhanging granite, has only recently been climbed, even though over twenty teams have tried in the last twenty five years. Our naivety didn't allow us, when we looked from the valley, to run away. We were proud and pushy and just like dishing out chips in the prison, I couldn't live with myself if I bowed to intimidation. A smack in the mouth was better than the self-loathing that would come from knowing I'd been a coward.

I jumared ropes for the first and nearly the last time on the Shark's Fin. We had fixed our four climbing ropes on the first attempt, and then run away when the regular afternoon snow began falling in the morning. We left the ropes in place for a return match. All four were stretchy rather than static lines and for a week, between the first abortive attempt and our second go, they swung in the wind, being chafed like a scab on a kneecap.

Jumaring with a 25kg sack on top of my 70kg bodyweight, and watching ropes just 8mm thick repeatedly stretching across a sharp edge far above my head left me terrified. Inexperience meant it hadn't occurred to us to fix the ropes tight, so the stretch was taken out of them, or duct-taping them wherever they ran over sharp edges. Thoughts of John Harlin falling from the Eiger when his fixed rope broke grated in my head. Every time I pulled up, images of chafed sheaths and long wriggling worms of pale rope-core knotted my intestines. I do not believe in any god, but unable to tear my eyes from the worn rope, I did pray.

Jones had opted to remain in the valley on our second attempt, considering the approach slopes too dangerous. Cartwright broke a crampon on the first day above the bivvy. He swore and yelled but continued. A second breakage slowed him further, but still we continued as a team of three. Cartwright's drive refused to allow him to accept the obvious and our blind faith in Cartwright refused to allow him to leave.

A testing traverse on ice at 6,100 metres on the fourth day was the deciding factor. Cartwright was jumaring sideways with no crampons on near vertical ice when an anchor pulled. He fought for a second, but then was off. Fixed to the rope by his two jumar clamps and nothing else, he swung like the pendulum of an old clock. As he smashed into granite thirty metres below, we heard the sickening smack of a body hitting rock. It was time to turn and run. Cartwright's leg was bleeding and badly injured. We were all mentally exhausted.

Reaching the base of the climb, two days later, nervous energy poured from us in gasps of laughter and relief. Just like after a battle in a cell, with the inmate now safely trussed up in a body-belt, face down and naked. The grappling and grasping, the smashing into walls, sliding in shit, spit and snot was over. But no matter how terrifying some of the situations on the mountain were, climbing was never as horrific as the worst times in prison. Facing the mountain's honest hardships always left me feeling cleansed.

After returning to prison from a long climbing trip, I needed to make up time with long stretches of work without any extended periods away. The constant grind from the inmates wore me down.

"No you can't leave the gym… No you can't come into the gym… Finish off and tidy your weights."

Some of the inmates had the option of leaving the workshop but instead of going on exercise, they would take the option of coming to the gym instead, which was allowed. Yet this was just a ruse to get out of workshop and after ten minutes they wanted to leave and go back to the wing. Phil was one of the more easily intimidated PE officers and would allow this, but I wouldn't. One day I thought I was going to get beaten up by a large ex-doorman from Leicester who was serving a life sentence for killing someone outside a nightclub. The ex-doorman loved to intimidate, but I refused to allow him out of the gym even though he towered over me, yelling only inches from my face.

The weekends at the prison were a solo affair; the PE officer on duty worked on his own with up to thirty inmates. I hated football and hated refereeing even more. Once a week on Saturday morning there was a game of football, which took place outside in front of half the prison population who were on exercise. It was a traumatic experience. I ran around the pitch refereeing but my mind would wander. Regularly I would come out of a reverie involving some climbing sequence, or imagining myself on a mountain summit, to see half the prison's inmates shouting at me, and the two teams screaming for a decision. Fights were de rigueur, usually between two inmates, although sometimes both teams weighed in. Inmates watching on the touchline yelled abuse and laughed. It might have brightened up their dull lives, but Saturday football gave me sleepless nights.

Arguing and being assertive all of the time is difficult if you are not naturally that way inclined. After a while it wears you down. I decided I had to leave. I desperately wanted to climb, but I loved my house and the village and I liked my privacy. Losing these things scared me.

One afternoon I spoke to an officer who had been given a sabbatical for several months to visit prisons in Australia and Canada. On his return to the prison service he wrote a report. The sabbatical idea appeared the perfect solution so I wrote an application to the governor. It was turned down. Unperturbed, I decided if I couldn't get the time off I would sell my house and quit and live on savings until they ran out. Then the housing market crashed and I couldn't get the price I had paid for my house seven years earlier. I felt trapped and disillusioned.

Returning from India with no leave left, I worked extra time, up to thirteen days in a row, which meant I could bank hours. Prison officers were not paid overtime but if I banked enough of these extra hours they could be redeemed as days off. I had arranged with Jules Cartwright to go to Scotland and this first trip after Meru was costing me two days of time off in lieu, known by the appropriate acronym TOIL, which gave me a whole week off work.

The day before I had arranged to meet Cartwright and drive north, I was at The Tower in Leicester climbing a route when someone stuck his head out of the office to say I had a call. It was Jules.

"The weather in Scotland's looking rubbish. I'll pick you up in a few hours and we'll drive to Chamonix. The Colton-MacIntyre on the Grandes Jorasses is in."

TOGETHER

Snow caught on wind-traced contours in the glacial blue ice before settling in crescent hollows in the lee of large granite boulders around us.
Cartwright, slightly bowed, was up front. There was no one else on the
Mer de Glace. In 1998, winter Alpinism on the harder mountains and more
difficult climbs remained the realm of the experienced. It was almost
unknown for Brits of our standing to entertain climbing one of the classic
north faces in winter, but here we were, stooped against the wind, heading
toward the mountain. Not much more than twenty four hours before
I had been locked away.

Jules, living in Sheffield and dossing free of charge at his sister's place,
had heard about successful ascents of the Colton-MacIntyre by British
Alpinists Al Powell, Rich Cross and the Benson twins, Pete and Andy.
Powell had forgotten his Gore-Tex jacket, so he completed the climb
wearing a poncho fashioned from a blanket swiped from the Leschaux Hut
at the foot of the climb, looking like Clint Eastwood in a spaghetti western.

Even though I had not yet met him, Powell was, in my mind, off the wall
– talented and tough. I heard all kinds of stories about him, the best being
the night he chased a burglar down the streets of Leeds brandishing an ice
axe. Powell was also a vegan and hunt saboteur who had won the elite class
in international fell races.

Conditions had deteriorated by the time Cartwright and I reached
Chamonix. We asked the lady in the Bureau des Guides about conditions
on the approach. She was dismissive.

"It iz winteur, you need skeez. The Grandes Jorasses are very dangereuses.
You do not climb in winteur."

I lost patience and left, but Jules, normally fiery and opinionated, took it
in his stride, thanked her, and joined me outside the building.

"Right then, let's go and find somewhere to pack our rucksacks. We have
to go today, the weather doesn't look so good in two days' time."

In the winter of 1972 the goulotte on the North Face of the Grandes
Jorasses that later became known as the Colton-MacIntyre was attempted

by Chris Bonington and a strong team that included Dougal Haston. An aircraft flew the climbers and a cache of equipment and supplies onto the Leschaux glacier, where, after seventeen bivouacs and using fixed ropes, they were still a long way from the ridge. A few years later, when Nick Colton and Alex MacIntyre climbed the route, they did it in summer and climbed it Alpine style, carrying everything they needed with them.

Attitudes had changed and with them the understanding of what is possible. We would be climbing in the same Alpine style, only in winter. Yet as we crunched across the rippled ice, I felt small and insignificant, surrounded by ancient mountains, exposed and vulnerable. I also felt privileged and a long way from prison and the traps of home.

We left the hut at three in the morning and ploughed waist-deep snow. This was the third time I had done this approach and it still shocked me how far it was from the hut to the foot of the climb. There was no one apart from the mountain and us with our dreams. Cartwright climbed the overhanging ice-wall guarding the start of the route and then we continued, keeping the rope tight between us. It was now light and the cold austerity of this place was everything I had hoped for while watching Nick Banks giving his lecture at Plas y Brenin six years before – no bullshit, no lies, just emptiness.

We climbed all day, swinging the lead, until just below a steepening in the ice that should have been the crux a third of the way up the face – only the ice wasn't there. We'd have to find another way. It would be dark soon and instead of continuing and being caught out, we stopped to bivouac, even though there was nowhere to sit. After cutting a small step, we emptied our rucksacks, attached them to an ice screw and stood in them. The next few hours were not a pleasant prospect.

Snow started to fall the next day but we continued. I swung into an overhanging groove to the right of where the ice pitch should have been and began to climb using axe picks in cracks and gloved finger tips on rock. I still wore my rucksack, but although the weight of it pulled me backwards, I continued and after what seemed like hours, reached a ledge and belayed. I was knackered but happy.

The rock was overhanging, and I had been so engrossed in the tech-nicalities of my dark corner I hadn't noticed the snow. Belaying, I looked out into the space dropping away beneath my feet down to the ice sheet at the foot of the face. Rivers of white were flowing down it and a maelstrom of fat flakes obscured everything.

"This is shit, what d'ya reckon?" Jules said when he reached me. "Shall we bail?"

I was suddenly in my circuit class, head filled with The Prodigy, sweat and iron.

"Let's keep going."

Jules led us out of the overhanging corner and belayed. I followed and we stood side-by-side on a small tabletop of rock. Snowflakes drove into us, pushed on by the strong wind – the thin runnel of ice I now had to climb was a moving, living thing, writhing and white.

A quick trip away from life inside. Jules Cartwright running away from the upper icefield of the Colton-MacIntyre route on the North Face of the Grandes Jorasses, France, during a storm – our first taste of winter Alpinism. We should have been climbing in Scotland, but the conditions were rubbish.

"We could bivvy here," Jules said, "see what the weather is doing tomorrow?"

"Let's keep going."

I set off into the flow, unable to see hands or feet, but the ice was better than anything below. Swinging, kicking, pounded by snow, I saw piss flowing under a cell door into the corridor at Gartree. Forcing myself on, I felt trepidation, excitement – fear. The afternoon light and the solitude were like patrolling the 40-watt dimness of Gartree. My imagination ran riot, the smell of sweat and wasted lives filled my nostrils. Maybe witnessing ruin and pain was what fuelled my drive, kept me going.

Kicking, swinging, snow thundered down the runnel. It felt as intimidating as Charlie Bronson. I swung my axe. Crash. Ice splintered, falling into the white. My lungs sucked in powder. Crash, another placement. Crash. I saw my stave breaking bone. Crash. One hit is self-defence, the second is assault.

Stalking the landing that New Year's Eve, I was convinced Charlie Bronson, all muscle and moustache, would break through steel. I held my stave aloft ready to strike. Crash, kick, kick. Ice. A skull. Show no fear, fear is weakness. Crash.

"So you think you're hard?"

The upper icefield, two thirds of the way up the face, was like a scene from *Aliens*. The walls, floor and ceiling moved with monsters. What were we doing here in these conditions?

But wasn't this everything I had desired?

Jules, up ahead, hunted for something solid and eventually found a collection of anchors that would hold the two of us. Hardly having had the opportunity to eat or drink since leaving the hut the day before, we both needed something, but the first night standing in rucksacks was luxury compared to this. Desperate as we were, we couldn't even light the stove.

I chipped a small foot-ledge into the ice and after about an hour of clipping everything to anchors, I pulled my sleeping bag and bivvy bag from the rucksack, immediately they became covered in snow. Then I started the exhausting process of removing crampons and getting into my sleeping bag inside the bivvy bag. Cartwright didn't even bother taking off his crampons.

"It's my mum's sleeping bag."

Snow filled and covered everything. The dark concealed the horror from view, but the sound could not be tamed. Every twenty or thirty minutes the rumble of an avalanche pouring down the mountain made me cower. I tried to pull the sleeping bag up around my shoulders but there was no chance of that. Fortunately I had a big duvet jacket Mum and Dad had bought me for Christmas and birthday a few weeks before.

The bivvy bag pulled over my head stopped most of the snow but I couldn't close it because of the ropes running from my waist to the anchors. I dreaded the hiss of powder pouring through the gap. Legs became numb, the blood cut off from hanging in my harness. Every twenty minutes I had to change position. Hanging, turning, I went through the night expecting to be picked up and thrown down the face.

Time passed, but at no time did I wonder why I was there. At no time did I think never again. This is what I had wanted, although I hadn't perhaps wanted quite this much. I changed position, face left, changed position, face into the slope, head resting against the ice, changed position, face right. If the snow continued there was a possibility we could be trapped – unable to move up or down. I stopped thinking about it and sung a tune between the bouts of shivering.

"You're no good for me, I don't need nobody, don't need no one that's no good for me …"

… Les Tyrell, the principal officer on duty that New Year's Eve was talking to me.

"You have to work on C Wing and take the place of an officer who has just gone sick. All of the cell locks have been filled with matches and broken so no one can be locked away."

There was obviously going to be trouble. C Wing had a reputation. It held one inmate who was very anti-authority having transferred to Gartree after starting a riot at Strangeways in Manchester.

Walking the corridor from the Block to C Wing, I hummed a tune one of the inmates had been playing. "You're no good for me, I don't need nobody …" Unlocking the gate, I stepped onto the wing and immediately felt the tension. Angry voices. A drunken shout. Posturing. Aggression.

I looked into the ground-floor office. An officer with less time in the job than me was acting as senior officer.

"What's happening?"

"Loads of cell locks compromised. The long leg of the three's landing is a no-go area, the inmates have barricaded it off. It's shit. Try and lock up anyone who wants to be locked up and see what happens." Climbing the stairs two at a time, passing two officers on the one's who looked like they had just survived a mountain epic. Three officers grouped together on the two's landing looked at me.

"Who did you upset?"

Three's landing had been barricaded at the top of the stairs with a pile of tables and chairs. Bang-up time came and went and the inmates above us grew loud and threatening. A chair flew past, then a table. There was a shout and a crash and another chair rattled off the banisters. All three of us looked at each other and then ran as steel food trays flew past our heads.

"Go on, fuck off! This is our wing now."

Inmates began climbing over the barricade. The thought of being taken hostage was scarier than the thought of being stuck on a mountain in bad weather. Three stairs at a time, I jumped onto the ground floor and sprinted past the hot plates before diving through the gate ...

Fat snowflakes swirled in a milky-red sky like an abstract painting. More snow poured down the face. Cloud and spindrift locked us away from the world. We needed to escape.

"Let's get the fuck out of here."

We packed soaking gear and started abseiling off old pegs, the odd rock spike and our own gear. Snow rumbled all around us. Reaching the top of the massive ice sheet, I began cutting ice bollards to wrap the rope around to save wasting hardware. Neither of us knew about Abalakov ice threads, even though just a year ago I had watched Valery Babanov abseiling down this very ice sheet using precisely that technique. We were still green.

At the bottom of the ice sheet Cartwright took us over the bergschrund and at four-thirty, just as it was getting dark again, we stood in waist-deep snow and hugged each other. Cartwright put his long legs to good use and waded to the hut down the glacier in two hours. In the hut I took my boots off and noticed my right foot, which had been numb from hanging all night, was swollen and purple. I went to sleep unconcerned. As long as I could just lie down.

In the morning, my foot had swollen even more and getting my boot on became the crux of the morning. Following the lanky Cartwright's foot-holes through thigh-deep snow came a close second.

"Wanker... wanker... Take smaller steps."

I had to jump from one hole to the other while Cartwright just carried on, looking like John Cleese from the Ministry of Silly Walks without ever slowing.

Stepping from the train in the middle of a wet Chamonix afternoon people milled around, stepping round puddles as they peered into shop windows. We crossed the street to the brasserie, where we dumped the rucksacks and slumped into plastic chairs sheltered beneath a red parasol.

"Deux grandes bières, s'il vous plait?"

Lifting the glasses, savouring the moment, I studied the amber liquid bubbling with life and energy. We looked at each other and the beer and at each other and clinked glasses.

"Cheers."

We had eaten and drunk almost nothing for three days, and after half a glass even Jules was drunk. We laughed and joked and ogled the college girls who were walking home wearing uniforms and short skirts, dodging the puddles. They looked young and we looked at one another, haggard and unshaven, and laughed some more.

"Cheers."

Two days after hanging out in minus twenty on the Grandes Jorasses, I was jumping on and off a wooden bench dressed in shorts and vest, while shouting encouragement at a group of new prison officers.

"Come on! Keep going."

One by one they gave up, fighting for breath. I couldn't feel my right foot, it was so swollen, even though my training shoe was only loosely fastened.

The doctor laughed when I showed him.

"Yes, Mr Bullock, you have a textbook case of frostbite."

He thought it quite amusing to treat someone with frostbite while working at a surgery in Leicestershire.

"Don't get it cold again for a while."

I neglected to tell him I was setting off for my winter mountain leader assessment in Scotland later that day.

FAITH

After qualifying to become a PE officer I had returned to Plas y Brenin and passed my summer mountain leader award. The next step up the outdoor instructing ladder was the winter version. I knew earning these awards would give me an out from the prison if I needed one, but as I became a more experienced climber, I also knew working as an instructor was not what I wanted. I didn't want to spend precious time in the hills leading strangers by the hand; I just wanted to climb with friends as often as I could. But the prison service was paying and gaining the winter award meant a week away training and another week being assessed all in Scotland. There was no contest.

Like most things in my life, I decided if I were going to do the winter award, I would give it my best shot. So I devoted a lot of time and effort on big winter walks in the mountains practising my navigation.

Michael Tweedley joined me on one of these trips, eager to find out what the whole winter game was about. We left Leicester in my small red Citroën and headed north. Over the next fortnight we camped and drove all over the Highlands, drying gear in our sleeping bags at night and cooking in the porch, before moving on next day. This spartan life was interspersed with a couple of nights of luxury in the Alex MacIntyre Hut at Onich near Glen Coe, a memorial to the man who had climbed my objective on the Grandes Jorasses and perished on Annapurna a few years later.

Sometimes the rain fell in torrents, and on those days we walked from before dawn until after dusk, over the Five Sisters of Kintail, including the Forcan Ridge and then the Horns of Beinn Alligin in Torridon. When the rain stopped and it froze hard, we climbed: *Poacher's Fall* on Liathach, a grade five ice climb and Michael's first winter route; *Chimney Route* on Stob Coire nan Lochan in Glen Coe, a grade six; and then soon after *Tilt*, also on Stob Coire nan Lochan, and an even more difficult climb.

Moving on from Glen Coe we camped for a few days behind the stone wall at the side of the car park at Creag Meagaidh, where we climbed *1959 Face Route*, a long and testing grade five and spent two days walking the peak's ridges. Finally we drove east to the Cairngorms and the peaks of Lochnagar and Creag an Dubh Loch. After a few days spent walking, one of them cut short when Michael forgot his crampons, we chose to finish our expedition with an out-of-condition grade six. The start, a thin icicle which should have been a fat icefall, broke and – whumph! – I hit a bank of snow and disappeared into a cloud of powder. Dusting myself off, I started again, sweating and thrashing, and this time succeeded.

The snow fell in buckets, large wet flakes tumbling down the overhanging head of the *Douglas-Gibson Gully* on Lochnagar. Michael stood patiently as the snow got deeper, concentrating on the ropes and encouraging me to keep going. I'd shouted at him when he forgot his crampons, but he'd forgiven me now we were climbing. Several hours later we both collapsed in the dark on the summit in a maelstrom of swirling snow. Steaming with effort, our arms cramping, I felt euphoric, and we doddered from the summit like old folk for another damp night in the tent before the long drive back to Leicester. Stopping at a petrol station somewhere near Stirling, Michael bought me an ice cream.

I lost several climbing days while completing the necessary walks in preparation for my winter award and at times I felt robbed. But those weeks with Tweedley were some of my best days ever in Scotland.

Later that winter I arrived at the Alltshellach Hotel in Ballachulish, on the road between Glen Coe and Fort William, for the assessment. I felt quite intimidated. Everyone else already appeared to be working in the outdoor industry. The assessors were from Plas y Brenin and I knew several of them, but that didn't settle my nerves. The winter mountain leader award is one of the most difficult to gain in the outdoor industry. Try as hard as I could, the feeling of being a fraud, of not been the right kind of person for this qualification ran through my mind, chipping away at my confidence.

The assessment lasted a week, starting with a few days' walking and navigation while illustrating competence at ropework, cutting steps and general basic mountaineering skills. Walking down an easy-angled snow gully on Stob Coire nan Lochan the first day, I caught the front points of my crampons on the leg of my salopettes, tripped and landed on my front facing downhill. Quickly, I swung my axe, driving the pick into the snow, spun around, stood up and continued walking and talking unconcerned. The assessor glanced my way and carried on walking without saying anything.

The meat of the course was a three-day expedition, which was to be assessed by Nick Banks, whose slideshow had first inspired me all those years ago. Also in my group was a tall guy from Northern Ireland called Tim Neill. I couldn't know it, but Tim, quietly spoken with a soft Ulster accent, was to become a great friend. For three days and nights the group walked miles and miles through the Grey Corries, along snowed-up rocky ridges, over wind-scoured summits and into snow-filled glens. The pressure to perform was constant.

On the first night I followed the others in the group while studying my map. I was sure we had gone wrong, but lacking their experience and not wanting to drop anyone in it, I kept quiet. When it was my turn to lead, Banks gave me a point on the map to locate, but starting from the wrong position, I couldn't find it. It then became apparent we had been wrong for some time.

DAY 1: Basic Snow Skills

SKILLS	GOOD	AVE	POOR
Kicking steps		✓	
Using the axe		✓	
Self arrest		✓	
Snow anchors	✓		
Holding sliding falls			
Belaying under winter conditions		✓	

Further details of above:

[handwritten notes]

V poor understanding of snowpack stability. Considerable risk Category 4? Step kicking OK. Step cutting could be better. —Very sloppy. Wrong direction off summit of Stob coire ran locher looking for broad gully. Snow belay OK. Tripped over crampons descending Broad gully. Too casual approach — needs to sharpen up.

A page from the MLTB winter mountain leader documentation. My footwork and axe skills are still something to be desired. Maybe when I grow up I'll get better. The name of the person who supplied this photocopy is withheld to prevent any repercussions...!

Back on course, everyone had another turn at navigating and this time we all did much better. Later, in a quick debrief, Nick asked me about the navigation error and I told him I was pretty sure we had gone wrong but didn't want to get anyone into bother.

"You should have spoken up," he said. "That's what being a leader is about."

I knew he was right, but it wasn't life or death and being loyal to the group was what I was about. Maybe my constant concern about not being the right material for the winter award was right?

The second day continued in similar vein. Banks asked me to take him to a small feature on a single contour on the map, which I did with confidence. Standing in a shallow windblown scoop in the hillside, he asked me if I was certain we were there.

"Yes," I said proudly. He then asked the group and some of them pointed to a feature about twenty-five metres to the right.

"Okay, do you still think we are where you say?"

"Yes I do."

"Well I think it's that feature over there."

"Okay," I said, "prove it." Which was impossible, and Nick agreed. You wanted assertiveness so now you've got it, I thought, but I was disappointed some of my fellow students didn't appear to share my sense that we were all for one and one for all. If this is what instructing is about, I thought to myself, then you can forget it.

Returning from the expedition, back in the warmth of the hotel, we were called one by one to receive our results. When my time came I still had no idea of how I would fare. Mike Turner, the course director, known by all as Twid, shut the door behind me and asked how I thought things had gone. I told him I knew I had made a few mistakes but, all things considered, thought I'd done okay. Twid then told me that of all the candidates on the assessment, I had been the most difficult one for them to judge, but they had eventually decided to defer me.

Twid made his case by recalling several of my minor mistakes. As far as I could tell, everyone had made similar mistakes but I knew they had passed, so I was confused. Twid then suggested that if I spent several days on the hill supervising groups under the leadership of one of the Brenin instructors, I could come back for a day and easily pass. The penny dropped. I realised I was being deferred because I lacked experience of working in the outdoor industry. I didn't have that day-to-day experience with groups on the hill. I had no experience or understanding of the kind of people a winter mountain leader would take up Scottish mountains.

I had to agree with Twid. I was a driven climber who loved mountains and climbing. I didn't have the right attitude or skills to be a group guardian, shepherding the inexperienced. But I did have a logbook jammed full with mountain experience that was more than enough to fulfill the syllabus criteria. So I had been allowed to train and assessed.

This annoyed me. They could have told me at the start that I was the wrong type of person for this qualification. They could have pointed out that I was a driven and obsessive climber, not an instructor. Straight talk is all I need. I told Twid that I thought that their deferring me on the pretext of a few small mistakes was somewhat unfair. And looking into his face I'm pretty sure he agreed. But quickly, perhaps making a joke of it to highlight the truth, he said: "Well you did fall down on the first day!" I had to laugh.

As I left the hotel Nick Banks pulled me to one side and said he would have no qualms going anywhere and doing any climb with me. I was happy about that. Banks was the guy who had inspired me, and here he was saying he would climb with me. But at the time, his words left me even more confused and frustrated that I had been allowed on the course in the first place.

My original plan had been to stay in Scotland and climb for a few days, but instead I drove back to Leicestershire disillusioned. I went to work to save my holiday, but then got a call from a friend who was spending the whole season at the Alex MacIntyre Hut in Onich. He told me it was freezing hard and that I should "get my arse" back to Scotland. I could stay in prison and mope, or I could take his advice. And so I drove north again.

Intent on soloing, I set out early for Ben Nevis. It was dark, clear and cold. The forecast said bad weather was approaching, but it shouldn't hit until the following day. Quietly passing the C. I. C. Hut, the crunch of my crampons reassured me. The approach slopes leading to the Minus Face were pristine. Streaks of light filtered through the grey, features formed, a dusting of snow whorled over the icy surface and in the half-light I saw two figures ahead kicking steps. There was no one else around but I knew the climbers ahead of me were heading for the same objective. I closed the distance between us.

"Hi, Twid."

It was the winter award course director from the week before, and his partner Louise.

"What are you doing?" I asked, knowing the answer.

"Minus One."

As I was soloing and wouldn't slow them down, I asked if they minded me going ahead. Louise told me that actually she did mind. Earlier in the week they had been first at a climbing accident where a solo climber had fallen the distance of the Orion Face.

"I wouldn't want you above me. If you fall off you might hit us."

Slightly put out by her lack of confidence in my abilities, I told Louise that was fine. I hadn't climbed *Minus Two Gully* either and so I would start there.

Starting *Minus Two*, I discovered it was not so much a gully as a sheet of ice, but I moved up anyway, warming my body and mind to the action, swinging and kicking until I built a rhythm. I carried a short rope after my experience on *Orion Direct* but, feeling confident, I continued higher and higher enclosed by steep, rime-encrusted rock.

Engrossed, the activity of climbing, the need for quick and efficient movement, helped to put behind me the disappointment of the last week and my slight feeling of indignation that Louise's comment had provoked. The higher I climbed, the more I knew this was for me. This was what I did. Topping out on the North East Buttress, I realised it was still early. The air was still and I breathed in the excitement of being back in the mountains.

Climbing back down the buttress and then *Slingsby's Chimney*, I was soon once again traversing under *Minus One Gully*. Twid and Louise were now out of sight, but there was another party climbing the first pitch, approaching the belay before the overhanging crux of the climb.

"Is it okay if I start soloing up?" I shouted.

"Is that Nick?" came the reply. The climber was Neil Stevenson, a friend I had climbed with in the past. I caught him up and with his blessing climbed past and into a big cave. The walls of the cave were bare except for blobs of ice on the left wall. I inserted a pick into a small hole in the first blob and pulled. Swinging my foot I pushed a front point onto a smear of rock. The gully dropped into the space beneath. Hook and pull, pull and hook, a roof now blocked my way.

Neil, below and to my right, watched while belaying his partner.

"Go on Nick, make it look hard."

I felt pleased by his comment. It restored a little bit of the confidence I had lost being deferred on the course. I reached around the roof and finding good ice, smashed in the pick and pulled. Above the crux, a silver twist spiralled through steep rock, hugging me like the four walls of a cell. I met Twid and Louise in a large snow bay.

"Do you mind if I come past?"

They didn't, and soon I was pulling onto the North East Ridge for the second time that day. Instead of climbing down again, this time I headed for the summit of Ben Nevis, climbing the awkward 'Mantrap', the crux of *North East Buttress*. On the summit, the emergency shelter was coated in rime while around me, as far as I could see, were snow-covered mountains. I stood by myself and laughed, happy that I never needed to prove myself by finding a ring contour or any other kind of finicky detail on a map ever again.

Later, sitting in front of the coal fire in the hut, Twid stuck his head round the door

"Hey Nick. I was wondering if you wanted to go out climbing tomorrow?"

Back from Scotland, the acting head of the PE department called me into his office.

"Do you still want a sabbatical?"

The prison service was having another of its radical reforms. For the first time in its history, each prison had independence from the suits at head office. Governors now had power over their own finances. Looking to save money, the governor at Gartree wanted to offer me six months of unpaid leave. So I rented out my house and left for Pakistan.

FEAR

——

After discovering climbing and in particular mountaineering, I found the straightforward challenge of the hills refreshing. The rules are simple. Walk to the bottom of a daunting face, start climbing and stop when you can't go any further, and then, hopefully, return safely. Sometimes you reached the summit, sometimes you didn't. Sometimes you felt you could have done more, sometimes you knew you had gone as far as you could. On every occasion you grew and learnt and unlike life in a prison, or even life in general, the experience was basic, uncomplicated and cleansing. My second expedition to the Himalaya was just such an experience – after a brief hiccup.

Paul Schweizer was forty one years old, ten years my senior, and lectured in Informatics at Edinburgh University. His formative climbing years were spent in that 1970s pot-smoking world of Yosemite, in the heyday of Jim Bridwell and John Long and the up-and-coming Ron Kauk, wild and free in Camp 4. We were on our second day attempting the first ascent of a mountain called Savoia Kangri, right next to K2 in Pakistan.

If this peak had been located anywhere other than near K2, then Savoia Kangri would have been considered just as intimidating. It had the classic mountain shape, conical and pointed. As an Alpine style objective it was perfect: two thousand metres of climbing up a long sweeping snow skirt topped with rocky ice-filled runnels, an ice sheet, and a final short fluted snow ridge leading to the summit at 7,263 metres.

Our trip to Pakistan came only ten months after we had backed off the Shark's Fin in India, right at the start of my sabbatical. There were seven of us on Savoia Kangri, more or less inexperienced at the expedition game. Two of the team I knew already, Jamie Fisher and Jules Cartwright, and they were the reason I was along. The other four were unknown.

The plan was to climb Alpine style in three pairs and I was teamed up with Paul, who was the oldest member of the expedition. He was also the most experienced, enthusiastic and fun to be around, so I was happy to be paired with him. The other two climbers, Andrew and Roy, were unknown to me, as was Roy's brother who was coming with us to manage base camp. Yet the more I got to know them, the more I considered Andrew and Roy were out of their depth.

This was rich, I know, coming from someone on only his second trip to the Himalaya, but I knew Jamie and Jules were solid and sensible with lots of Alpine and Scottish experience and I knew Paul had climbed the Cassin Ridge in Alaska among other routes. I knew I was fit, had been rock-climbing for years, and now had four intensive Scottish winter seasons behind me, as well as a few Alpine routes and the Shark's Fin expedition.

What worried me most were some of the decisions Roy and Andrew were taking. Andrew nearly collapsed the day we passed beneath the vast Trango Towers on the trek to base camp, suffering from hypoglycemia. Just before flying to Pakistan he had been diagnosed with diabetes and his sugar levels were all over the place, and he had exaggerated when he told us it was under control. Andrew also had a barrel of his own food, he said because of his condition, but I suspected he wasn't happy eating spicy food. He'd modelled himself on Don Whillans, the tough, pie-eating northerner, but he couldn't live up to it. While acclimatizing, he forgot to use sun cream and his face became crisp and swollen, so much so that he couldn't eat any of the food from his barrel.

Roy's personality concerned me even more. He appeared to see himself as the modern equivalent of the leader of an old-school Himalayan expedition, rather like Chris Bonington, even though he was the most inexperienced climber at base camp.

At the time I was too intolerant of people who I considered fools, a habit made worse by dealing with prisoners. So I gave Roy short shrift. Things came to a head when Andrew was hit by a rock while climbing an avalanche shoot and ruled himself out for a week. Roy announced he would be climbing with Paul and me. It wasn't a request, it was an instruction.

"I will be climbing with you."

I informed him that at no time in his life, my life or the next life would he be tied on a rope that was tied to me. Roy threw a pot of mayonnaise across the mess tent and stormed out. I thought his response both funny and sad. Funny because I was used to dealing with real aggression, not public-schoolboy hissy fits, and sad because we hardly had any mayo and I loved the stuff. A few days later, the three of them left and the four remaining expedition members breathed a huge sigh of relief.

Our first attempt on Savoia Kangri stopped abruptly on day two when a rock rattled down the gully and glanced off Jamie Fisher's bicep. This was quite fortuitous. I had been suffering from giardia and dysentery after drinking from a stream on the final day of the trek to base, which on further inspection I discovered was filled with human waste. My stomach was in bits and as we abseiled, I doubled up with cramps until I could hold on no longer and shat myself. We stood in the burning sun on a snow ledge and laughed, but the stench was awful.

The second attempt went better. Having taken industrial amounts of antibiotic bought from a Swiss expedition on nearby Broad Peak, Schweizer and I climbed through the night. We pulled from the twisting gully onto a large rolling cornice of snow at the top of a ridge. The cornice overhung so far it could have formed the roof of a semi-detached house. Beneath our feet, a cliff of black blocks jutting from rotten pebble-dashed snow plunged to the Savoia Glacier a thousand feet below. It was late in the afternoon, so we hurried to cut a level platform on top of the cornice. In the fading light we moved around, each with a long lead of rope attached to rock anchors fifty feet away. We tried not to think of the gaping void beneath our snowy floor.

Tent pitched, I stood and took in our situation. Gasherbrum IV, colossal and glowing red in the evening sun at the end of the rippled Godwin-Austen Glacier was a formidable prospect. I pondered what must have been running through the minds of Robert Schauer and Voytek Kurtyka the day they set off to climb the mountain's West Face, the 'shining face' I was looking at now. Were they similar thoughts to those I experienced, thoughts of doubt and trepidation, or did men of their ilk not feel emotion?

Broad Peak was a massive snow lump with little in the way of lines. It did not interest me, but K2 grabbed my attention. It towered above our viewing platform, a vast pointed big brother to our mountain, so big it poked the sun in the day and cradled the moon at night. The mountain seemed the ultimate in Himalayan challenges.

The sweeping curves of the Godwin-Austen cupped the bases of these mountains, squeezing with cold hands, guarding their approach with monstrous icefalls. The French guide Eric Escoffier and his client were missing on Broad Peak – presumed dead. I turned and stared intently at the West Face of K2, so big it looked like a trick of the imagination. Above the summit a snow-plume was a howling spectre. On reaching K2 base camp I visited the Gilkey Memorial where silver plates with hammered inscriptions recalled the many climbers who had died there, starting with Art Gilkey himself in 1953.

I tried to imagine the avalanche that had swept Nick Estcourt to his death in 1978 and the deaths in 1986 of thirteen climbers, including Julie Tullis and Alan Rouse. I thought of Alison Hargreaves lifted up and swept away by hurricane winds. I felt scared and intimidated. But it wasn't the same as the fear and intimidation I felt in the prison.

We anchored the tent to the same rock to which we had leashed ourselves, fifty feet away. There was nothing else. The ropes ran in a curving arc and grew heavy as ice gripped their colourful sheath. To pin the tent to the top of the cornice we drove the shafts of our axes into the snow at each corner.

As night took hold, we brewed up and survived. The wind was tearing across the cornice and battered the little single skin tent so that it flexed and rattled. Noodles and soup boiling in our hanging stove spilt and soaked into our down bags. The litre pan, full to the brim with gruel, swung and rattled like an incense burner in an Orthodox church. Slop slithered down the outside of the pan baking to a dry crust. As we settled down, snow began to fall in large flakes, threatening to bury us.

Fully zipped up, arms trapped against my sides, I was warm but unable to move. I thought of the inmates I had fought and held face down in the Box, my hand pushing into moist hair, the inmate's warm cheek crushed so hard into the concrete floor that its crazed pattern would be etched into his skin. The inmate's wrists were handcuffed to a six-inch leather belt strapped around their waist. Trussed, with arms straight against their hips, they would be left to contemplate the errors of their ways.

More than once, even after being trussed, the inmate would attack us as we entered the cell. On occasion they were ferocious. We would have to go in as a team of three, in arrowhead formation behind a shield. Spitting, headbutting, kicking and charging were all part of the inmate's repertoire.

There wasn't an inch to spare in the tiny single-skinned tent. I wondered what went wrong in people to make them so violent. I wondered what crime I had committed, to put myself through this torture.

Schweizer began to snore, he always snored and it really pissed me off. I lay there in the dark with my sleeping bag tight around my face, listening to the wind and the snow and the snoring. I must have dozed off, but suddenly woke with a jolt. Paul stopped snoring. I lay frozen to the spot.

"Did you feel that?" Paul whispered in his Californian hippy drawl.

"Of course I felt it. You know what's happening don't you?"

The cornice was loaded with fresh snow and the extra weight had caused it to crack and settle. It was two in the morning. Frantically we pulled on frozen boots without tying our laces. The inside of the tent was as cold as a freezer, but we had to leave its shelter – fast. I imagined the cornice breaking off, and the tent, with us wrapped inside like chickens in cling-film, left hanging on a thread, unable to escape.

Snow was blasted into the tent as soon as I unzipped the door. Heavy flakes slapped my face. I crawled from the entrance, floundering on all fours into the teeth of a blizzard, through deep snow lapping cold against my thighs and waist. I edged away from the overhanging section of the cornice and balanced on the crest of the ridge. I was unclipped, but the only anchor was the one the tent was fastened to, and I wasn't keen to clip into that.

Schweizer joined me, a snow-covered apparition crawling from the dark. His goatee's whiskers stood clear of the ice encrusted on his face, his round John Lennon glasses steamy and lopsided, hiding his eyes. No doubt they were wide and wired like my own.

"Fucking hell, man, this is not good."

Schweizer's understated drawl would have been funny had I not been terrified. We crouched side by side, scared we would be snatched away by a gust of wind. What could we do? The cornice had dropped a foot. A crack had opened running along its length. Soon we were both shivering uncontrollably. It was obvious we couldn't stay alive out in the open. Cautiously, clipping into the rope, we stepped one at a time onto the cornice, expecting it to collapse. But it appeared to be solid, so parking my imagination we began to clear the new snow to lighten the load. An hour later we crawled back into the tent to start the long wait, punctuated by several more snow-clearing sessions.

Schweizer didn't snore again that evening.

Escaping from our deadly cornice camp the following day, we met Fisher and Cartwright retreating from the summit ridge. They had been battered all night, but had found a good bivvy site and left behind a stash of food and gas. All four of us retreated and returned several days later, reaching 7,000 metres.

For four days, we barely existed, perched on a narrow ledge dug into the summit meringue snow-crest, battered once again by high winds and snow. The cold left my bones numb. We stretched two days of food into six, but our chance to rush the final 250 metres to the summit never came. On the evening of day eight of our third attempt, we made it safely back to advance base. The following day Schweizer led the rest of us, now suffering from snow blindness, down to base camp. The expedition was over.

PAROLE

In the months building up to the sabbatical I had been receiving phone calls and letters from solicitors. The inmate who had attempted to murder the paedophile in the gymnasium had been charged. Another inmate, a quietly spoken man who had found religion, had spoken up and agreed to stand as the sole witness. I was sick and disillusioned with the legal process. Having already been called as a witness, I'd been made to feel small and watch this obviously guilty man nonchalantly lounging in the dock. I was refusing to have anything more to do with the proceedings.

Governors visited the gym adding to the pressure for me to conform, telling me I would be subpoenaed if I continued to refuse to attend. In the end my sabbatical proved to be perfect timing as I was in Pakistan when the second hearing took place. The final outcome turned out much as I suspected. The case collapsed when the inmate standing as a witness refused to testify for a second time. I couldn't blame him. He could no longer mix with other inmates in the prison for fear of being attacked because he had spoken out.

Several years later, the paedophile brought a private prosecution against the prison service. Again I was told I had to attend court and again I refused and yet again I was threatened with a subpoena. This time I was not away and was forced to attend. Everyone turned up at court but minutes before the start of proceedings the prison service settled out of court for a total of £17,000.

If I needed more evidence that something was seriously wrong with certain aspects of our society then this was it. We were living in a country where the system stood up for violent, crack-addicted men who attempted to murder while convicted child-abusers were receiving almost my year's wage in hand-outs. I couldn't side with the attacker because his victim was a paedophile, and he wasn't doing what he did through any feelings of disgust. It was purely to pay for his habit. I could not help but think the prison service had got off lightly. They have to protect everyone no matter what their crime.

Home from Pakistan and still suffering from dysentery, it wasn't long before I was driving out to Chamonix with Cartwright in his old Ford Escort. Rattling down the French motorways, I was filled with a sense of escape, of living beyond what had been mapped out for me. I had only just returned from an expedition and here I was setting out on another trip. This wasn't how things usually worked. It was almost too good to be true. Life was brilliant and my life was even better than brilliant.

Driving up the road between Chamonix and Argentière, heading toward Bernard Ravanel's campsite, we both stared longingly at the pointed monolith of the Petit Dru. Too late we noticed a car had stopped in front of us, waiting to turn left. Stamping hard on the brake pedal it was immediately clear we were going to hit it, so Jules yanked the wheel to the left. We were now speeding toward oncoming traffic. I screamed, Jules screamed and then swerved. Somehow we avoided a head-on collision, but still sideswiped the car driving toward us.

"This is going to be an interesting trip," I said, when I was sure we were still alive.

Two days later, after sorting out the not-so-insured-car-insurance with Cartwright's mum over the phone, we reached what remained of the Ghiglione bivouac hut on Mont Maudit's Frontier Ridge. It was now little more than a snow-covered wooden platform.

"Jules, you said it was a hut."

"Well, last time I came here it was."

Next morning we abseiled down the other side to the Brenva Glacier and waded through deep snow to reach the foot of the East Face of Mont

Left: Jules Cartwright studying Lindsay's *Book of Lies* for 'what next' while sitting on the crest of the Grand Pilier d'Angle after climbing a new link-up of the Cecchinel-Nominé into the Boivin-Vallençant. The Central Pillar of Frêney and the Right-Hand Pillar are both in the background. *Right:* "We have to do something else, I still have a full packet of Marlboro."

Maudit, Mont Blanc's near neighbour whose name translates as the 'cursed mountain'.

Our route comprised rock low down and snow higher up, but it was cold and ice plastered the pink granite.

"You feeling okay?" Jules looked into my face. At first I thought he was concerned, but then I realised he was just worried I may turn around and climbing would be put on hold.

"Why?"

"You're not moving very quick."

"Yeah, tell me about it. You should try throwing up and shitting yourself for two months and see how well you go."

I wasn't used to not performing well, but more than the physical suffering, the feeling of not pulling my weight, of not doing my bit and letting people down was bothering me badly.

High on the face, after climbing for over eight hours, we were moving together joined by the rope with a few runners clipped in between. A heavy crashing noise yanked me from my thoughts. I looked up and screamed at Jules:

"Watch out, avalanche!"

He sprinted to the side of our gully but I was stuck in the middle. This is it, I thought. But the avalanche slid to one side, missing us both.

"Christ, I don't need any more of that."

The following day, we topped out on the summit of Mont Maudit in a blizzard, sat down and shook hands. Cartwright had a goofy grin, his long legs dressed in yellow windproofs stretched toward me and he gave the double thumbs-up.

"This is the first thing I've got to the top of in two years," he said. "It feels good." It felt great to me, but being there with Jules made it more special, especially since he knew the way down and neither of us had a compass or a map.

Traversing from the summit of Mont Maudit, heading to the summit of its lower neighbour Mont Blanc du Tacul, clouds swirled and the wind gusted. Fresh snow, getting fresher and deeper as we watched, covered the mountains. We were inside a time-lapse world of accelerated weather. The sun, hidden behind thick cloud, was setting for the second day. A glistening skin of verglas covered the slope beneath us. Every step had to be stamped.

While driving to France, we had listened on the radio news of seven people slipping from near the summit of Mont Blanc after encountering similar icy conditions caused by rain freezing as it hit the snow. All of them had died.

Reaching the summit plateau of Mont Blanc du Tacul we looked down into the misty gloom and began descending the loaded slopes. Heavy snow continued falling and the lower we climbed the more the danger of being avalanched grew. There was nothing to do except keep going and pray. A few hours later we floundered into the Aiguille du Midi cable car station to find two Brits ensconced in the corridor near the toilets.

"You made it then. We were running a book on how far you'd get before being avalanched."

After so much snow, Cham was out for a while so we travelled to Zermatt and walked up the snowy trail to the Hornli Hut below the Matterhorn and settled into the winter room. The vast pyramid, that mountain of dreams, including mine, twisted into the sky. But after four days of waiting for the wind to drop we bailed leaving its North Face for another time.

Driving over the Col des Montets back to Argentière we couldn't believe the change in the weather. The hills were sparkling and white – full of possibilities.

I sat in the car looking at the Petit Dru and the North Face of Les Droites, but I was a million miles away, thinking about the past. Thinking about Gartree.

The Block was quiet. Tim and Kev sat next to me and across the desk the senior officer was filling out adjudication papers. The alarm bell rang followed closely by the red phone.

"It's A Wing."

We'd been expecting it. Michael Peterson, also known as Metal Mickey but more commonly Charlie Bronson, had been on 'normal location' for at least two weeks, which was a long time for Charlie. As soon as the senior officer said A Wing, we all knew what was heading our way. The phone rang again and an officer on A Wing told us Bronson was on his way down, escorted by several staff, but not 'wrapped up', meaning he was walking and not under restraint.

Standing outside in the corridor, the four of us waited until a group of officers and Bronson came around the corner. Bronson looked like a character from a Dickens, upright and strutting, barrel-chested with thick arms, his head shaved and wearing a large moustache. His eyes were blazing.

"How's it going to be Charlie?"

"No problem, just get me a medicine ball and give me some exercise."

Someone had upset him on A Wing and received a sack of potatoes over their head for the trouble, but this was mild fare compared to what Charlie usually dished out. In the past he had beaten, kidnapped, threatened and blackmailed anyone who crossed him. He had staged rooftop protests and intimidated officers. He had first been banged up at twenty two and since then had only been released from prison twice, each period of liberty lasting just a few months before he was arrested again.

Bronson was forty when I met him and the only thought that crossed my mind was what a waste of life his had been. Here was a man, who for whatever reason – mental illness, lack of treatment and support, lack of education or just from being bad – would spend the rest of his life locked away in prison. It depressed me to think that we still cannot find a way to look after and treat people like Bronson. That all we end up doing is to lock them away.

Soon after his spell in the Block, Charlie was ghosted to another prison, at short notice, and I never saw him again.

The weather was set for at least five days so as soon as we reached the campsite we packed our rucksacks for the mountains.

"It's got to be the Grand Pilier d'Angle."

Cartwright's confidence was infectious.

"Okay." At that time I would have followed him anywhere.

Standing once more in the cable car to the Aiguille du Midi, with every metre we rose into the sky I felt a little more free, a little further from bars and walls and the aggression of men like Bronson. Crossing the Vallée Blanche, now familiar territory, I began thinking about what it was in my character that made me feel alive and free when I was climbing and why others appeared fulfilled in secure lives and secure jobs while never apparently challenging themselves.

Behind me, Jules kept the rope tight as we passed through a heavily crevassed area between the Gros Rognon and Pointe Lachenal, but the crevasses were easy to see and we were soon heading downhill towards the Grand Capucin and the Combe Maudite. My mind drifted away from the slog and I found myself thinking again about Bronson and Price, and why people like them found it impossible to live any kind of life except in an institution – and why I craved uncertainty and adventure. Even then, the route we were making for was unusual, not something most other climbers would choose, being more obscure and wild and a risk. For me, all these things made life more thrilling, less certain.

Reaching the Combe Maudite we climbed a steep ice slope in the evening light to stand on the metal balcony of the Col de la Fourche bivouac hut. Perched among rocks and balanced on the crest of the ridge, the tiny hut, like a gardening shed, was surrounded by mountains and snow. The hut only slept a few people but it was empty and a whole lot more comfortable than the wooden platform of the nearby Ghiglione where we had slept just a week ago.

Jules stood looking over the Brenva Glacier toward the Grand Pilier – the great pillar.

"It looks good. Can you see that curving white line? That's the Cecchinel-Nominé, that's what we are going to do."

He pointed at a ridge of snow between us and the Grand Pilier. "That's Col Moore. We have to climb up and over that and then drop onto the glacier below the Grand Pilier."

"Looks great Jules, want a brew?"

Truth be told, in the fading light I wasn't sure where we were going or what I was supposed to be looking at, but I knew Cartwright had everything figured out and that was enough.

Standing on the balcony a few hours later, waiting for Jules to finish the first abseil, I looked at the stars filling the night sky in their thousands. The night shrouded my mind and the cold penetrated inside my skin and into my bones. The rope came slack. I clipped in. Living life through careful and cautious calculation, with no risk and as little uncertainty as possible, might lead to a ripe old age but I'm not sure longevity necessarily means happiness. For some, I suppose it must do, but as I slid toward the glacier and deeper into the wild night, I knew I was finally on the right path.

Cartwright forced the pace with his familiar long stride, swerving around crevasses to reach the slope of Col Moore. We took the rope off and began climbing until we stood on a wide snow ridge.

"How many Marlboros did you bring?"

The number of cigarettes Jules had brought was the best indication for how long he thought we would be out climbing.

"Forty."

Dropping down the other side of Col Moore we discovered rocky slabs which made abseiling the only option.

"Forty. A pretty short outing then?"

Sneaking around and sometimes under seracs, we traversed a snow slope, heading toward the dark outline of the Grand Pilier. An orange glow emanated from the valley far below. I imagined all of the people sleeping in Courmayeur, safe and warm under the sulphurous lights. I imagined the inmates asleep under the near-daylight orange of the high-level lights that shone over Gartree, making it look like a birthday cake. For a moment I could smell slop-out and sweat – and fear.

We stopped beneath a sliver of ice stuck to the back of a gully and pulled the second rope out of the bag, and the climbing hardware too. Then we had a drink, tied on and began climbing.

Ice creaked around us. Our exhaled breaths condensed on the frozen air. *Thwunk.* The ice was perfect. I swung my headtorch beam around me. It caught on granite and ice. To the right, halfway through the third pitch, I spotted a mixed line, which may or may not have been a variation climbed by Mick Fowler and Phil Thomas. We weren't even sure if we had found the right start to the Cecchinel-Nominé, or were instead on the Czechoslovakian route farther to the left. Wanting something interesting and different, I climbed to the right, belayed, and hung in the dark watching Cartwright's torch-beam swooping around the gully.

"Shall we head out here? Looks more fun."

The ropes moved steadily. I stood in the dark belaying. The lights in the valley looked appealing but a long way off. I envisaged myself doing this over and over again – and again and again. For many, climbing was an escape, for me too I suppose, but it wasn't the only reason. Why did so many of the people I knew from prison return time and time again? Drug addicts, joyriders, fighters, gang members and armed robbers. Growing up in run-down areas with limited or no opportunity while suffering that sickness of wanting more and more material goods beyond their means. That must have something to do with it too.

I wanted climbing but I was prepared to put in the time and effort to gain the experience. But then, for repeat criminals, there's also the thrill of the chase, the uncertainty, the tension and the excitement – how much is that a part of their drive? Crime or climb? Were they just two intoxicating drugs to get some of us through the sterility of modern life, the consumerism we learn in our schools, from parents and on TV. It seems this is what is expected of us.

Climbing can have fatal consequences – a severe price to pay, but so obviously worth the risk for many of us. The criminal also faces consequences, and yet so often returns to crime.

As daylight strengthened it became obvious we had started up the Cecchinel-Nominé and were now climbing new ground on the buttress to the right. Thinly iced corners led directly up the face. We shouted and laughed, moving easily and quickly. The sky was clear. Pitch after pitch, ice, rock, then ice again, a sticky veneer left by the storm that had chased us down Mont Blanc du Tacul.

We climbed higher and higher, and then faced a decision – straight up or slightly right into the Boivin-Vallençant. There was no choice really, the gully of the Boivin-Vallençant looked to be in perfect shape.

The long ice sheet at the top of the face felt never ending but it was only two-thirty in the afternoon when we stood on the crest of the Peuterey Ridge.

Jules sat smoking, leaning against a massive gendarme balanced on the ridge.

"What do you reckon?"

He was looking down to the Frêney Glacier, and, pointing with a Marlboro Lite, he traced a smoky line up the right-hand pillar, the less famous sister of the central pillar, climbed in the 1960s by a British and Polish team that included Chris Bonington and Don Whillans.

"It'll be more interesting than going up the Peuterey and, let's face it, after the effort of getting this far we might as well do something else. And I have a full packet of cigarettes left."

We set off at one in the morning, once again starting with an abseil, but unlike the previous morning, this was followed with four more abseils. Unlike the difficult traverse to reach the Grand Pilier, the traverse to the right-hand pillar was considerably easier. Cartwright led off, up into the dark, climbing the first few metres of the thousand we had left to climb.

We finished the pillar in the late afternoon and continued to the summit of Mont Blanc de Courmayeur where we scraped a shelf to sleep on just beneath some rocks. The sun set and we settled in for our third night since leaving the Aiguille du Midi. Clouds had bubbled up in the valley but the weather was good. We joked and laughed. Jules was nearly out of cigarettes, a sure sign we had done enough.

In the morning we set off before daylight and reached the main summit of Mont Blanc. I stood and looked around, taking in the view for the first time. Others who had been guided up the normal routes milled and chatted. It was a shock to see so many other people and we soon began the jog downhill towards the train.

"Do you want a beer?" Jules asked a few hours later.

"How much is it?"

"Does it matter?"

Fair enough, I thought, as Jules walked to the small wooden café at the top station. Waiting for the train, we leaned back and clinked bottles.

Driving to Britain a few days later, I knew continuing with the cold stuff would be an anti-climax. I played with the idea of travelling to Canada for the final three months of my sabbatical, but I craved warm rock, and the thought of being fit and strong was too much of a draw. When I got back to my parents' house in Cheadle, I booked a flight for Melbourne.

I spent three months in Australia, most of the time climbing at Arapiles and the Grampians. I enjoyed my time there, but the difference in attitude between cosmopolitan Melbourne and the farming areas where I spent most of my time climbing was a shock. The racism I experienced away from the city was appalling, and the attitudes of many Australian people made me despair. If this was how Britain was through the 1950s and 1960s, how would it be now if Enoch Powell had had his way? After three months, I was glad to leave, but not happy to be going home to Gartree.

Back at work, many officers said to me: "So now you've got that out of your system, what's next?" Now I had been away, they assumed I would want to settle back into the routine, as though I'd been a student on a year out, a final fling before following the same path as the rest of society.

The other officers couldn't appreciate that being away from the prison's claustrophobic undercurrent of hate and aggression had shown me another way. I was now more determined than ever to leave for good. Sometimes other climbers I knew would say they wouldn't be so keen to climb if they had nothing else. But I was convinced I would remain motivated. My eyes had been opened and my hunger sharpened for travel and adventure and for meeting people who were bold with their life choices.

The big problem was still my home, which gave me my independence and sanctuary. I was happy in my small, safe home and was scared to let go of it, but knew I must if I wanted to act on my dream. Since my house had not sold I decided to save and then pay off my mortgage early. Making a decent living and having no family made that easy. It also helped that I've never been materialistic.

My house was tidy but basic. I had never seen the point in moving and increasing my mortgage. I had a portable TV, no central heating, one bed-room, and the car I drove had more than a hundred thousand miles on the clock. I had no interest in buying a new one every three years or so. I'd then be beholden to a bank, and I wasn't having that.

What I really craved was time and freedom; for me these were the most valuable possessions. Drinking every night in the pub didn't interest me, and after working in a prison for ten years, the thought of going out at night concerned me – even frightened me. I had met too many inmates that were average people, family men working their way through life, until one incident had changed their life forever. It could be a friendly night in the pub, or larking around in a nightclub but it would just take one person to start trouble, start a fight, a single punch which could result in a fall, a skull hitting the kerb and suddenly a door is being slammed on you at the start of a long sentence. By now the horrors that could be inflicted by other humans was, for me, far worse than any terror I felt among the mountains.

It may be the same for everyone, but it felt to me that trouble followed me around. When I worked at Alton Towers I began seeing Sheila and eventually we became engaged. At the start of our relationship her ex-boyfriend turned up at the house one night holding a wheel brace, but we talked and the situation was defused.

Later another ex-boyfriend of a girl I had only recently started seeing turned up at her house and began to smash the front door down. The police were called. Several months later we had split up and while visiting my parents, walking back from the centre of Cheadle, a car screeched to a halt and the same ex-boyfriend, who was now back in a relationship with the same girl, jumped from the car and knocked me through a hedge.

"What's up with her then, isn't she good enough for you?"

Even the friendly village pub in Burton Overy where I lived could turn scary. One night two brothers, local farmers, came into the bar where I was having a quiet pint and offered me out. I couldn't believe it. They were both in their late forties and the smaller one was nasty. He leant toward me, his face inches from mine.

"You think you're hard, don't you? I'll have you any time." I could see flecks of saliva caught on his lips, smelled his beery breath, his aggression, his own insecurity. I looked at him and said nothing; he swaggered off feeling superior. I'm not a scrapper and apart from when I was young and didn't know better, I've never wanted to be known as a hard man.

Then again, I have always known I would rather face my demons and stand up for myself than feel a coward. This attitude has at times helped while climbing and mountaineering but it made working in the prison a constant stress. I would never back down in the face of bullying or intimidation.

I sat in the pub drinking my pint slowly, calculating, simmering and waiting. Eventually the farmer left the bar for the toilet. I gave him a few seconds and followed. The toilet was empty except for the farmer who stood at the urinal with his back to me. I approached, and knowing he had one hand in use, stood right behind him.

"Right, it's just you and me now, so if you want some trouble I'm ready."

He turned his head but carried on peeing. I was on my toes knowing that if he said anything remotely aggressive I would punch him in the back of the head. I could see in his eyes he felt vulnerable, as any man with his penis in his hand would when confronted with aggression.

"I'm sorry about that, I didn't mean it. It was just the drink. No hard feelings."

I walked out of the toilet knowing I wouldn't have any more trouble. I couldn't care less that no one had seen me standing up for myself. I knew, and that was enough.

LOSS

Finding climbing had brought profound changes in my outlook on life. It changed how I thought about other people and how I saw myself. When I got back from Australia, the decision was made. I would pay off my mortgage and leave the prison service. Then I would sell, or better still, rent out my house and I'd become a climbing nomad.

Returning from Australia I had enough saved to pay off three-quarters of the sum, and each month I managed to save several hundred pounds. But I still had a little way to go. Leaving Burton Overy on my regular run, up the small hill past the large house with its herringbone brickwork and weeping willows, crossing the cattle-grid and out into open fields, I would work out how much I needed to escape, to pay off the mortgage, buy a new van and still have enough left over to climb full time for two years.

Jogging down the narrow lane, past the skeletal stands of hawthorn and blackthorn, I'd be plotting how I'd survive. Half-listening to a noisy wren, I'd reach the spinney and scuff through its carpet of dead leaves. I'd often startle a cock pheasant, hear its whirring wing-beat, the kok-kok-kok of its call fading as the bird sped downhill toward the muddy banks of the stream. My life as a gamekeeper seemed to belong to someone else. It would be a few years yet, but I knew my climbing life would happen. It had to, if only because I was becoming more intolerant and cynical, and the more I fought against that, the more difficult work in prison became.

In the gym things took a turn for the worse. Clive, who had run the gym in a way that suited me, had been promoted and in his place came an ex-army, short-back-and-sides jobsworth, who was set on change and told me I trained too much. Inevitably, we clashed.

One of the changes the new senior officer introduced was limiting the gym sessions each inmate could take part in. All of a sudden, the inmates who worked as cleaners and were able to come to the gym every day, were restricted to three sessions a week. This included my training crew, who I really cared about. But if I couldn't allow other inmates extra time in the gym, then I couldn't allow my crew extra time either. That would have been unfair and hypocritical of me. This new regime piled extra stress onto my daily life. Arguments not only with the inmates but also with the new senior officer became routine.

One by one my friends in the PE department transferred. Rich Sawbridge moved to Welford Road Prison and Mick Greenslade set up his own department working on a drug rehabilitation programme. I needed out. I took my physiotherapy study farther until I was qualified to work in national football clubs and applied to several universities to study physiotherapy but none accepted me, even though I had two diplomas. I became frustrated with what I saw as a narrow and hypocritical system, that couldn't get past its box-ticking to see that I had potential.

I could hear Dad moaning about it all. "Bloody degree in social work, students coming in with no experience, no idea how to talk to people, telling me what to do." Only now that's what I sounded like too.

One possible escape was a vacancy I knew would be coming up in the gym at Welford Road Prison where Rich Sawbridge was now working. I put all my hopes on this vacancy, while all my physical efforts went into working on fitness for rock-climbing. For the first time since starting to climb and for one winter, I took a conscious decision to leave the cold stuff alone and train until the weather improved and I could climb outside.

Sitting alone one evening in the gymnasium office, I rang Jamie Fisher who was living in Edinburgh. It had been a few months since we parted company at the end of the Savoia Kangri expedition and we hadn't spoken since.

"Hi Jamie, what you up too?"

"Who's this?"

"It's Nick you idiot."

"Nick who?"

"Nick Bullock."

"Ah, you want the other Jamie."

It seemed Jamie was now living with another climber called Jamie – Jamie Andrew. When Jamie Fisher came on the line he buzzed with vibrancy and excitement. He was packing, and about to leave for the Alps with the other Jamie. We chatted for half an hour and at the end of the conversation I told him to take care and have fun.

During the Savoia Kangri expedition I had grown close to Jamie. I'm not sure it was a change in him or me or both of us. On the Shark's Fin I had found him pushy and driven almost to the point of selfishness. At times he seemed to bulldoze his views through, taking the attitude that he would do it his way and you could like it or lump it. In Pakistan he appeared more relaxed and content. I grew to like and respect this easier-going version and I looked forward to spending more time with him.

A week later, leaving the warmth of the climbing wall, stepping out into the cold and dark, my mind flitted between the Shark's Fin and Pakistan and Bernard Ravanel's campsite in Argentière. Crossing the wet road, the yellow glow of the streetlight reminded me of the sun shining through mist as we left the Concordia to cross the Gondogoro La, heading toward Hushe village at the end of our Savoia Kangri trip.

Driving through Leicester centre I passed abandoned, graffiti-daubed hosiery factories, kebab houses, papers blowing in the gutter, the high walls of Welford Road Prison and the dark deserted park. Driving out of the city, the van's headlights picked out leaves being blown across the country lane. Trees stooped either side of the road against the wind, twisted. Sleet struck the windscreen and I switched on the wipers. I was half-listening to the rolling news reports between songs on the car radio.

"British climbers are trapped on a mountain in the French Alps." I arrived back at my red-brick labourer's cottage, the windows dark, the living room cold. I switched on the TV and closed the curtains, looked at the books piled on the shelf, at my randomly hung black and white pictures, turned on the fire, sat in my chair and waited.

Jules and Jamie were both in the Alps and we all had the same distinctive yellow jackets that had been given to us for the Shark's Fin climb. Watching the news later that evening, shot from a helicopter that could get close but no closer in the high winds, I recognised the jacket of one of the two climbers trapped at the Brèche on the summit ridge of Les Droites. I knew it was either Jamie Fisher or Jules pinned down by the atrocious, freezing weather. I spent the rest of the evening listening to the rain lashing against the window, waiting for an updated report.

When the news came it confirmed my fears. The climbers trapped were the two Jamies. Jamie Andrew was still alive and had been rescued; he had severe frostbite to both hands and feet. Jamie Fisher was dead.

At the time of the tragedy, Jules Cartwright had been in the Chamonix valley. I asked him afterwards if Jamie Fisher had a sleeping bag with him. I was trying to make some sense of what happened and knew Jamie was an advocate of moving fast and light. It turned out he did have a sleeping bag and proper bivvy kit. People, myself among them, are always trying to find reasons and place the blame for accidents in the mountains. Sometimes there is no blame. The mountains may have been tamed with time, experience and better equipment. But sometimes they fight back and it is this uncertainty that keeps people like me returning.

Being a climber and in particular a mountaineer the thought of death is never far from my thoughts. This may sound melodramatic but it isn't; the death rate in the Greater Ranges is high. I've never been of the 'it will never happen to me' school of thought. In fact, I'm not sure any mountaineers I know are. Most of my friends or fellow climbers appear very aware that life is a one-way road and because of this awareness they generally have that vibrancy and energy which is so evident.

At times I sit and wonder what life actually is about and I always return to the same answer: it isn't really about anything other than existence, and existing honestly and fully is the best for me. I will always be questioning, pushing, striving and challenging. I know this is how Jamie Fisher lived. What is sad is a life so full of energy being cut so very short. But to dwell too long on this is to wrap oneself in a blanket of fear.

FLIGHT

Staying away from winter climbing in Scotland and winter Alpinism paid dividends. My first route of the summer was *Linden,* a hard and bold Mick Fowler route on the gritstone edge above Curbar in the Peak District. I was climbing with Jon Read, who had become a good friend. Jon worked at Leicester University counting flies for research purposes and was a doctor in something very intelligent. He was also a very competent and gifted climber.

Jon loved the technicalities of hard grit routes, but his intelligence didn't help him in climbing them in good style, without first trying the route with the safety of a top-rope. I think his imagination, which was immense, could see a whole load of the bad shit that might happen, something my mind mostly chose to ignore. More often than not, Dr Jon practised hard climbs on a top-rope, checking every gear placement before attempting the lead. It was all very scientific.

Jon's tactics suited me at the beginning of the summer, when all I wanted to do was get climbing and measure my fitness, but later I preferred to climb 'on-sight' without practising climbs before I lead them. On-sighting a climb, in my mind, is what climbing is about. It's battling the voice in my head that says, 'No, this is too dangerous,' but then discovering that, in fact, I am good enough and I will attempt it, that I won't be intimidated, or even if I am, that I refuse to give in. These psychological journeys are the most important thing for me, not just doing the moves of a particular climb.

That attitude has consequences. In the six years since I'd started climbing I had taken quite a few big and scary falls attempting to climb, on-sight, routes I knew were within my capabilities. One of the biggest had taken place the previous summer.

North Wales had become my favourite hunting ground for pushing the grades, particularly Dinas Cromlech in the Llanberis Pass, a crag best suited to climbers with strong fingers and lots of forearm stamina – perfect then for a climber who regularly trained on Slawston Bridge. The ability to push on above spaced protection was also a bonus on the more difficult routes of the Cromlech.

Romping up the steep, scree-covered path to the crag, I followed in the giant footsteps of Tim Neill. Tim and I had become good friends since our first meeting in Scotland on the winter mountain leader's assessment. Unlike me, Tim had continued on the outdoor professional path and was now a qualified international mountain guide.

The sun shone, the crag was dry. Both of us had ticked nearly all of the routes on the open-book walls of the crag's main feature. We had spent the previous evening in Tim's small house in the Llanberis Pass poring over the guidebook and delving deep in the hunt for the esoteric – and we came up trumps.

Ivory Madonna, (E5 6b). A rising right-to-left girdle of the Cromlech walls, starting at Cemetery Gates. First climbed by Ron Fawcett in 1980.

Tim Neill sporting the trouser style of the day while leading the 'easy' second pitch of *Ivory Madonna* (E5) on Dinas Cromlech, North Wales. Skyhook non-essential for this pitch.

If Fawcett's name got my attention, the route description took me into blessed ecstasy: *An adrenaline pumping twenty-foot sequence of 'brick-edge' climbing enables non-flyers to gain the sanctuary of Cenotaph Corner.*

This was a red rag to a Bullock.

Quickly climbing up the polished rock step, avoiding the dribbles of water darkening the grey rock, a short grassy walkway led to the large sloping shelf in the corner below *Right Wall* where we made base camp. Big Tim asked if I wanted the first pitch – the bold, potential-monster-lob pitch. Even though Tim and I had not known each other that long, Tim obviously saw in me a good person with whom to climb those routes he didn't particularly want to lead himself.

"Yeah, I'll have a look."

Some strange trait in my psyche was taking over. My climbing had been heading in this direction for some time. People climb for a variety of reasons: exercise, gymnastic movement and the camaraderie to name just a few. I climb for all of these reasons, but I especially climb for the head games. The ability to cross barriers inside my head, to push it out above suspect protection, to climb technical, difficult moves at my limit.

I had been accused of chasing big numbers, of not enjoying the natural environment. Wrongly so, but how are others expected to understand that the very type of climbing that scares me is what attracts me? That the battle between the sensible voice and the voice that cries, 'Go on! Push yourself. Challenge expectation,' offers the greatest reward?

I soloed the start of *Cemetery Gates*, climbing through its overhang before placing protection. Easy climbing followed, albeit easy climbing with the prospect of a ground fall. I climbed through the line of *Precious*, another Fawcett route of the same grade which I had climbed the previous year with Michael Tweedley, including John Redhead's difficult direct start. Then I climbed into and out of *Right Wall* only to slow as *Lord of the Flies* approached, Fawcett's most famous creation in North Wales.

I knew the rock here intimately, its small but positive finger jugs. Looking right, the ropes ran in an arc unbroken by the comfort of karabiners. I knew the protection to come was also terrible but I had to try to place something, if only to delay the inevitable hard climbing. The pocket for a skyhook, which protects the crux moves on *Lord of the Flies*, was just above me. I placed this desperate measure, a bent piece of metal originally made for aid climbing, onto the lip of the pocket and, to stop my ropes flicking the hook out of the pocket, I hung it with heavy wired nuts to weigh it down.

Now I shake out my arms and dip into my chalk bag as I try to fathom the sequence of moves I'm required to perform. I try to clear my mind, switch off the dissonance of my brain that's ringing in my ears. I seem stuck to the holds so I dip into the chalk again, as my head screams, 'Commit! For God's sake, just get on with it.'

The holds are tiny but positive and sharp, a match on a match, a side-pull, rock-over on my left foot, then swap the hold to my right, pull with the left hand, skip my feet across. *Cenotaph Corner* is near – just a move away. One more foothold, one more handhold. I begin to lean towards safety…

The crag is now deathly quiet. A climber on *Cenotaph Corner* is just above me. I could've whispered sweet nothings and then he fades like a memory into the distance.

Arrrrrrghwhooooohoooo!

I wave farewell. The rock is a blur, flying past me. The ledge Tim is sat on grows larger, until it fills my vision. Spinning like a bullet, my trajectory is set.

I flash back to our gang of grubby kids growing up in Cheadle. Strange how some things from childhood re-emerge when you least expect them. We're perched in the tree, which leans over the dirty brook. The rope hangs down straight from the branch to which it's tied, and then curves back up in a great loop to a kid, me, holding the end of the rope.

Count to three and launch. Gravity. Acceleration. The loop in the rope allows me to free-fall. It's freedom. Escape. But distance and time destroy the fantasy. Rules apply. Knots creak and tighten. The tree complains. I see green weed, woven by the brook's brown hand, threading the spokes of an old bike wheel. Gradually I come to a stop. Who dares jump from higher up the bank?

Tim throws himself backward in an attempt to pull in the rope. It works, *just*. I whizz past, skimming the ledge, which the big man is now hanging below, by mere inches. I lift my legs, but for a moment I am tempted to see if I can run along the top. We exchange greetings as I fly past. Then I leave as quickly as I've arrived.

My journey of discovery continues with a vengeance. A party climbing *Cemetery Gates* are looking distinctly unhappy as the Bullock bomb heads in their direction. The leader holds on hard and prepares for impact. Gracefully I swing to greet him, introduce myself and wave goodbye. This is fun. Whooping and laughing, I swing across the right wall for a second time. The crag is in uproar. What a blast.

I look up and realise that the rope holding my roller-coaster ride is passing through a single point of suspension – the skyhook. Hypnotised, I watch as the hook swivels in the pocket. Whispering, scared my voice will shake the hook free, I ask Tim to lower me. Carefully.

Since coming home from Australia, I had begun climbing regularly with the former England wicketkeeper Bruce French, now working as a builder. I had known Bruce for a couple of years, first meeting him when he worked drilling a load of new holes to add more screw-on holds to the wall at The Tower Climbing Centre in Leicester. We had climbed in the Peak and Wales and in winter climbed in Scotland. He was the polar opposite to Dr Jon. I was not often allowed to work routes before leading them when climbing with Bruce, which was great, as the experience gained from falling and climbing, more climbing and more falling, gave me an instinctive understanding of when to push and when to hold back. Unfortunately, my head often overrides the catalogue of epics stored in the recesses of my memory. Skin-of-the-teeth escapes or last-ditch dynos before plummeting are conveniently forgotten.

This forgetfulness does have a down side. I've had very scary experiences after forgetting important factors like an early-season inability to place protection, or tiredness at the end of a long day. Combine either of these with an exceptionally driven personality, throw in my regular I'm-going-to-the-mountains-soon-but-still-want-to-knock-off-several-more-hard-climbs-before-I-leave issue, top that off with a whole winter's manic training and – hey presto! – an epic is guaranteed.

As on the occasion I climbed with Bruce at Stoney Middleton, a former limestone quarry in the Peak District. It was still spring and all my focus for that summer was devoted to climbing my first E7, although the E7 that had piqued my interest years before, *The Bells! The Bells!*, was still a distant prospect.

Bruce was often a steadying influence, especially when my enthusiasm threw unforeseen hardship in his direction like the time we were battered by bad weather in Scotland or the time we were gibbering up a route too difficult for us both. But when rock climbing in England, and not winter climbing in Scotland, Bruce changed. Good weather, a short walk to the climbing venue, a cell phone with a signal, a single-pitch climb, all these luxuries seemed to remove Bruce's boundaries. And then he was transformed, from cautious, patient Dr Jekyll into Mr Hyde, the Evil Belaying Bastard.

The day's loosener had been *Wee Doris*, not the easiest climb by any stretch of the imagination, first climbed by the abnormally strong Tom Proctor, who had trained on the walls of his parents' farm near Chesterfield. Bruce had pointed to it with an evil glint in his eye.

"Your lead," he said, and laughed in his impish wicketkeeper way.

I slithered up the polished holds, reaching the top hyper-ventilating and unable to make a fist. The second climb of the day, also a Proctor classic, was *Bubbles Wall*, with its direct start. I climbed up and down several times trying to fathom the sequence before finally committing to a series of semi-dynamic pops to reach a break above. I was pleased to place some gear, but even more pleased that I had found such strenuous moves reasonably easy.

What should have been the final climb of the day was *Scoop Wall*, a classic route of medium difficulty taking the airy upper wall of Stoney Middleton's Windy Buttress. Sustained at the grade and exposed, I followed Bruce, loving the route's feeling of space. At the top of the climb, Bruce's big smile beneath his dark curly mop said all that needed to be said. It was like Ian Botham had bowled the perfect medium-paced outswinger and Bruce had snaffled the catch.

Bursting with enthusiasm and confidence from successfully climbing three very good routes, it should have been time to call it a day. True, the sun was still shining and lots of daylight remained, but I reasoned the climbing must have taken a little energy from my arms. And then I questioned myself. Had it really? Because it would be a shame not to add one more route, wouldn't it?

The evil one sat contentedly, his climb in the bag. The pub would be open for a long time yet. He left the decision to me. So it was back to *Bubbles Wall* then, since the voice in my head wouldn't let me settle if I didn't try at least one more climb. I had spotted a great line out to the right while climbing earlier in the day and Bruce, having completed his transformation into the Evil Belaying Bastard, was demonically encouraging.

I should have read the warning signs, but, of course, I didn't. Bruce merrily dropped poison in my ear, much, I imagine, as he once did to Australian batsmen as Graham Dilley pounded in to bowl at them.

The route was called *Black Kabul*, a hard climb put up by Jerry Moffatt in the 1980s. Yet *Linden* at Curbar Edge was more difficult, and so *Black Kabul* didn't cause me concern. It had protection, although spaced, but it was good gear, definitely good. The crux sequence is high in the climb and rather run-out, but I wasn't worried. A great big pocket offered protection before I set off into the sea of nothing above it. 'If the unthinkable happens, I'll be fine,' I thought. 'There aren't any large ledges or lumps of rock to hit on the way down.'

Black Kabul starts by climbing the route to the right, a crack line above a large hole at the foot of the crag. The hole is the entrance to one of Stoney Middleton's underground tunnel systems. I minced around the wide mouth of the hole, avoiding mud and patches of wet stinging nettles. A cold stale breeze emanated from the bowels of the crag. Stepping onto the foot of the route and making one move to the right immediately placed me fifteen feet above the ground. Bruce stood to the side holding my ropes. He wasn't that tall, but was now at the same level and fixed me with an evil stare.

"Get on with it Bullock, the pub's waiting."

I climbed the crack glancing occasionally at French, imagining his dark curly hair, like a clown's, springing from beneath his white bush-hat, crouching in his pads and thick gloves with his devil's horns and tail. The climb was as intimidating as a fast bowler and as polished as a cricket ball, just the sort of thing to fall from and wreck months of training along with my confidence.

At the top of the crack, *Black Kabul* traverses left. The moves to reach the large cam guzzling pocket mentioned in the guidebook description looked steady. There was even a small break to stand in. Before setting off and leaving the crack behind, I placed a nut high up that sank into its placement. That should stop me, I thought, and then noticed that Bruce's partner Andy and her daughter had appeared. The two of them, both climbers, sat down to witness a climbing display of consummate skill.

Leaving the crack, I locked off my fingers, caught a ledge with the heel of my rock shoe and rocked over onto my foot and reached out my hand to catch the pocket. 'Cruising,' I thought to myself.

Andy quietly explained to her daughter the reasoning behind some of my actions. Why, for example, I had placed gear high in the crack before leaving for the traverse, to protect me should I fall while traversing – and the reason I had placed a piece of gear on the second rope at the end of the traverse to protect the hard move reaching the pocket without causing the rope to drag.

It felt nice to show off my hard-won skills to a younger generation, to be a role model demonstrating expertise. The warm glow it gave me was tempered only slightly by the heat being generated in my tiring forearms. And so, pushing the thought of my dwindling arm strength to the back of my mind, I continued with an air of confidence, even as my forearms ignited in agony.

I took the large cam from my harness, glad to be rid of its weight as my arms began to melt, and stuffed it into the depths of the pocket. A perfect fit. Confident the cam was solid, I studied the crux section. Then I asked for the Evil One's eye to be fixed on my progress. I didn't catch the full reply, but I did hear mention of the pub. I heard a voice in my head and it screamed: 'Back off! Run away!' I calculated this was going to be a skin-of-the-teeth affair. My arms told me so. I joked with the ground support; asked for mobile phones to be at the ready.

The first move away from the pocket was powerful and energy-sapping. The hold I aimed for, the hold in which I had placed all of my hopes, was small and crimpy and facing the wrong way. I slapped for a better hold out to the right. It was good but I realised instantly there were no more footholds.

The next move was a long reach I'd spied from below. I smeared my right foot as high as my flexibility would allow, stretched up – and was short by an inch. Using as much strength as I could possibly muster, I jumped my right foot higher and pulled hard enough to rip the crimp from the wall. I began shaking, the remaining power in my arms drained. My head was on fire, my eyes wide. I needed to run my feet up the rock but there were no footholds. The next move would have to be dynamic. But I was spent.

"I'm off."

The cam is quite far below, but the distance will cushion the fall as the rope stretches. The female contingency start talking excitedly. Here is a chance for Andy's daughter to witness the reliability of modern protection. Throwing myself back into a crouching position, like ducking a cricket ball, in a flash I am falling earthwards, the trees and rock a blur. My eyes fix onto the cam as I fly past. The rope comes tight and I prepare to slow. The rope stretches. And... the cam rips straight out of the pocket.

My speed increases. The ground looms closer. The Evil One is trying to take in as much rope as possible. As a last ditch – and saintly – effort he runs backwards and jumps like I imagine he would do for a difficult catch. I think the wire I placed what feels like a year ago in the top of the initial crack might just save me.

The rope twangs taut when I'm ten feet from the ground. Still I plummet. The rope stretches. Five feet… three feet… I hit the muddy ground with my heels, the rope at full stretch. I surf the mud. The Evil One is catapulted into the air as if rejoicing at his catch. The mud disappears as I swing out across the hole in the ground below the crag, my feet now skimming air. Crashing into the rock at the base of the crag, the impact is cushioned only by clumps of nettles.

The Evil One is left hanging halfway up the face. I am hanging below ground level in the hole. Obviously there is a god. I begin to crawl out of the pit, fighting nettles, slipping and sliding in mud. My legs are jelly. Popping my head above the edge of the hole, a gopher on the prairie, I look up and ask the onlookers if they had any questions now that the Bullock masterclass of modern climbing techniques had finished.

They didn't and so we all went to the pub.

NORTH

────────

"Visit yourself someday on North Stack and ask for some scissors, because if your mate's a mate, he should have an axe."
JOHN REDHEAD

Cartwright has just returned from another expedition. If anyone will climb with me on Gogarth's North Stack Wall, it'll be him. While Jules has been exploring the planet for unclimbed lines, I have remained true to my word, confined within the shores of Britain, building on my Australian fitness. I have climbed many routes with Bruce and Dr Jon, including a line on slate called *My Halo*, given the grade of E7, the magical standard I had been aiming to climb for six years. But it isn't Gogarth and it isn't *The Bells!*.

Unfortunately, my Gogarth plans have hit a problem. Climbing partners are falling by the wayside, especially at the mention of North Stack. Now Cartwright has come to my rescue, agreeing to climb with me before his next mountaineering trip.

Jules and I leave Breakwater Quarry to walk the steep track heading toward the foghorn station on top of North Stack. How will North Stack appear to my more experienced eye? Will the routes I yearn for disappoint? Names of climbs and descriptions swirl inside my head like flecks of lichen in an updraft: *The Bells!*, *The Long Run*, *Art Groupie*, *The Cad*, *The Hollow Man*, *The Clown*. Conjured images of tortured, tormented souls battling on a vertical field draw me towards them. I know I am physically good enough to climb these routes but do I have the skill? Will I be mentally strong enough?

Once again, staring across the zawn, the cliff appears green, but I refuse to allow my enthusiasm to be dented. Where are the lines that I know exist, the lines that weave their way through all that lichen? I wonder about the others who have shared my viewing platform looking with longing and confusion… and fear. The sea crashes into the base of the crag throwing clouds of spume into the air, rumbling rocks in the mouth of Parliament House Cave and mixed amongst the clouds of spume I see climbers battling on the edge, battling life and questioning their mortality and I need to be there with them battling and freeing myself. We will have to wait for the tide to turn, but that's okay. An hour or two hardly matters after four years.

The rock is sticky; smells of salt. Limpets cling to the base of the wall, still wet from the sea's recent withdrawal. We uncoil the ropes beneath the start of *The Cad*, Ron Fawcett's route at North Stack. The wall is just off vertical, but bulges in places, with overlaps, arêtes and corners. There are sharp edges and positive side-pulls. Movement must come easy – for the confident, for the questioning.

Waves lap the rocks, the evening sun reflects white and green. Somewhere in this vertical maze I hunt three spikes upon which to drape thin slings. Not the greatest at finding sneaky gear placements, I press on unconcerned. The climbing, or what over the years I have imagined the climbing to be, is too good to let a lack of protection spoil the outing.

Skipping quickly up to the right, I reach the old rusty bolt. Slipping a wire around its broken head would be easy but I wouldn't get the E6 tick. My original dream all those years ago was never to use the bolt and I don't intend to change my mind now. This is as much a retrospective journey of discovery as it is also a test of nerve.

Clinging to tiny edges, twenty five feet above gear placed under a hollow flake near the bolt, I don't feel confident now. Through the lichen, like a spider on its silvery web, my hand creeps in search of deformities.

Hallowed ground with a foghorn above it. North Stack Wall, Gogarth, Anglesey, North Wales. *"There are lines there somewhere amongst the lichen."*

My questing fingers escape the trap, the evil spell is broken, both hands wrap around a hold and I drape a sling over the spike. Having grasped large comforting holds above the spike, I lean out and try to judge the distance of the fall should I miss the last hard move. There's no point dwelling on the past, on what would have happened if I'd tried *The Cad* in 1995. But I can't stop my mind playing out the scenario of a body falling and screaming. Sitting on the edge of the crag as I belay Jules, I watch the sun set and listen to the lapping waves.

Returning to North Stack next day, there is so much to do and the lack of time in life weighs heavy. The success of the previous day bolsters my confidence. The need to push myself is strong, but I don't yet feel ready for the intense outing one of the harder climbs will give. Redhead's routes are calling. They dare me to test my fate. Seagulls circle and cry. Jet-propelled guillemots scoot back from fishing trips. The cliffs across from North Stack swarm with hungry chicks. Tiny wings, sprouting from plump bodies, flap madly. From the ledges run long streaks of shit. The colony's chatter is raucous and ever present.

Sliding down the rope once again to the base of North Stack the decision is made. I choose a Redhead route, a great line that is preparation for harder climbs to come. Redhead's own description of his route *Birth Trauma* in his book *…and one for the crow* made no sense at all. But the picture of him climbing the route – like the Son of God, spread-eagled, nailed to crumbling quartzite – drew me in. The line it took was direct, obvious but uncertain. I wanted this experience.

Boulder-hopping at the base of the wall, we head into the non-tidal corner below the abseil point. We have used this approach so I don't see the moves before I climb them. My obsession with on-sighting the route has taken hold; rational thoughts have left my head. I recall a conversation with Owain Jones after I told him I wanted to climb *Birth Trauma*.

"No you don't," he said.

"Yes I do."

"Believe me, *you don't.*"

The consensus of opinion in the pub that night was that *Birth Trauma* is a pile of loose choss, and not to be considered under any circumstance. I left the pub with people shaking their heads.

Cartwright uncoils the ropes. I clip gear to my harness – a few wires, a few cams, nothing excessive. The route has two pegs, for heaven's sake, although the condition they are in is anyone's guess. I suppose checking the quality of the pegs for corrosion would have been sensible. Stormy winter seas have slapped the cliff repeatedly over the years, but as the climb was falling down anyway, according to the pub's clientele, Redhead's book, and the guidebook, the sensible option would be not to climb *Birth Trauma* at all.

The start is surprisingly steep. A flake succumbs to bridging and powerful laybacking. Level with a handrail of sharp positive edges, I question the need to place a small wire before setting off; I can see the first peg at the end of the traverse. Yet for once the voice of reason speaks loudly, and for once I listen – and place a nut.

Cutting loose, legs trailing and hands slapping for holds, alarm bells start to ring. Whole lumps of rock are detached, and some that look solid break with the slightest touch. Milking the good holds becomes imperative. Redhead's words begin, most worryingly, to make sense.

"One wishing to attempt this line should follow along the lines of karma!"

My feet cut loose once again, fluttering like my heart. Why did I choose to on-sight a pile of shit? Rocking bodyweight onto a high foothold finds me perched studying a dirty shallow crack. I have failed to clip the peg; the karabiner would not fit through the eye, which is now below me. I press my face to the rock – it smells of iron, salt, earth, life, fear and desperation – before seeking a nut placement in rock that isn't crumbling.

"I think this is the most friable of my routes at North Stack, and as such, gives an unsurpassed experience."

Higher now, I'm looking at a ground-fall. Bridging a faint corner-line, I place a cam and a wire. Their placements are separate; I'm gambling the rock around one of the pieces will hold should the time come to test it. I reach the top of the corner and snatch greedily at the first really good hold I've had for a while… but in an instant… I'm flying. The large lump of rock that was my handhold is flying too, flying into space until it smashes into the boulders.

Shocked at the speed all this happens, I take to the air in pursuit of the falling rock, arms windmilling, legs cycling and… time… so… much… time. Cartwright jumps from the rock and falls on his back clinging hard to the rope. The gear holds. Slamming into the rock below the handrail I'm shocked and angry that I've completed so much of the climbing, and good climbing at that.

"What are you going to do?"

"I'll show you what I'm going to do!"

Untying the ropes at the bottom of the route, I pull them through. Tumbling, they land strewn across the boulders, colourful felt-tip squiggles getting wet in the small rock pools. Ten minutes of ranting pass, and now the game is on more than ever. I won't be beaten, so launch myself once more onto the climb.

"The image is one of easy chairs, flickering televisions and shaking bits of anatomy, of padded cells and largactyl."

I refuse to be dictated to by this climb, but anger and aggression do not work and soon I'm flying again after ripping a handhold.

"This is ideal terrain to measure one's free will against predestination!"

My predestination at the moment appears to be down by the quickest and most direct route. I pull the ropes for a second time.

The initial steep corner is easily dispatched now, having completed the moves twice and knowing which lumps of rock to avoid. I quickly move up the handrail and clip the first peg. I have persisted this time knowing how poor the gear above is. I complete the mantel and slither up the loose corner to clip my highest gear, still in place from the first fall. Finally, new ground. Scary, loose uncharted ground. I make hard, contorted moves and establish myself in the second crack system out to the left. There is no protection.

"Birth Trauma connects with the institutionalised."

Twenty feet, thirty feet, the wire and cam are left behind. I carefully pull every hold before trusting my weight to it. Every foot placement is lightly pushed with a toe, gently weighted, kicked and STAMPED ON, before very slowly I stand on it. A rust streak runs from the highest peg and dribbles down the corner in front of my face, but still I can't reach it. My legs are spread across the wall, a hold breaks, clatters ninety feet down the face.

My forearms ache. Cartwright disappears beneath the overhang to avoid the rocks. Eventually, the peg is reached. Bridging wide, looking up the groove, my head spins. The cliff sways and twists like I'm standing beneath an electricity pylon on a windy day. I grasp a ledge and mantel, arms straight, shoulders locked to hold my position before I throw a foot up to the ledge and stand. Years of circuit training in the unnaturally dark and aggressive environment of a prison gymnasium have prepared me physically and mentally for this climb.

Hunched, but balanced on the ledge, I'm gripping small but positive holds above me, when the ledge decides to give up and tears itself from the cliff without warning. I'm left hanging from two crimps, my feet dangling. The ledge crashes, ricocheting and splintering into a thousand pieces. The rockfall echoes off the walls, off the walls, around the gaping mouth of Parliament House Cave and off the walls. A smell of cordite and sulphur fills my head. I am going to fall. I am going to fall for miles. The thought galvanises me but, before I can move, I have another more shocking thought.

"Jules, are you still alive?"

"Just get up the fucking thing!"

This is all the incentive required. I beat the hell out of every hold and eventually slither like a battered newborn over the lip of the cliff.

"Visiting times can be fun, if as a visitor, you can establish yourself inside…"

The following morning I ease out of my sleeping bag. I'm still tired and aching, but I have to return to Leicestershire tonight and I can't leave North Wales and North Stack without one final visit. My head is fried by images of deadly moments. But the thought of returning to the Midlands, to car fumes, McDonald's wrappers and people who don't climb threatens me much more than staying. Climbing life is cleansing. It is both life-threatening and life-enhancing and, I have discovered, my life is especially enhanced by this kind of threat.

Comfortable now with the crashing sea and the exposure, we have just climbed *Zeus* on Wen Slab. The wind has picked up; a change in the weather is imminent. Walking across the top of the headland North Stack Wall comes into view. Water is lapping at the foot of the climbs, and out to sea a bank of thick cumulus is building. My head is pleased for the excuse to cheat, and I ask Jules if he minds belaying at the top while I look at *A Wreath of Deadly Nightshade* on a top-rope.

I climb *Wreath* with one rest on the first attempt, and clean on the second. The route is definitely on. But not today.

DEVOTION

Early morning. Wrapped in a duvet jacket, I sat in the prison gymnasium office, cradling a cup of coffee and listening to the muffled train-rattle of food trolleys being shunted along cold corridors, ra-ta-de-tat-ra-ta-de-tat, first loud, then not-so-loud – and then nothing. Thirty minutes left. It seemed I was always counting down.

First class on Mondays, Wednesdays and Fridays was running. Over the years, prisoners in the running class had learnt to appreciate my early morning idiosyncrasies, and I had learnt to understand theirs. We ran three miles around an oval cinder track bordering the muddy football pitch. The track was surrounded by a tall fence, and beyond that the prison's wall. Thirteen laps run with the strategy and cunning of an espionage plot.

The speed would increase with every lap while we pretended not to be concerned, while we pretended to look at the ground and not to have noticed the opposition. I kept an eye on Mike, slightly chubby when first sentenced, lean and fit now. Mike pushed the pace along. Gary pushed also, but only for himself. He was not concerned in the slightest about where in the field he finished. Barry was the competition. Barry loved racing. And so did I.

Lap thirteen. We had reached a lung-bursting crescendo of effort. The last lap was always a sprint that tore our lungs to shreds. But no matter what the end result, we all returned to the prison laughing and joking. Me and my training crew. We would have been called friends if the situation were different.

The second class of the day was circuit training; time for more machismo-fuelled competition, more brutality in the guise of getting fit. Heavy house music shook the walls, echoing off the cavernous roof of the sports hall. My life was strip lights and plastic floors, and me and twenty or so inmates beasting ourselves into a frenzy of competition. Star jumps, press-ups, burpees, squat jumps, shuttle runs, sideways ski jumps over benches, sprinted laps of the hall and double bench step-ups. We were nearly fighting each other to get past to the next discipline. Even Gary was more competitive.

Sweat sprayed the floor, and our eyes darted from side to side as we worked, to check no one cheated. Our pounding feet became sticky, the air thick with hot body odour.

"You didn't do all your star jumps, cheating wanker."

"Fuck you."

My third class was in 'Four Shop', an industrial workshop stripped down and converted into a weights room. It was a filthy, narrow room with a corrugated asbestos roof, illuminated by more fluorescent tubes. There were no windows. Metal electrical ducting and heating pipes ran like veins across painted brick walls lined with fading crumpled posters of men and women with ripped bodies, with scribbled arrows pointing out their massive muscles.

The weight-training equipment was old school, as though I'd never left the Cheadle Health and Strength Club. There were racks of matt-black dumbbells, plates of iron disks stacked like pyramids, bars, cables, slides and springs, skipping ropes hanging from nails, benches made from angle-iron topped with blue PVC, brown leather medicine balls, scuffed and worn, a canvas punch-bag, well-patched and re-stitched, hanging from a chain. The room had a sound; it was the sound of human bodies making metal creak.

Then it was lunch.

At noon, I would race into the daylight. Often, a fresh wind would come slicing across the open farmland surrounding the prison. The hugeness of the sky always came as a shock, the vast puffy cumulus. In spring, the lapwings would skim low over ploughed fields and then soar into the air before flopping and folding downwards in their strange ritual flight.

As a teenager, I used to listen to their 'peewit' call walking along the lane towards Alan Johnson's farm on the edge of Huntley Wood. I would lean against the wooden five-bar gate in the oak tunnel's shade and watch the lapwings striding among the squelchy holes made by the cows and perform their flittery aerial dance. Lichen green from the top bar smeared the sleeves of my combat jacket. I remember thinking birds must have a simple life. Innocence. Peace.

During lunch, I drove down similar narrow country lanes away from the prison and out of Leicestershire altogether. On either side, clematis entwined with flowering hawthorn became a creamy-purple blur. A buttery scent poured through the open window of my new van. Fat flies popped against the windshield, their lacey wings fluttering from the blue and red pulp. Within twenty minutes of leaving the prison gates, I arrived at my destination, deep in the rolling countryside of Northamptonshire:

Slawston Bridge, the old disused railway bridge, a crossword puzzle of blue brick and large ironstone blocks daubed with grafitti, white aerosol exclamations like 'Rat Boy,' 'Jew Boy,' and an 'A' enclosed in a circle. Anarchy.

Many years ago, at the annual fair in Cheadle, I'd worn my red jeans and green combat jacket, the same white A painted on the back, and stood feeding copper coins into one-arm bandits. Bunches of raspberries, cherries, crowns, grapes and the word BAR spun by. Next to the arcade, dodgem cars jerked across their rink, contacts sparking on the metal mesh overhead. Flaking hand-painted light bulbs flashed in sequence: red, green, yellow, blue.

Glittering goldfish with big dark eyes swam in bags of plastic tied at the top with string. On the waltzer, girls with spiral perms and platform shoes squeezed into the hand-painted carriages, a metal bar closing across their thin denim thighs. Tattooed, unshaven men in leather waistcoats spun them until they screamed. The tattooed men looked at each other laughing as they rolled up and down standing on a sea of spinning wood.

Jimmy McCausland leaned against the wooden barriers, watching the girls spin past. Jimmy was twenty and came from Hammersley Hayes, the Wild West as far as I was concerned, a pebbledashed council estate at the top end of Cheadle. I was in awe of him. Jimmy was a proper punk rocker with a proper punk motorbike. He and his mates noticed me at the slots wearing the combat jacket with the big letter A. They laughed. The PA on the dodgems played The Undertones. "Ooh, Jimmy Jimmy."

"What's that A on your back mean?"

Jimmy prodded me in the centre of my back in time to his question. He already knew the answer. His mates laughed.

"Anarchy. It means anarchy."

"Yeah and what's that then?"

The laugh from the pack grew louder. Their chains and tartan bondage straps rattled. I was thirteen. I hadn't grown strong; I wasn't yet an individual. I just wanted to belong. Uncle Dave had just been killed. Jimmy, in his cool leather jacket, walked away, shoulders shaking, still laughing. Job done. I felt like a fraud. A few weeks later Jimmy was killed on his motorbike.

"Poor little Jimmy wouldn't let go." But he did, just like Uncle Dave.

By the time I was twenty nine, already a year older than the age Uncle Dave reached, my own chances of falling hard and ending up like roadkill were high. I'd only just discovered climbing when I began visiting the bridge. I felt an immediate ache in my forearms as I learned to read the rock and brick, the coarse, sharp, crystalline grit, the orange ironstone calcifications, the bubbles and waves and embedded lumps, the smooth, shiny, blue rectangles and the positive edges in-between, where rain and wind and probing fingers had worn away the yellow mortar. I was full of fear, but also thrilled, teetering beneath my stone summit, seven metres high. The rutted and potholed road seemed a long way down.

Yet in time, after many lunch breaks and evening sessions, Slawston Bridge became an old friend. And I noticed other things: the nesting blue tit, the aggressive robin. When the grass around the base grew, it covered the lowest edges and squelched between my feet and the brick so my nose filled with the scent of crushed green goo, like the smell of long grass growing in the hayfield near Cheadle, beneath the broad leaf canopy and white candles of a flowering horse chestnut, where as a boy I lay side by side with Jacky, my first girlfriend.

Cumulus bubbled on the horizon. Bees worked the pollen. My green combat jacket insulated us from the damp, and from the holly leaves, bluebell stalks and conker shells that crunched when we turned to face each other. I remember the tree roots poking through the soil.

Her hair was long and black and shone like a freshly peeled chestnut. Brown freckles smattered her pale cheeks. Staring into her wide, dark eyes, I felt scared and exhilarated, shy and inexperienced. I felt in love. I pretended I knew what to do but having lain there for over an hour all I'd done was talk. She spoke of friends who were flattening a patch of field not so far away, how they would be removing their clothes. Touching. The smell of crushed grass, rich with green, caught on the evening breeze. The smell was sharp. I kissed her for the first time. She asked, "Are you trying to eat me?" Terribly embarrassed, I kissed her again, but this time opened my mouth a little less wide.

A short time afterwards, Jacky and I split up, and she spread the word that I didn't know what to do with a girl in a hayfield. I felt betrayed. At school, heads from the front of the class turned to look. I heard whispers from behind cupped hands. The foundations of my young adult world seemed fragile.

But Slawston Bridge was solid. It was El Cap, the Shark's Fin, the Sex Pistols singing *Pretty Vacant*, it was Savoia Kangri and the Grandes Jorasses, it was the Ruts and lying in the grass with a girl I thought I loved. The bridge was honest and dependable, but it demanded commitment. I knew each hold intimately, and each hold knew my touch: rusty iron edges, deep positive pockets, ornate nubbins, chalk-smeared pinches, fins, ripples, slopers and crimps spread in more random patterns than could ever occur in nature. A single finger pocket in the middle of a blue brick was, perhaps, my second favourite feature. A small slash, a tiny imperfection hidden around the arête that balanced my body just enough to enable a foot-swap, a pull, a smear and a quick shuffle of feet – this was my favourite. But it only succumbed after months of devoted attention.

During the summer, the barley in the surrounding fields swayed in the sun, and in the sun, it was a shimmering ocean of burnt gold. The rustle of stalks in the summer breeze was the sea, the soundscape to my progress over the orange, into the yellow and across the blue. The bridge became North Stack Wall, but instead of the choppy Irish Sea that sucked at North Stack's quartzite, a narrow road skirted the base of the bridge's walls. I was free to top out, just as long as I could mantel the sloping coping stones at the rim, trusting to my dwindling strength – and believing in myself.

The sun shone more often than not at Slawston and sitting on the grass at the top I would breathe deeply. I'd watch the rabbits and the sheep, and the floating clouds.

So easy to watch.

WIRE

———

A week has passed. I'm back at Gogarth. Bruce French has agreed to climb with me in return for holding his ropes on *Quartz Icicle* in Wen Zawn. I enjoy Bruce's company, his no-bullshit attitude, and feel lucky to be contemplating such a serious climb as *A Wreath of Deadly Nightshade* with someone who instills so much confidence in me.

We climb *Quartz Icicle* and move to the top of North Stack. Wind hammers the cliff. Yelling for Bruce to take the rope in tight has no effect. I'm in the middle of North Stack hanging on to thin flakes of lichen-covered rock, and the rope runs in a huge flying loop from my waist up to Bruce who sits at the top.

Having cheated by practising *A Wreath of Deadly Nightshade* with Jules a week earlier, I now have no problem with the ethical issues raised by top-roping. Who am I anyway? Does it matter if I top-rope a climb? Is it important to anyone other than myself? Who cares? Practising and completing these less important climbs, graded at the top of my ability, is a stepping-stone to more important on-sight attempts.

The problem, though, with practising a climb, is the loss of that thrill you get from uncharted ground met in the moment. Where will the next rest be? Will the gear be good? Being impatient and driven has left me believing that there is never enough time to complete all the routes I desire, and this means not spending long on any individual climb. Having practised *A Wreath of Deadly Nightshade* twice today and twice before, I decide I have already spent enough time on it.

Bruce offers his usual encouragement.

"Get the bloody thing done then."

Wind blows off the Irish Sea. Each wave is white-topped froth. Seagulls skim the boiling water, others bob between crest and trough. A large grey head pops up from the dark below, and casts a sad interested gaze, big eyes gleaming. So at home and safe in the water, I conclude that the seal's sorrow must be for me.

The line of this route follows a series of leftward rising undercut flakes.

159

I'm not even a third of the way along when, hanging from an energy-sapping hold, I place a couple of nuts, one of them a 'micro' the size of a dot. It's the last protection on the whole climb that's likely to hold a fall. Wasting no more time or precious energy, I press on, undercutting the inverted 'V' of the flake until I reach its apex. Here an overhanging step on an arête leads to the upper wall. I cling to undercuts, walk my feet high, and pull, managing to wrap two fingers over a square razor edge. The edge bites into the skin of my fingers. Closing my head to the pain, I rock-over slowly and try to stop my leg from trembling.

At the top, I feel cold pricks of rain on my face but the weather has held off, even long enough for us to coil ropes and pack rucksacks. *Wreath* is in the bag also. Pink thrift dances in the wind, and the rain joins the party. I'm one step nearer my goal.

It's an obsession-filled fortnight. I train continuously, hanging and pulling from the smallest of edges I can find, the best being the edge of the doorframe of the prisoners' shower room. In the prison gymnasium two queues would form outside the showers, one of people wanting to shower and the second of inmates determined to complete a single pull-up using the doorframe.

Mornings were spent running and circuit training. I would escape from work at lunch, drive like a lunatic through the country lanes of Northamptonshire to climb at Slawston Bridge. After an hour, back in my enclosed world of gates, walls and the rattle of keys was torture. I had been given a brief taste of how good life could be and was now teleported back to real life, the life I seemed destined to live.

The senior officer's attitude made life even more difficult. An hour-and-a-half session of pull-ups with weights attached to my waist eased the torment and always attracted a crowd. As usual, in an attempt to validate my position as an instructor, I tried and failed to convince the clientele to join me.

On the hunt for climbing partners and not having a phone at home, I walked past the thatched post office to the red phone box in the village centre. I rang Tim Neill and he promised two days in the week. Gripping the phone a little more tightly, I asked the dreaded question.

"Do you mind climbing at North Stack?"

I realised I was holding my breath.

"No problem. I'd love to."

I burst from the phone box cheering. The pedigree sheep in the field neighbouring the phone box lifted their heads to look. Arms held aloft, if the grass on the verge had been muddy, I'm sure my celebration would have rivalled any goalscorer's corner-flag skid.

It's calm today. Peace and quiet has fallen onto North Stack. I'm not afraid of falling, but I'm terrified of failing. Anyway, the chances of surviving a fall today are actually good. Tim and I have decided to attempt *Stroke of the Fiend*, a Redhead route that traverses the wall from left-to-right. The first pitch starts by climbing an E3 called *South Sea Bubble* but after the first few metres the route begins traversing rightwards, aiming for the undercut flake of *The Cad* and finally the old bolt.

Using this, we set up a hanging belay, backed up with the static abseil rope, which we have left in place. The second pitch is sustained climbing following a break in the rock below the upper traverse of *The Bells!*. It's a big run-out protected by just the rusty old peg on *The Bells!*, until I can place gear in an arête at a junction with *Wreath*. Then we follow *Flower of Evil* and *Blue Peter* to the top. Tim is hanging from the belay at the top of the first pitch. I join him and my eyes scour the rock beyond. Hanging in the middle of the wall, wires are exchanged and a few words shared until it is time for me to leave. Cautious and calculating, like a sloth I move away from Tim and creep towards my destiny. An hour passes before I heave onto the flat platform at the top of the wall. I see the grass tousled by the breeze, and a shout of triumph escapes me.

A voice from behind the fog station's wall makes me jump. "You've done one of the hard climbs then?" It's the woman who lives in the station. I'm embarrassed at my blatant outpouring of emotion.

"Yes!" I say, "hard for me, anyway."

The stream running down from the hillside above Tim's cottage in the Llanberis Pass gabbles through the long hours of darkness. I lie awake and listen. I can see the water twisting and surging past rocks in the stream, cold and clear as glass, pouring over boulders polished smooth by its passage. Falling, the water churns violently. Bubbles spin a wild vortex.

Next morning, the smell of fresh sea air fails to clear the poisoned lethargy that has settled on my body and mind. Quietly I walk. My sense of freedom, my driven psyche, seem to be missing today. I've spent a miserable night without a moment's sleep turning over thoughts, a slow unravelling of dull terror. Still, opportunities have to be taken. And today it's *The Bells! The Bells!*.

I have no qualms about abseiling the line of the crux section of the route. The flapping scarf of salted tat hanging from the peg must be replaced. Yesterday I clipped the peg and its tat without a thought for its age and condition. But today is different. I am riddled with doubts. Have I blown an on-sight ascent because I've looked at the line? I reason with myself. Who cares? Really, only I should care. This is about me, and my life. My real life.

I try to stay apart from the tittle-tattle of points and numbers, grades, on-sights, flashes, redpoints, pinkpoints. What does it all mean? Does any of it matter? Staying alive matters, but staying alive right at the very edge of where you are capable matters more. Living with hope and positive energy, that's what I need.

Arriving halfway down the abseil rope I reach the peg. The eye is broken, rusted through. I clove-hitch flat tape around the rust where it protrudes from the crumbly rock. The peg bends as I tighten the knot.

Sliding further down the rope I look at the rock I have to climb before I reach the peg. It's sandy and gritty. Snappy. I watch a spider crawl across the quartz. I need a particular line but that could be anywhere. Like the spider on its silk, I slide to the sea-washed boulders below, and yet I feel the route wrapping its finely woven shroud around me.

Starting up the familiar line of *The Cad*, I start to climb, stepping into the vertical parallel life that gives me so much more than that other enclosed life. Tim is nestled amongst the boulders. I quickly cover some distance and am now beneath the undercut flake of *The Cad* – it would be so easy to step up there and fill the flake with protection. When climbing *The Cad* the gear felt frail and dubious, but now that gear seems as certain as a fat bouldering mat filled with sponge waiting for me just a few feet below. The flake's temptation has to be ignored, so screwed up are my ethics. I've already sneaked a preview of the crux section, would it now make such a difference if I stray a little and place some protection off route?

THE PEG. Life swings in the balance and, when it comes down to it, it is decided by the thickness and the strength of a piece of rusty driven metal. Terror, or a release into life-enhancing horror.

Well yes, it does – to me. So I pass, leaving the flake alone and empty of gear.

Reaching a good foot-ledge beneath the crux section is a slight interruption. I can shake blood to my arms and try to relax. Three skyhooks and two RPs, brass blobs the size of pink matchheads, are placed with great care. And now I move on and try to focus. Making one move, and another, I'm suddenly surprised the climb is not following the direct line I'd seen earlier. It is revealing itself, unlocking secrets. With arms spread wide, I hold myself using side-pulls. Doubt crawls through my mind. I reverse.

With new resolve, now determined, I set out for the second time. My head is turned sideways, the soft skin of my cheek is rubbing against the rock. The smell of the wall and its sunned warmth are as familiar as a lover's skin. Silently I pray and stand. The skyhooks glint in the sun. Tim's face is turned toward me. He shuffles on the top of the boulders. The sea is radiant, reflecting light onto the wall like a shoal of small fish. Another inch... just another inch to be level with the rusty old peg… it may as well be a mile away, a country, a world, a lifetime.

I'm snatching at holds, not flowing free. My body is stiff and cautious, every movement is guarded. The consequences of falling here are congealing in my limbs. My style is grinding – laboured. If only I could free my mind from the prospect of a fall. The right hand hits a hold. Instantly my thumb, which doesn't seem like my thumb any more, wraps itself over the top of this stranger's fingers to create more pressure.

To clip the peg I need to swap hands and feet. Sinking low over my feet, I negotiate with my fingers, ease them to the left of the hold until no more space is available. A single finger of the right hand pushes alongside the fingers of the left. My glasses are smeared with droplets of sweat, making the rock and the muddle of my clumsy fingers appear warped and shaky. The tape, clove hitched around the protruding peg, hangs in a loop. It doesn't help, it doesn't reach down to me. It just hangs. My nerves are nailed out on a wall of rock. I can't reach the loop. I reverse to a pedestal out from the rock to watch myself. The years preparing me for this climb appear to be catching up. Is this where it will all end?

It takes two more attempts before eventually the peg is clipped and I snatch an edge, and then another. Time is running out, my time is running out. My fingers begin to unfurl. I am racing against a tide of ebbing finger-strength, their inevitable refusal to grip. The traverse line of *Stroke of a Fiend* comes into view. I gaze at it trying to will myself into another life where I'm just over there, but it seems to be decades away. I hear a very faint crack and suddenly the wall accelerates upwards. I'm no longer touching it, I'm…

…falling…

…flakes of rusty metal spring from the peg as it twists like a rotten torn finger. My body scrapes down the surface of the rock. I hear the smack and chafe of skin, the drag of fabric. Green, yellow, white, all the colours of the wall explode. I can't kick out and push away. I'm terrified the peg is going to break. It is going to break? Very soon my body will be just another piece of flotsam, dragged endlessly in and out with the passing of the tide, the turn of the planet…

Sitting in the dark confines of Tim's living room, we shared war stories. A foothold had broken as I'd rocked onto it. Tim had given me a massive dynamic belay passing rope out through the belay device in time with my fall, which almost certainly saved my life, keeping the forces on the pathetic peg to a minimum. And it had held. I asked him what his plans were for the weekend after next.

"I think I'm free – why?" He already knew the answer.

For a week I trained feverishly. The climb consumed me every day, every hour, every minute. My elbows complained with chronic tendonitis that was quelled with anti-inflammatory tablets. Obsession consumed me until I phoned Bruce and Tim who were both keen to belay. But now both were working and the forecast for the weekend was fantastic.

By Saturday morning I could take no more. Instead of Gogarth, I was still in Leicestershire. Pulling my road bike out of mothballs, I pumped up the tyres, ate an extra piece of toast and cycled to my parents' house seventy miles away. Lorries thundered past missing me by inches. I swore and shouted, my tension eased with every wave of the fist. Flashing a V-sign at drivers who showed no regard for my safety sweetened my bitterness. After four and a half hours of riding and ranting, I rolled into Cheadle and relaxed into an evening of pasta, red wine, and rest.

The return journey the next day evaporated my tension. I could now take a more realistic view of events. It was still only August, and I was still alive, and with a little luck the climb that had become the focal point of my life should still be on. But worryingly, since returning from my bike ride, my fingers had become numb. My hands jumped and shook spasmodically.

Two days later, unable to grip a can-opener, Mike Allen, my friendly doctor, confirmed carpal tunnel syndrome, a trapping of the nerves in the wrist due to inflammation of the fascia. A test revealed I had lost sixty percent of use in the right hand, and thirty in the left. An operation was the only certain cure, with rest being a poor second choice. I chose rest.

In one fell swoop my year of rock-climbing was over. It was shocking to be climbing the routes of my dreams one day and struggling to hold a toothbrush the next. The bitterness and concern about not climbing paled into insignificance when the whole of my climbing future was in jeopardy. But still, as I lay half-asleep, half-awake in my bed, in my small safe cottage in the country, in the small dark hours, the wall called.

"The Bells! The Bells!"

WORDS

After several months working with the new senior officer at Gartree, it was obvious something had to change. He could never be flexible. Rules had to be followed without question. He was the type of person who would have murdered hundreds of innocent people in a war if instructed to do so by his superiors. Either he could not or else refused to look outside his narrow world, and was the polar opposite of me. We hated each other.

"You've got your transfer." It was the best news I'd had since hearing that my carpal tunnel syndrome had sorted itself and I wouldn't need an operation. I moved to HMP Welford Road, the castle in the centre of Leicester, without ceremony or even a leaving party soon after.

Welford Road would be classed by most as a Victorian prison even though it was opened before the start of Victoria's reign in 1828. The gatehouse, from the outside, looks like a castle with crenellated columns made of sandstone, large wooden doors that resembled a drawbridge, arrow loops, a false portcullis and a postern gate, the small entrance which pedestrians used.

Inside was a scene straight from *Porridge*, the TV programme starring Ronnie Barker. Every space was utilised, with prisoners two or three to a cell, narrow corridors, tunnel walkways like the passenger ramps used to board an aircraft. It felt very different to Gartree.

Welford Road also housed a contrasting assortment of inmates, some of them sentenced and some on remand. Many of the inmates were in their early to mid-twenties, which also felt different to Gartree's more middle-aged clientele. Many of the inmates were local, from rundown parts of town – drug users, repeat offenders, thieves, gang members, people who had little consideration for anyone else but themselves.

Some of the inmates were okay, and then, of course, there were the characters. Buster was from Chesterfield and a similar age to me. He looked like a teddy boy, with dark hair, short at the sides, longer on top, and after a few months of prison, a few good meals and no drugs, he developed broad shoulders but always kept the skinny legs. A smattering of prison tattoos dotted his pale muscled arms. On his knuckles, in blue, he had marked LOVE and HATE.

Buster was from quite a good background. His mum sounded like she was a decent woman who despaired of her errant son, but he was addicted to drugs which led to burglary and then prison. Buster immediately took to me; he watched me train and then pestered to join in. At first I wasn't sure, but he talked and pestered, and talked some more and cajoled me like an enthusiastic puppy wanting to play. Once I became accustomed to his pestering, I grew to like him, especially when he joined in with a pull-up session.

It wasn't only the inmates who differed from Gartree. The gymnasium facilities were a big change. There was a very small weights room and a small sports hall big enough for one badminton court, although you couldn't play badminton because the ceiling was too low. There was a caged area outside with basketball hoops, like you would see in an American jail, alongside a large three-storey wing, which towered above us as we exercised. On the other side was the high red-brick prison wall.

The rubber all-weather pitch was large enough for five-a-side football, basketball and circuit classes and in the summer months, the sun found a way around the walls and razor wire to shine on us, lighting up the cage. Inmates locked in their cells would look down on us, yelling their special type of encouragement as we circuit trained.

The gym was joined to the main prison by a warren of low-ceiling corridors, which, like the bulkheads of a submarine, were sealed with several locked gates and thick wooden doors. The gym was dusty, dirty and basic, reminding me of Cheadle Health and Strength Club – and like the club from my childhood it generally had a good vibe, even if no day passed without confrontation.

Bob McFadden, the senior PE officer, was a friend, who had done me many favours over the years, and pushed for me to work at Welford Road. I had a lot of time for Bob but he could be fairly volatile, placid one moment and then blowing up at an inmate the next, adding to the uncertainty of each day.

When I went for my interview at Welford Road, Bob told me I would get the job on one condition, that I didn't take more than five weeks off at one time. Even this could only happen with the full support and agreement of the rest of the department. I agreed, knowing I wanted to go to places like Peru, Canada and Alaska, places where I could climb successfully in a shorter period of time than that required to visit the Himalaya. It would do for now. I had a good chunk of money saved and reckoned it would take me another three years before I had enough saved to pay my mortgage and fund two years without work. The only problem with moving to Welford Road was the Alaska trip I had already arranged.

Since returning from my Himalayan expeditions I had read about Alaska, about the convenience of the climbing and the ease with which it could be arranged. This really appealed to me. In particular, I read the American climber Mark Twight's book, *Kiss or Kill*. Twight's uncompromising, angry prose roared at me from the page and left me inspired. I read of his route *Deprivation* and single-push climbing, by which he meant starting at the base of the route and continuing to the top in a single effort without stopping to sleep. This bold approach was virtually unheard of at the time.

I also read about Greg Child and Michael Kennedy's route *Wall of Shadows* on the North Buttress of Mount Hunter. Hunter appealed both to my nature and to the demands of my new workplace. It was convenient to reach but as uncompromising as Twight's writing. Ribbons of ice separated bands of steep rock, so that Hunter's North Buttress appeared to be everything someone needing to challenge all their skills as a climber could desire.

After two long expeditions where the days of actual climbing could be counted on the fingers of two hands and recuperation could last months, I needed something simple but challenging. Looking at pictures of the North Buttress of Hunter and researching the established climbs, I discovered obvious gaps for high-quality new routes.

On holiday with a broken ankle from my first full winter season in the Alps and spending time with the Pretentious Poet, Mark Goodwin; writing mentor, teacher, inspiration and nagging pain in the arse.

I told Jules Cartwright about my plan and he agreed to join me. Then I drew lines on my photographs and sent them with an application to various grant-making bodies. Unfortunately, my switch to Welford Road happened just before we were due to leave and Jules decided six weeks was the minimum time we required. I really wanted to go but I didn't have that kind of time. As the departure date drew near and with Jules intransigent, it was easier for me to send him all of the paperwork so he could go on my trip with someone else.

I chose instead to throw myself into shorter trips: ice-climbing in La Grave, mixed snow and rock in Scotland, waterfall ice in Canada and the *Dru Couloir* in the Alps with Paul Schweizer. Returning to Bernard Ravanel's campsite in Argentière, after the ascent of the Dru, I sat in my new Citroën van and for the first time since my English teacher had accused me of being sly and copying someone else's work, I began to write.

Having no writing paper, I scribbled short punchy sentences on used envelopes I had stuffed beneath the dashboard. There was no editing or re-writing, misspelt words tumbled from my pen without punctuation or much concern for grammar. Back in Leicester, I gave the envelopes, covered in scribble, to Mark Goodwin, a rather individual character I knew working at The Tower climbing wall in Leicester.

Mark was a climber, but more than this, a writer, mostly of poetry. He had badgered me to write about my experiences after I had acted out my *Orion Face* epic for Mark and another instructor, Rob Cooper, in The Tower's tiny office. Both of them sat amazed as I whirled my arms like a madman, miming climbing moves and ranting. Yet afterwards both insisted I had a talent with words. It felt odd; I'd never been encouraged like this before. But I could see they really meant it, and so I took them at their word.

"Here you go," I said, handing Mark a bundle of creased envelopes. "You asked for it. Do something with this lot." Mark, who I had dubbed affectionately 'the Pretentious Poet', seemed delighted, and told me how impressed he was that I'd started to write. He took the bundle home and went to work on it.

One morning at The Tower, and bored of bouldering, I felt I needed to challenge myself. So I went into the empty leading wall and began climbing solo up and down the wall's fifteen-metre overhanging section. Mark, the instructor on duty, was used to me soloing and let me get on with it. I started by climbing up the easier routes with the biggest holds but quickly abandoned them for the hard routes. Two middle-aged climbers arrived, and seemed a bit bemused by my antics, so I sloped off to the little office.

I stuck my head round the door and found the poet poring over his laptop. I asked him if he'd had a chance to look at my bundle of envelopes. He replied eagerly, explaining he'd been through the lot, and seemed rather pleased. We sat side by side in the little office in front of his laptop and discussed what I'd written in detail.

For the first time in years I began to trust someone outside the confines of climbing. Over the course of a few sessions together, Mark listened to all my suggestions, and I listened to his. All the changes made were negotiated, and he was careful to point out that what we were doing was collaborating. I learned a huge amount, and suddenly another world of challenges opened before me.

I was excited about the discovery but also a little angry. I might have found this sooner. My English teacher's words still taunted me. "At least with the others," she had said, meaning the trouble-makers, those who were disruptive, or noisy, "it's obvious." She knew what they were, and so could handle them – by labelling them and putting them in a box. But I was something different, and all she could do was suspect me of being a sly cheat. She refused to believe I was capable of writing anything worthwhile.

Working on words, with words, expressing emotions, sharing my experiences with others lifted some of the secrecy with which I had surrounded myself. I found the experience cathartic and enjoyable. After this first collaboration with Mark, I began to write avidly. I found writing to be a release. But much the same as with climbing or politics or teaching, there appeared to be those who thought you had to stick to the rules to get proper results – and that nothing else would do.

Time and again I hit a wall when I sent my essays to editors. But Mark, a somewhat unorthodox and non-conformist poet, kept offering me encouragement and advice. Besides, writing had got hold of me in a similar way to climbing, and so, as with my climbing, I pushed on with my typical, driven enthusiasm. Just as climbing had allowed me the freedom to grow in one direction, writing helped equally in another. I could now not only express myself physically and freely in the mountains, but I could also express my thoughts and speak to people.

During that same summer of discovering writing I travelled for the first time to Peru. And as I travelled the words came with me. I saw and experienced the world in a new way. I travelled and I climbed knowing that I could – and would – write about it.

It was dark and murky when we landed in Lima; I felt edgy with new-country nerves crackling through my body. Yet forty busy minutes later, Bruce French, Bruce's partner Andy, his brother Dave and I were on the night bus heading to Huaraz. Lima was awash with life. The bus nudged through streets teeming with people and cars and their screaming horns, the atmosphere heavy with the heated stink of over-crowding, the brightly painted buses bumper to bumper.

I pressed my face to the steamy window, overwhelmed by the smell of the bus, its dusty upholstery and sweating passengers. Dim streetlights couldn't match the bright flames of open fires. Ghostly crowds stood at street corners, waiting and watching or else busy buying and selling. It was all a blur of humanity, of survivors in a crumbling city tacked to the edge of the world. I felt transported to another planet. Life is short, but as I wiped condensation from the bus window and looked out, I knew life for some was even shorter.

At dawn, our bus pulled into the kerb. After eight hours spent bouncing across Peru, weary passengers climbed down, staggering a little on stiff legs. I looked up at the snow-covered mountains surrounding Huaraz. Men in worn dress trousers pushing bicycles milled around in the cold air of 3,000 metres, shouting their wares through megaphones fastened to the sides of the bikes.

Women hidden beneath broad-brimmed felt hats stood by carts lined with bottles of fluorescent blue, dayglo green and pomegranate pink liquid. You chose a flavour and it was added to boiling water from a blackened kettle. Dogs hunted rubbish from between the cobbles. Pigs squealed. And cockerels crowed a welcome for the Westerner who had escaped – for the time being anyway.

I spent a month in Peru, most of it with Bruce climbing Ishinca, Ulta and Alpamayo. After Andy became ill and left with Bruce and Dave, I climbed Tocllaraju and Pucarashta Oeste on my own. Making my way around Peru alone, I felt satisfaction that I had the courage to stay on in a country where I couldn't speak the language. Peru appeared to offer many mountaineering possibilities. Walking out of the Santa Cruz valley, with an *arrero* leading a single donkey carrying my bag, I took a shot of a mountain, a snow-encrusted pyramid I thought offered more potential than most. Gaining the *arrero's* attention I gestured towards the hill and shrugged a question – what was its name? His answer, when it came, was an unintelligible jumble of words that spoke of dust and donkey hooves. It sounded like: "Quitaraju."

CONFRONTATION

I remember a steamy ski chalet in Chamonix, clothes hung on every available beam, the windows running with condensation. It was crowded with people enjoying the skiing but I was there to climb. I had driven to Chamonix on my own to meet Jules Cartwright who was promising a new route on the Aiguille Sans Nom. It hadn't happened – thanks to the weather. Outside, snowflakes smacked against the windows, hung there for a moment, and then slithered down the glass to be quickly replaced by others.

It was here I had met Al Powell for the first and only time. We'd spoken a few times over the phone since then, but that doesn't help much when it comes to recognising your climbing partner to be.

Now, several months later, I was waiting at Manchester Airport, looking around for a face I recognised while recalling my last conversation with Al. His parting shot was still running through my head.

"This will be the ultimate blind date."

After visiting Peru with Bruce French the previous summer, I was determined to return and try something challenging and new. I discovered the pictures I had taken while walking out of the Santa Cruz valley were of the South Face of Quitaraju, which only had one route. I had rung Cartwright, but his answer was typical, delivered in his blunt style: "It looks too white for me." Cartwright was not partial to a bit of ice or snow, preferring steep and technical mixed climbing. Instead, he put me in touch with Al Powell, one of a strong crew of British Alpinists knocking off hard stuff in Europe and attempting inspiring new lines in the Greater Ranges. It was Powell who had climbed the Colton-MacIntyre wearing a blanket as a poncho. I was sure we would get on.

In Peru the year before, I had been surprised with the speed and ease of getting into and out of the mountains. It seemed the perfect country for two climbers with limited time. We spent the first week getting to know each other, doing things that most new couples don't normally experience – getting ill, arguing with donkey men and carrying monstrous bags to base camp.

We acclimatised in the beautiful Laguna Parón valley. At its northern limit was Paria, our first warm-up peak, at 5,600 metres in altitude as good a starting point as any. The guidebook said it should take three days. We set off from our base camp at eleven in the evening and were back from the summit at ten the following morning. Al is a brilliant hill runner and very fit. He also acclimatises well but I seem to have acquired the right genes for rapid acclimatisation and so the unspoken competition between us was intense.

Our next peak was the nearby Artesonraju. The climbing this time was a little more sustained than on Paria, but still relatively straightforward. At 6,025 metres, though, it tested our lungs. Al told me later that when a friend heard about my acclimatisation schedule, he told Al he should have pissed in my sleeping bag for making him go that high so soon. I think if he had we might have fallen out.

From the top of Artesonraju we got views of many of the Cordillera Blanca's finest mountains, including the very objective we had come to Peru to climb – Quitaraju. I looked across at its huge South Face, ice-coated, steep and rocky, with white runnels in its upper section leading directly to the summit. Al and I sat together staring at this monster and growing excited about what lay in store. Then we jumped to our feet and ran back to base camp to catch a taxi to Huaraz.

Tucked up in my sleeping bag for the night, I stared at the roof of the tent and wondered what the next few days would bring. Spending four days in Huaraz and then walking into the Santa Cruz valley had been relaxing and enjoyable, although Al had been ill. But camped now on the wide plain with lakes and mountains surrounding us, I was worried.

Originally, we had planned a recce into the hanging valley beneath Quitaraju's South Face, but because the hillside was so steep we chose to just go for it instead, and not bother. Having scoped out the face the day before, Al sounded suitably impressed: "It's like several *Galactic Hitchhikers* stacked one on top of the other," he said, comparing our route to somewhere we both understood – Ben Nevis. I was pleased with this appraisal. I didn't want Al to think I had dragged him all the way to Peru for some boring snow plod – as Cartwright had suggested it would be.

The following afternoon we flogged up the steep hillside, and then continued on into the hidden, hanging valley of the Quebrada Quitacocha. The sun shone through the quenal trees, their bark peeling, and their vibrant limbs prickly and green. Long marsh grass swayed in the wind. We descended to a dry lakebed, its surface baked and cracked by the hot sun into millions of herringbone lines. Following this crazy paving at the lake's edge, we picked our way to its end and then, entering a line of trees, we began the long climb to the head of the valley.

Unfortunately, we had more pressing concerns than the scenery to occupy our thoughts. Above our heads lurked the gigantic broken icefall spewing out from the bottom of Quitaraju's South Face. During an interview in London, a panel of eminent mountaineers at the Mount Everest Foundation had dared to suggest that this icefall might explain the lack of previous action on the face. Now we'd find out if they were right.

The more I grew to know Powell, the more similar we appeared to be. We were both equally driven and ambitious, although friends would probably describe us as being pigheaded, perhaps even bloody-minded. However, there are times when such traits may be deemed advantageous – and the icefall looked like one of those times.

The closer we got the more difficult it appeared. In fact, it looked almost impossible. It was two, perhaps three football pitches of ice-block jumble that was creaking, breathing, moving – a belching monster. This would have been a good moment for any sensible party to look at other objectives, to lick wounds, to laugh a little at how blind they had been, even a little arrogant to think they could get through where others had failed – to run away. We were not that party.

After resting, then eating the only proper food we had brought, we set off in the dark to find a way through the icefall. Our plan was a good one, but it depended on our ability to move quickly and continuously. We took only food we could eat whilst climbing: chocolate, biscuits, sweets and a malt loaf. We took no food for cooking and so needed no fuel. We wouldn't be stopping, so there was no need for sleeping bags or duvet jackets. We took just one homemade Pertex bivouac sack, which I found out was called 'The Coffin' and designed by Al himself.

We'd climb quickly through the icefall, move together on the route, use our recently gained acclimatisation to reach the summit speedily and abseil down the opposite face, which is the standard route and would hopefully be equipped. There would be a cold and hungry bivvy, or more likely we'd keep moving to reach base camp late, knackered but safe. It sounded a great plan.

Al started into the icefall. His headtorch beam picked out small blocks of ice, and we found it easy enough to hop from one to another. But as we moved further into the icy maze, the blocks grew as though on steroids to gigantic proportions. We were diverted repeatedly. Often unable to go around the towering seracs, we had to tackle them head on while hoping the whole lot wouldn't tumble over and crush us.

On the sharp end, I found myself beneath an overhanging ice-wall. Getting started was difficult and the climbing steep from the first move. The ice was so hard and it took several axe-swings to get a placement. Bludgeoning got me over this first hurdle and at the top I threw a boot heel over the edge and slithered onto the top.

I now found myself sprawled on a shelf, with a curving chimney above me. I placed an ice screw, and began to follow this icy fault-line upwards. As the chimney leaned towards vertical I started to bridge across its dark interior. Nearing the top, I found a huge rounded block of ice was wedged into the chimney. I moved onto the right wall to bypass this obstruction. Just a few more moves would put me on top of the serac.

Planting my right axe I leaned backwards and began to move the left pick towards the top of the block. The pick touched it and the block suddenly fell, plunging into the darkness below. My left axe had ripped free from the ice-block's soft outer layer. I hung from my right axe, panting in the freezing air, stinging inside my lungs. Sweat froze. The block landed and I heard echoes of ice shattering in the dark. Then – quiet. Reaching the top I quickly set up a belay.

"Safe! SAFE!"

Safe?

Through my small door, a glow of wan light melted into the wet pavement. That morning, like every morning, I pulled the latch shut on my small cottage in Burton Overy, to drive the dark lanes to work. It was raining. The hawthorns were bare, a few brown leaves clung to the skeletal oaks.

I barely noticed any of it. I was lost in my usual fantasies about quitting the Prison Service to climb full time. I was lost among the high peaks of the Himalaya amid plumes of spindrift and clouds and the sound of yak bells. I was touching warm rock and bright water in Spain. I was held by the blue ripple of an icefall in the Alps and the crumbling quartzite of Gogarth.

One path had been instilled in me from a very young age. You work hard, you take the job that pays the best whether it gives satisfaction or not, you meet a girl, get married, have kids, support your family and buy a house. A quotation my grandad knew from Shakespeare was, "Neither a borrower, nor a lender be."

No one resigns. No one gives up security. Routine is safe, but safe is minutes, hours, days, weeks, months and years. Safe is a quick existence. My mind jumped in and out of dreams of escape. Climbing seemed like freedom, another life. Just a few more miles to dream.

All too soon, HMP Welford Road rose up in the yellow streetlights of

Leicester's city centre, the solid sandstone fortification, the castellated towers, the large wooden double entranceway – and the small postern door, with its pallid glow. Got to leave, time is running out. One last deep breath of exhaust fumes, then I stepped through the ghostly light into the shadow of cast iron girders, steel stairways and exposed pipes, of polished handrails worn smooth by weary, desperate hands.

"Three's landing unlock for slop out and medication, bang up the one's, unlock the cleaners." The shout came from the senior prison officer, in the centre of the two Victorian wings. Echoes bounced off the walls like the calls of climbers. Three levels of railings, thick metal doors and wire netting stretched across the void like trampolines to catch falling bodies. Which of my worlds was the dream? I'd entered a space turned inside out, where everyday values were a sign of vulnerability, where the rules of survival kept changing. The smell of waste was as pungent as the sea. Flotsam and detritus. Unwanted lives, unwanted hours.

I inserted the key into the lock of a cell door. In a dark corner, a shadow waited. "Just another dreamer," rattled in my head. Security is a sentence.

The icefall levelled out. Snow had settled, but not consolidated. Al now took over trying to find a way through. His headtorch swept from side to side and in its beam ice crystals sparkled. The snow deepened. When it reached my thighs, the snow became a tedious struggle. At shoulder-depth it became the new senior PE officer at Gartree – an annoying bastard.

The ice creaked as the temperature dropped. Every so often, the sound of a collapsing serac shattered the silence. Carefully, we inched upward through the icefall. There was no respite. The water we had melted for when we reached the climbing on the face was already drunk. Our muscles ached with effort, but the wading seemed never to end. Our plan was ruined.

Finally, at 8 a.m., we emerged from the icefall. Eight hours of continuous climbing and wading had made serious inroads into our reserves. We talked about traversing the base of the face, and so escaping. The most obvious line looked steep and hard. If it were covered in powder it would take forever. Yet after all the hard work getting through the icefall, we had to at least take a look at the face. If the snow was névé, perhaps we could make up the lost time.

We made the decision together. If the ice was anything but perfect, we'd scuttle off to the left and escape.

Crossing the steep rocky bergschrund proved awkward but I pushed on, climbing furiously up our chosen line. The snow was generally good – patches of névé mixed with water-ice over bulging rock. Al moved up, collected some gear and climbed on.

The cornice bivvy/tent spot on Savoia Kangri, in the Karakoram, Pakistan. A fine place to have a night-time epic. In the background, just left of centre, is Broad Peak (the rounded summit), one of the world's fourteen 8,000m mountains. Lower down the Godwin-Austen Glacier is Gasherbrum IV (the wedge-shaped peak right of centre), scene of one of the most important and historic ascents in Alpinism – the first ascent in great style of the West Face in 1985 by Robert Schauer and Voytek Kurtyka should be an example to all of the peak baggers who cheat and cut corners by using fixed ropes and performance enhancing oxygen on Everest and the like. Style is everything; anyone using engineering can climb anything – where is the challenge in that? *Photo: Paul Schweizer*

Al Powell on the first ascent of Quitaraju's Central Buttress, Peru. We went equipped for a twenty four hour, single push; no bivvy food, just a few bars and a malt loaf, no fuel for the stove, no sleeping bags or even a duvet jacket, no sleeping mat. We drank our one litre of water each before starting to climb. Three days later we returned to base camp with a new route, twenty four frost-nipped digits between us and a radical new method for weight loss. It took me six months to recover from this one, but it remains in my memory as one of the best climbs and experiences ever, and with a great mate.

The snow-hole on the summit of Quitaraju. One of the few times I've spooned a bloke and enjoyed it, although Powell needs to put a bit of weight on.   *Photo: Al Powell*

The end of moving together. This was just a temporary stop as I pulled in the ropes before finding a proper belay, but Al has never let me forget that this spike was slightly dodgy. In my defence, the axe placements were very good.   *Photo: Al Powell*

Al Powell, with the cause of his frost-nipped toes in the background. Quitaraju base camp in the Santa Cruz Valley, Peru.

Another year, another Peru expedition with Al Powell. L–R: Yerupajá, Siula Grande, Jirishanca, in the Cordillera Huayhuash.

Avalanched from Jirishanca. No, it's not set up – this is how I was, waiting for Powell to get the snow off my back so that I could sit up. "I'll just take a picture." "Bastard." *Photo: Al Powell*

The family who farmed the ground at the foot of Jirishanca were extremely friendly. Every day they would come by to sell us eggs, cheese, milk and fish. Al christened the father 'Daddy Cool' due to his trendy sunglasses.

Al Powell surrounded by Queropalca children on the way out from Jirishanca in 2003. *"He's a person, but he's a lot taller and more gangly than anyone we have ever seen."*

Me and Al Powell about to set off and be avalanched on Jirishanca. Death Lob 2002 attempt. *Photo: Owen Samuels*

Jirishanca base camp 2003. The helicopter lands bringing the Peruvian search and rescue police. Powell, Mark Richey (American climbing legend who happened by!) and I led the police through the icefall so they could start their search for the missing Austrians.

Jirishanca South East Face. Later in the summer two more lines were climbed on this face, both teams sadly using bolts and fixed ropes. Not having the ability to safely slide to base camp at any point on the climb would result in looking like a member of the HMP Welford Road detox!

My lead on day one, approaching the crux of what was to become the climb *Fear and Loathing* on the South East Face of Jirishanca.   ***Photo:*** *Al Powell*

Al Powell before the weather closed in, early on day three of *Fear and Loathing*.

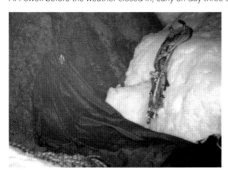

Al Powell in the trusty homemade 'coffin' bivvy bag. This was the bivvy before being avalanched in the 2002 attempt of the South East Face. *"It shouldn't be this warm at five thousand metres should it?"*

Al Powell on the summit ridge of Jirishanca, 2003. Here comes the bad weather.

Me leaving the first bivvy site and beginning day two of *Fear and Loathing*, Jirishanca. This was made into a great big wall poster by Rab – it always made me laugh looking at that yellow piss stain where we had spent the night.
Photo: Al Powell

Above us sweeping vertical sastrugi stretched upwards as far as the eye could see. Moving together we climbed on, pushing ourselves relentlessly – on and on and on. We had been moving together now for a while with me out front. Below me Al was following with all the gear, the extra weight causing his calves to scream. He had to traverse from one side of our gully line, teetering on front-points, over to the opposite side, recovering running-belays as he went. I was oblivious to him, pressing on, pressing on, urgently, the rope tugging at Al's waist.

"What the fuck are you doing?" Al yelled, yanking at the rope.

I guessed what was happening below, but the steepness of the face and lack of anything solid to anchor forced me to continue.

Stopping at the first available belay, an exceptionally poor spike with only my axes as a back up, I waited nervously for Powell to join me. When he arrived, I knew his anger was justifiable but with a great deal of climbing left, we were going to have to make up quickly.

The nature of the face now changed. Thin hollow ice took the place of névé. Powder concealed rock. The angle of the face steepened and unknown to me the crux pitch was just ahead of us. At least the confusion of the previous section was over; we would be pitching the climb from here on.

I'm twenty feet above my last protection, a camming device I know won't stop me if I fall. I can see rock above and around me where the picks of my tools have shattered the skin of ice. I scrabble urgently and huge sheets of scabby ice peel away. My forearms and shoulders are hot as coals. Up is impossible. To the left there is a better looking line but reaching it means reversing. Teetering on crampon points, expecting my axes to rip, I fight to control the tremors shaking my limbs. Al looks down, checks the belay.

Back at the cam, I now begin the traverse, which is even more difficult. But at least the cam has a better chance of holding a fall. The ice rings hollow as I tap my picks into its skin. All my weight is on my arms; there's nothing for my front-points. I give a gentle kick aiming for an overhanging corner and the ice-skin peels. The trick is not to let the mountain know I'm here.

Al gives a loud sigh as I pull through the overhang.

"Fucking nutter."

The crux pitch was over, but that didn't mean the climbing was easy. For rope-length after rope-length we continued into fading light and then the deep red of sunset and finally the dark. At last, after seventeen hours on the go, Al fixed an anchor-point while I dug a snow step on which to spend the night. Huddled under Al's bivvy sack, cramps racked my body. Al's eyes streamed with water. Above us, high on the summit ridge, cornices collapsed periodically sending avalanches crashing down. We were still only halfway up the face.

My bedroom was still dark. Ten minutes, just ten more minutes. Please. I dragged the covers over my head. How do you prepare yourself? Soon I knew I'd get up and make the daily prison commute. Soon ten heavy steel doors would open, then close – clunk – and I'd be escorting ten inmates to the gymnasium.

Each time I supervised in the gym, hours felt like days. I jumped on and off the benches, on and off, my head numbed by a pounding bass line, the house music cranked high. Inmates' feet in blue denim plimsolls hammered on and off the flaking varnish of the wooden bench. The bench creaked. Blue cotton shorts. Thin white legs. Blue cotton vests. Soft, drug-wasted shoulders. Hollow cheeks. Sunken eyes bobbing up and down.

Wind pushed snow across the green gymnasium floor. A soft drift of deep powder built against the painted wall. I tilted the angle of the running machine so it steepened. A summit twisted into cloud above me, an unclimbed mountain face appeared through a hole in the mist. I heard a glacier stretch and groan.

During my dinner break, I ran along the canal bank. A dealer stood in the gloom beneath an ornate cast-iron bridge. Scum and wrappers floated on the surface of the canal's stagnant water. My feet skidded in the mud. Or is it snow? Shards of glass glitter. Or are they slivers of ice? Derelict red-brick cotton mills, now empty, tower over the canal. My lungs are burning, sweat stings my eyes. Broken windows, rusty frames, graffiti dissolve into mountains.

Just a few more minutes.

Behind the clock hands, arcing shadows trace their own time, flexing to a silent rhythm. Better to stay asleep. Better to hide. Better to dream.

Climbing the first pitch of the morning, Al shakes the stiffness out of his legs. A steep, fluted snow-runnel leads to a rib of bulging snow. It is like *Point Five* on Ben Nevis. Both of us stare longingly up at the ridge. It's visible now, but so far away. Spindrift pours down on us but the flurries eventually slow. We crawl up feeling imprisoned by bulbous mushrooms of ice. Al looks at them, weighing them up. I can tell he is thinking about finding a way off the face, a way to reach the summit.

Still alternating pitches, the climbing is still consistently hard. Nothing quite as tenuous as the first day, but nothing is easy enough that we can relax.

Entering a large bay, Al sets up an ice-screw belay. The summit looks very close now. Continuing direct looks to be the best bet. Two pitches. Three, maybe.

I hope the ridge I can now see is the summit ridge, and not some subsidiary, which leads to yet more climbing.

"Surely it can't lead to more climbing. Can it?"

Ahead the bay steepens to a rocky wall with only one possible exit – an ice-runnel guarded at the bottom by a rock overhang.

Confrontation was unavoidable. "What the hell have you done?" Tall prison walls loomed above us, the inmate and me. In the rafters of the cavernous warehouse, fluorescent tubes hung from chains. Their glow projected shadows of railings on the painted brick walls and painted doors around us. It gave an eerie radiance to the white fatty fascia protruding from the length of his forearm

"What the hell have you done?"

He smiled at my question. He seemed pleased with my shock. He appeared pleased with the attention.

"I cut myself."

Tattered with scar tissue, the inside of his forearm turned inside out revealing a crisscross of welts, fat, and bloody congealed skin. He'd repeatedly cut into the largest wound, through stitches and his veins. Prison officers walked past, too burdened to be interested. He'd been a regular in the gym. I thought the exercise was helping his confidence.

"The doctors can't sew it together anymore," he said. "The skin isn't strong enough."

Together we stared into the inside of his flesh, neither one able to move or speak. In the streaks of red and white, a hidden universe had broken free. Another life beckoned. A better life.

I place three screws, more than on any pitch so far, conscious of how weak I feel. The effort required for this is going to be more than my body wants to give, but my mind will not back down. Placing my left axe high, beneath the overhang, I close my eyes, force air from my lungs… now! Step up, lock off, reach above the overhang, swing the right axe and get a placement. The ice is hard. Swing again. Again. And again. At last, the axe is in. Pull, pulling, my upper body is past the overhang. The next placement needs to be as high as possible. The next placement needs to be good. I swing and my feet stay put while the left axe is driven home. 'Thank you.' I straighten my legs and retch.

Powell watches as I set up the last belay on the route. Then he climbs up to meet me. Eagerly he moves past, without saying a word.

Now he's wading, forcing a trench through unconsolidated sugar for fifty metres. And then, finally, he is rewarded. The mountains all around are deep red as the sun dips below the horizon. He looks across the whole of the range, re-born into the horizontal world. The sky turns dark and stars appear. The wind whips up spindrift, stinging and sticking to his face. He shivers, the snow on his face melts. The spell breaks.

We spend the third night on the summit in a snow hole. It is unfathomably cold.

After dinner, the prison gym was empty, the inmates locked inside their own heads behind their heavy cell doors. I lay on a bench. Sweat from my head smeared against blue plastic. I held a knurled Olympic weight bar with silver 10kg plates at arm's length in the air. I lowered it, until the bar touched my chest. I pushed, looked at the ceiling, and dreamed. Bend, dream, push, dream, bend, dream, push. Dream. Routine is a quick existence. I smell sweat, shit and fear.

At 8pm, I threw my keys down a slot in the gatehouse. From behind thick Perspex, other prison officers waved goodnight and pushed the button that opened the electronic door, which creaked and slid open.

"Come again soon, dreamer. No one resigns."

At dawn, we quickly set off. Packing is a short affair when there is nothing to pack. By midday we've reached the bottom of Quitaraju's North Face. We've found no abseil anchors so we've been down-climbing, first passing Swiss climbers, who gallantly feed us tea and chocolate, and then a French team at the Alpamayo high camp who give us all of their spare food.

Having an epic going the wrong way while soloing in the Alps in winter. I took this self-portrait to remind myself never to do this sort of thing again.

Then we drop down to the very busy Alpamayo base camp, sneaking through without talking to anyone.

Having just spent the last three days on a big mountain we suck in the scene. Our senses are amplified. I see hundreds of lupines, forests of quenal with bark peeling and branches covered in thick damp moss. I savour the scent of earth and water – and life. Mountain streams gush down the steep slopes and join the swollen river running through the centre of the meadow. Even the dust we kick up by our weary feet, as we head back down to the Santa Cruz valley, is refreshing. A condor swoops overhead, wind scouring its outstretched wings.

We reach the rock with our kit stowed underneath at 8pm, three and a half days since our departure. The first thing we open is the food bag.

A week later, on the bus from Huaraz south to Lima, we're rumbling over high grasslands. In the distance, a snow-covered range of mountains turns the horizon jagged.

"There's a hill over there called Jirishanca," Powell says. "Its South East Face has been tried a few times. It's really technical ice and rock up this amazing face. Maybe we should try that next year?"

Back at work, I stood in the gym office and took my top off to change into a vest.

"Fucking hell Nick, look at you! Where have your shoulders gone?"

Bob was right; I looked into the mirror and saw a skeleton. I had lost twenty pounds of bodyweight in three days on Quitaraju and then, instead of staying in Huaraz and resting, instead of walking the bustling streets, eating cake, drinking beer and watching the women in tight jeans and guinea pigs spinning on their skewers, we walked into the Ishinca valley and climbed Ranrapalca, a six thousand metre mountain. Why? Just for something to do. I felt sated, but knew the feeling would not last.

It took six months for my body to recover. Powell sent me pictures of the hill he had spoken about on the bus from Huaraz. I was transfixed – and terrified. I printed the picture and pinned it above my desk. "What's that?" Bob asked pointing at the picture of Jirishanca.

"That's what we are going to try and climb next summer."

"It looks like death, where are you going to climb? Not straight up the middle, surely?"

CRASH

Kicking a step in the snow to stand and sort gear, I glance once again back towards the start of Tower Ridge, towards the C.I.C. Hut. The climbers trying to catch me up have now decided the race is lost. With no rope, no rack and hardly any weight, I have the advantage. Finally, after six months of hard training after returning from Quitaraju, I now feel fit enough to start climbing the cold stuff again.

Unfortunately Paul Schweizer had run away the day before after we climbed *Astronomy*, a long and seldom climbed mixed route. He claimed illness, but after too much sport climbing in the warmth of Spain, I suspected he had gone soft.

My slog uphill ends at sheer cliffs, silver-streaked monoliths rimed in history. Legends of old – the likes of Jimmy Marshall and Robin Smith, Hamish MacInnes, Tom Patey and Mick Geddes – look down and watch with interest. I sense their anticipation. Tightening laces, swapping ski poles for axes and struggling into a climbing harness, I take a final look downhill. The coast is clear. Dipping into my anorexic rucksack, I retrieve the Ben Nevis guidebook.

The steep corner dripping with icicles above me is definitely my route. I'd decided on this line before reaching the C.I.C. Hut, but what of the two climbers about to start the steep slab directly below it? Maybe they are aiming for a climb to the right, called *Pointless*. That made sense. They were gearing up beneath a slab that was definitely not the start for *Galactic Hitchhiker*. The leader quickly starts the first pitch, seeing me climbing up towards him.

"Hello!" I yell, closing the gap between the remaining climber and me. "Great day to be on the hill."

The climber, belaying at the base of the slab, turns and mumbles something unintelligible.

Not one to be put off, I try again. "Great conditions, eh? So what route is this then?"

The remaining climber weighs up the options; I can see it in his face.

He is thinking whether he should ignore this buffoon, or throw him a thrilling morsel to scare him off? He decides on the scare tactic, and announces sullenly: "This is *Galactic Hitchhiker*."

"GREAT! This is my line as well. But are you sure? This line doesn't appear to match the route description."

"Yes, quite sure."

"Oh. Okay, I'll just follow you then. I'll stay out of your way. You don't mind, do you"? Obviously he didn't, as no reply was forthcoming.

Waiting and waiting, stomping my feet and standing around, the cold begins to get a little tiresome. The leader has placed four ice screws, and the thought of teetering on front-points waiting for the second to remove them doesn't make any sense. To top it all, the second hasn't even started to climb. It will be much better to bash on and get out of their way. So, without any further delay that's exactly what I did.

The waiting climber hurriedly re-arranges gear, hastily strips the belay, and now, with the frenetic movements of the ultra-stressed, fumbles his hands through the loops of his leashes.

"I thought you were waiting!"

"Yes, I was, but then I thought it would be much better to just get on with it… no ropes and all that. I'll soon be out your way." I continue to climb, followed closely by the indignant second who is now determined to show me up once and for all. However, light and partnerless pays dividends; with no gear to place or remove the distance between us grows.

The climbing isn't that difficult, but my axes and crampons are blunt. The ice is glassy-hard and nearly vertical. To the right is an arcing left-facing corner that sweeps into an overhang, protecting the top of the slab. I aim for an exit to the left of the overlap. Bringing both feet up together, I tap, tap, tap with my axes… Tapping gently is not normally my way, so I commend myself quietly for being so considerate to the climber below. Then suddenly and without warning, both sets of dull front-points shoot from the ice to leave me whimpering. I hang from both axes hyperventilating. I kick again and again to settle my nerves. 'Stuff the guy below,' I think, swinging an axe. Splinters and large lumps of ice fly. The gushing relief of a deeply bedded pick vibrates through my body, drowning out the remonstrations from beneath.

The leader is now near enough to talk. He makes an attempt to ask about my intentions, but I ignore him. Talking will upend my balancing act. At last I reach some security. Rather than simply talking, I yell. Yelling breaks the tension.

"Sorry for gatecrashing the route."

The reply, from the leader, is succinct: "Just don't fall off."

Thanking him for his concern I add that I will try my hardest not to.

It's steep, there's no disputing that, but unlike the open expanse of the slab below, the tight corner I now enter feels almost comforting. The eyes of the belaying leader burrow into my back, but soon he will be out of sight. A dagger of ice flows from the top of the corner to touch the slab below. I climb to within touching distance; its perfect plasticity gives me confidence. Hanging now in the middle of the rippling icicle, I guzzle the exposure, pulling crisp air into lungs, the effort scorching my heart.

In the distance, I see black specks move slowly up snowfields as weak winter sunlight ignites the top of Tower Ridge. Looking across into *Point Five*, I recall the classic account of Joe Brown and Nat Allen hurtling out of the gully to be held by Nip Underwood. Then I remind myself I have no Nip Underwood to stop me.

Shimmying up the icicle, I'm thankfully no longer above the other climbers, so I can fully employ my beloved technique of bash-and-crash. A short section puts me at the side of a second, even longer icicle. The next sequence of moves is obvious, but it's also obvious just how committing the moves are. I step left, burrowing into a small cave behind the tree-trunk of ice at its steepest. Then I bury a pick deep in the ice and lean out. I swing and swing, but the right axe's blunt pick bounces. Eventually I find a high placement. Jabbing with my feet… front-points bounce… the pillar is narrow and I inch upwards like a caterpillar watched hungrily by the crow's eye of the long drop below.

Hours after getting home, sitting in my cottage in front of the fire, the phone rings. I pick up the receiver but before it reaches my ear I hear an unmistakable voice booming at me. I wonder if there is any need for the phone at all. Ken Wilson had been at Riasg, the Climbers' Club hut where I had stayed in Scotland and I had told him about my solo. Ken is now talking forcefully and with increasing volume. He tells me I had not climbed *Galactic Hitchhiker*, I had instead inadvertently climbed a new route. And what's more, the climbers I had passed were making their long-awaited first ascent. Then – click! – Ken's gone.

TIME

Fresh from our success the previous year, Al Powell and I returned to Peru in May 2002 along with Jonny Baird and Owain Samuels. After an acclimatisation climb near Huaraz, we caught an early morning bus to a small town in the middle of nowhere and then spent two days inside a succession of cramped VW Transporter vans called *colectivos*. *Colectivos* are the ubiquitous mini-buses used by locals and we shared ours with the young and old, goats, net bags of guinea pigs, chickens, bundles of grass, boxes of eggs and our own high expectations.

We drove along the edge of muddy precipices, past vultures hopping out of our path, alongside grassy plains partitioned with stone walls, through small towns on the edge of nowhere. And eventually we were dropped after dark on the muddy streets of Queropalca, a small town straight from Sergio Leone's *A Fistful of Dollars*. There were no other Westerners – there rarely were. Leaving the following day we left behind narrow streets with gangs of curious, dirty-faced, wide-eyed children who swarmed around us, laughing in our wake.

Burros marshalled by a cheerful and portly *arrero* took us alongside a fast-flowing river. Grass-roofed huts spewed smoke that weaved its way through the thatch. People worked the steppe, their ploughs drawn by cows cutting the brown crust. The men stopped work to watch us, their deeply creased faces shaded by wide-brimmed hats, their trousers held up by string. Kids ran to meet us.

"American?"

"No, *Inglese*."

At its head, the valley is guarded by a small chain of steep and impressive mountains. To the left is the East Face of Siula Grande, this side of the mountain less well-known than its opposite West Face where Joe Simpson and Simon Yates had their well-documented adventure. To the right is Yerupajá, known as the K2 of the Huayhuash, a vast mountain of 6,617 metres, with several unclimbed lines. To the right of Yerupajá is her little sister, Yerupajá Chico and to the right again is our objective, the most beautiful mountain in the range, if not the whole of Peru – Jirishanca. The final mountain, which Baird and Samuels were hoping to climb, is Jirishanca Chico.

Jirishanca is not as high as its relations to the left, standing at just 6,126 metres. But what it lacks in height it makes up in beauty. Describing it as the Matterhorn of Peru sells it short. Jirishanca is an icy, towering skyscraper fringed with latticed icefalls. The formidable and very experienced Slovenian, Pavel Kozjek, had been into the valley several times to attempt this face but each time he was thwarted by weather and conditions only managing a high point to the shoulder on the left of the face.

Snowy ledges and steep compact rock form the upper three-quarters of its concave South East Face, while overhanging mushrooms and fluted honeycombs of snow protect Jirishanca's pointed summit. Reaching up from a massive snow-cone into the unclimbed central area of this extraordinary face was a tight chimney. This was our planned route.

Having set up base camp at the head of the valley near a large lake, we made a good recce of the face. The chimney was full of snow and it had a constriction halfway up that looked difficult to climb. But we felt sure it would go, as long as the snow was continuous and nothing poured down on top of us.

Our first attempt ended almost before it started. We bivvied beneath the face and approached in the dark, but the snow in the chimney had melted. The steep smooth rock that was now revealed looked impossible to climb. We explored other possibilities but it soon became apparent that the chimney would be the only way onto the face without bolts and aid-climbing gear and neither Powell nor I were interested in beating the mountain into submission.

To further rub salt into our wounds, clouds rolled in across the plain and the temperature rose. We didn't think it possible; it was already so warm. Getting comfortable in the bergschrund, we sat around waiting for daylight and when it eventually arrived our fears were confirmed. This wasn't going to happen, not today anyway.

Four days of stormy snowy weather followed. Baird and Samuels left after a brief attempt at Jirishanca Chico failed when Baird suffered altitude sickness. Edgar, the son of the family living by the lake, brought us fresh trout. His gran visited next day and offered us milk and cheese. We hung out and for the whole four days Jirishanca remained shrouded in swirling cloud. When the veil eventually lifted, the face had changed. After being lashed with snow and hail, the chimney had refilled and was now stuffed full of snow. The whole face seemed to be wearing a pristine white coat.

Clear blue icicles were now coated with snow and the large mushrooms at the top seemed fluffy with it.

The weather over the previous four days had been wet and warm and so a period of freezing could turn the climb into an easy romp up squeaky névé. This was our rationale for getting back on the climb. The pressure of our time at base camp running out also weighed heavy on our minds. Nobody else was climbing in the valley, but how long this would remain was anybody's guess. We swore about an article published in a climbing magazine that had given away all of these hidden, unclimbed gems that only a select few knew about. But at least we were here now and we were determined to try.

I couldn't believe it when a storm blew in at 10 p.m. Our alarms were set for one the following morning, but we ignored them as snow, hail and even rain fell heavily.

"We're at 5,000 metres for God's sake," I said. "It should be freezing."

Eventually the storm passed, but it was now 5 a.m. We packed quickly and set off. The new snow dragged at our legs. Maddeningly, the sky now cleared of clouds; it would only be a short while before the early morning sun began to melt the face. The chimney was already softening. Water poured down giving the rock a tiger-striped appearance. We were too late, too late at least to be there safely.

Both experienced climbers, we knew the sensible things to do. We could wait in the bergschrund for the sun to go off the face or return to the bivvy and try again later. Unfortunately, neither of us voiced these options. There was a very real chance the snow in the chimney would melt leaving us stranded, waiting for it to refill – or else the weather would turn for the worse again. We badly wanted this route. Too badly. So quietly we carried on.

I took the lead.

Climbing the chimney I repeatedly told myself, 'Two pitches, that's all, then we'll be onto the face, in amongst it.' Our intended line was on steep ground out to the right. Here a headwall protects the climbing. 'We'll be safe then.' We had both taken risks before, all climbers do. 'The climbing to come will be worth this moment of madness,' I said to myself. 'We'll laugh about this later.'

I moved fast, placing just two pieces of gear. The climbing wasn't hard. Our safety lay in speed – keep moving and get out quick. The rope tugged at my waist. I'd climbed sixty metres, but there was no belay. I shouted for Al to move up and then shouted again, impatient, scared. I needed to move and attach myself to something solid. Flurries of snow flew past. Occasionally, larger lumps rattled and whizzed.

The rope came slack and I moved towards a small rock in the middle of the gully. Reaching it, I shouted to Al that I would belay, but before I could attach myself a deep throaty growl belched from the belly of the mountain.

Instantly, I know its source. I desperately look around for shelter but the only option, the single rock immediately to my right, is too small. The ropes snake down the gully, useless. I drive both my tools into wet, melting ice and cower like an animal trapped in the glare of headlights. The heavy snow hits me square on. It's like wet concrete. I'm plucked from the middle of the couloir and thrown down the face. I scream from deep inside me, from my guts. I know I am about to die.

Tumbling, cartwheeling, smashing into the rock upside down, my body crumples – concertinaed. My knees smash into my face splitting the soft skin. Air is forced from my lungs. My ribs, chest and back feel as though they are tearing apart. I black out for a second then regain consciousness, horrified to find I am still falling.

Let the next blow end the pain, I plead. I've suffered enough now. Please.

I hit deep, soft snow – hard. But I'm alive. Then the joy of surviving gives way to panic as I begin to slide and I hurtle another two hundred feet down the hard snow cone at the base of the chimney.

Spinning, twisting, pushed on by hundreds of tons of wet snow, I struggle against the current. Surfacing, I gulp air and pull hard for the side of the avalanche. My legs are twisted into unnatural angles, the joints forced the wrong way. Still I fight, clawing, flailing. My resolve strengthens. I refuse to be dragged under. The avalanche slows. I claw and swim. As the snow starts to set, I pull hard to get on top of it, pushing an arm into the air in the hope of leaving some part of me visible, something for Powell to dig out.

It never enters my head that he could be buried as well.

The shock of surviving the fall was too much to comprehend. My chest heaved but moving was impossible. Large blocks of snow covered me, my body tangled in the ropes.

Luckily, Al had been spat out sideways from the avalanche. He climbed across the debris and freed me. Sitting up, it was soon apparent that I was battered, but not broken. I had wrenched ligaments in my shoulder and knee, torn muscles in my back, hips and ribs. My head pounded. Sitting on my rucksack, looking at the world with the eyes of someone who should not be alive, the whiteness of the snow, the savage beauty of the mountains, I wondered what made me different from my friend Jamie. I couldn't come up with an answer.

"What are you doing next May, Al?"

Powell looked at me like a patient, someone to be handled with care.

"Climbing this bastard with you, of course."

Having received the answer I needed, and filled with painkillers, we started our descent. I refused to let Al carry my rucksack, although he took our karabiners and protection and both ropes, until we were two hundred metres from base camp. Feeling nauseous I ate humble pie and reluctantly passed the sack over.

Al stacked it on top of his own and set off at a blistering pace. Some warped sense of competition took hold of me as I attempted to restore some pride, jogging to keep up with him.

Travelling back to Huaraz, I constantly reminded myself I was lucky to be alive. We were not yet robbed of the route. I began planning my early departure from Peru; I wouldn't stay in Huaraz for a week feeling sorry for myself. Al had the chance to salvage the trip with a quick climb in the Cordillera Blanca but even he was talking of an early flight home.

We retreated to Edwards Inn, our usual lodge recommended to me by Joe Simpson. Here we caught up with Owen and Jonny Baird, who had had difficulty acclimatising for the whole trip. One of their objectives had been a new route on the North Face of Ulta in the Cordillera Blanca. Al had given them the idea and so they checked it out only for Baird's lack of acclimatisation to put an end to it.

However, they had given the face a good looking over and both men enthused at the possibility of a new route.

"It's amazing Nick, just like the Eiger North Face," Bairdy told me. "An ice streak runs the whole length, from the middle of the face at its base to the summit. I think the line will go, but the sun will soon melt out the bottom unless it's done quickly."

I could see the plan hatching as though I were psychic. Powell had a partner who was smashed up. Samuels had a partner who couldn't acclimatise. There was a simple solution – Powell climbs new route with Samuels. Nick goes home early with Baird.

It was a neat solution but there was no way I was going home if others were staying and climbing. The thought of being back at work, knowing Powell and Samuels were on a mountain, would have driven me crazy. It wasn't a matter of jealousy, it was simply knowing how much I gained from the experience. Time is too short to squander opportunities.

Powell and Samuels climbing together made sense, although I was miffed because I could sense scheming. But I couldn't blame them for wanting to team up and not wanting a broken Bullock along. Eventually I could take the atmosphere no longer and made it easier for both of them by suggesting they should climb together if they didn't mind me coming to base camp with them. Deep inside I knew I was capable of something, I just wasn't sure at what level and I didn't blame Al for taking the guaranteed partner.

Frantically we all packed, Baird for the trip home, Powell and Samuels for the climb. I packed for a stay at base camp, or a lightweight solo mission, and in the evening before setting off I fattened up on apple pie washed down with a cocktail of painkillers and prayed for quick recovery.

Crammed into a taxi, the three of us rattled past the white bulk of Huascarán shimmering in the heat. Pigs squealed as they scurried out of our way, dogs yapped, chickens strutted, people pointed. Huascarán grew bigger with every mile, dominating the skyline of the Quebrada Ulta, but eventually the valley opened and Ulta came into view. The ice-streaked North Face looked grand, but it wasn't for me. The north ridge, a bastion of rock sweeping down from the summit, separated two faces, the North from the North West. I studied the area to its right, the North West Face. There was only one route here and it looked reasonably safe for a solo climber to approach. Only days after a fall I thought would kill me, I was back.

The sun dropped low on the horizon and the shadows lengthened. I had left Al and Owen contemplating their line, edgy with anticipation. Now on my own I crossed beneath their North Face looking for a bivvy spot. I needed somewhere that offered quick and easy access to the ice slopes beneath the North West Face.

Making sure there was nothing rattling down from above, I picked my way across a boulderfield sometimes looking up to see if I could fix a line of ascent in my mind. All I could see were icicles falling from the crest of the ridge forming caves that looked like prison cells with icy bars across their windows and in the dark behind the bars something unseen held captive. Over toward the right side of the face, a bulbous mushroomed ridge ran its whole length. Somewhere between the two I would make my attempt.

Below me, the dust road our taxi had driven along snaked back down the valley. On its far side, Huascarán's lower slopes, seracs and snowfields swept up to the summit still deep crimson in the last sunlight. Stars started to appear and then the night wrapped its freezing arms around me. I found a good spot with running water to my right and a wall behind that offered me protection from anything falling from the face.

At 11 p.m., I spotted pinpricks of torchlight flickering off the ice and rock at the base of the North Face. Al and Owen were on their way. Tucked up in my sleeping bag, I imagined the energy they were using plodding the snow slopes toward their climb and I gave myself a little longer in bed before making a brew to wash down another fistful of anti-inflammatory tablets. Flashing my headtorch on and off hoping they could see it, I wished them good luck.

Starting an hour later, my legs and lungs soon found their rhythm but I stopped regularly to control my breathing, which in turn relieved the pain from my injured ribs. Zigzagging, I looked over to the left hoping to see some evidence of my friends, but there was none. I was now hemmed in between the two ridges. I was completely on my own crossing large crevasses. I tried not to think how difficult it would be to return once the sun got to work on their thin snow bridges.

Crossing left into the centre of the face, the climb started in earnest. I entered a very typical Peruvian snow fluting. With steep walls on either side, hard snow at the back and occasional bulges to turn, it reminded me of a route on Alpamayo I had climbed with Bruce French on my first trip to Peru. Stars flickered but the moon didn't make an appearance to guide me. For almost the first time on the trip it felt really cold. The face, broken rock with slivers of white, was steep. The dark had a peculiar way of distorting.

The original route up this face followed a fluting on its right, and at halfway doglegged further right to avoid the steep ground near the top. I couldn't make this line out, but my best bet appeared to be to the left. I recalled a continuous line of snow and ice I'd seen the previous day as I approached the peak. This line also appeared to offer a way through the billowing mushrooms of snow directly below the summit. It was a gamble. Should I forego known ground and try something new?

Pulling out of the fluting I traversed left, my decision made, and joined a system of shallow runnels. Thin ice over hard compact granite made me think back to the year before and Quitaraju. My initial plan for descent had been simple – down climb the route I went up. But the more I climbed the more it became obvious this wasn't going to happen. However, Owen had lent me a light rope, fifty metres of seven millimetre cord. Since I hadn't climbed any bulges longer than twenty five metres, I knew I had enough rope to abseil over the steep sections. This thought kept me going.

After climbing for a lifetime, the angle of the face steepened and I sensed the top was close. Large granite blocks perched precariously one on top of another and dusted with snow guarded the summit ridge. I slotted the picks of my axes into the cracks between them and levered the shafts, the torque sufficient to hold me in balance.

Standing with my feet together, the front-points of both crampons teetering precariously on an edge of granite, I reach up to another vertical crack and, pulling back on the torqued pick, I lift my right foot high. I can just position it onto an edge. Rocking-over onto this, placing all my weight onto my right leg, I'm suddenly shocked as I catch a glimpse of what lies below me. It stops me dead. I'm looking straight down for a thousand metres.

It had been light for two hours now, perhaps more, but I wished the sun was gone. Time continually ticked and the earth continually spun and my mind continually whispered. I looked down on the brightly lit icefall. No doubt the sun was melting everything. I began to worry about getting down. The sun would hit the whole face in two or three hours and the thought of being in the middle of it as the sun's heat worked its destructive power on the cornice mushrooms above me was terrifying. Having been hit once by an avalanche on this expedition, I wasn't keen to repeat the experience.

To compound my fears, abseiling from ice-screw threads cut into a melting slope didn't thrill me either. But I was nearly there. Clouds whipped above my head near enough to touch, a sure sign the summit was close. An off-balance mantelshelf onto a powder-covered slab made me question my enthusiasm but after this I arrived at a corridor between two overhanging mushrooms. This led to easy-angled snow. I could see the slope leading to the summit and I weighed up my options: go to the summit and wait there for the face to re-freeze, or go to the summit and put myself in danger of descending in the heat of the day. In my mind I'd done enough. I decided it was time to go down. I was glad of the experience but I didn't want it to be my last.

Carefully climbing down between the mushrooms I made a grave discovery – I couldn't lower myself. My shoulder was too painful. I was going to have to abseil the whole face. This required me to make two ice-screw holes that joined inside the ice. I could thread these with thin cord and then abseil off it, but all this was horribly time-consuming. But for once the unsettled weather was in my favour as clouds rolled in, blocking the sun. I abseiled over and over again, trying not to look down because the distance I made with each twenty five-metre rope-length was heart-breaking.

At last after six hours of abseiling I reached the bergschrund at the bottom of the face and jumped across it. It was still only two in the afternoon. I was slowing now, picking my way back through the icefall, following steps where they hadn't melted out. I held my breath while levitating across the smaller crevasses until I came across a monster I knew was waiting to get me. Looking down the face at the start of the descent, this was the obstacle I had been dreading the most. I remembered the size of this first crevasse from the climb up. I also remembered the extremely thin snow-bridge I had needed to cross. This was the sort of crevasse that featured in every Hollywood mountaineering film ever made – *Cliffhanger*,

Vertical Limit, K2, they all had a crevasse like this one. It had personality, a sort of deadly charm, and it sat waiting to welcome me with open arms.

Icicles hung like piranha teeth from its mouth that became a huge black void. This monster could have swallowed a London tube train and still have room. The snow-bridge I'd crossed in the night had melted away. Looking left and right, it was clear the icefall became more chaotic. There was no way I would explore elsewhere; it was too dangerous.

Decision made, I plodded a few steps back, turned and ran. In flight over the crevasse's dark maw, I wondered how painful it would be hitting the slope on the opposite side – less painful than it would be if I didn't reach the slope that was for sure. Thumping into snow, I slid down the slope on its far side, gathering speed. Swinging an axe with my good arm, the pick ripped through but eventually I slowed and then stopped. The muscles and ligaments I'd damaged on Jirishanca complained – but I was alive.

Soon after, I lay in my sleeping bag, content and exhausted, and watched the sun set as I ate the last of my food. Settling back, a crashing noise destroyed the stillness. I whipped round to see ice blocks bouncing towards me. I dived for cover behind the wall of rock. Ice smashed all around me. Something huge had clearly broken away from the face. Minutes passed and still the ice fell. I had had enough. It was time to go.

Next day, sitting waiting for a vehicle to pass and the chance of a lift back to town, I thought about my climb and its worth. It was becoming more common for climbers operating in a world of sponsorship and commercialism to promote their climbs even if they had failed to reach the summit. Part of this philosophy comes from climbing in the European Alps where it has long been recognised that the natural place for a climb to finish is on a summit ridge.

More recently this same philosophy has spread to Peru where, similar to the Alps, the summit ridges are often not much different in altitude than the actual summit and getting to a lump just a few metres higher could involve days of difficult traversing. If someone is climbing just for himself or herself and not for a headline in a magazine, it shouldn't matter where they stop as long as they have lived and learnt and grown.

But I couldn't get away from the feeling that if you don't reach the summit, then it is only an attempt. The climb I had planned in Alaska with Jules, which he completed with another Alpinist, Ian Parnell, when I pulled out, was a great route. Yet it stopped hundreds of metres short of the summit, just like many others on Hunter. It didn't even finish on a ridge. It is easy to say this is the style of the area, but I would always have a nagging doubt in my mind that I had not done enough.

As I sat, basking in the sun, I felt ready to return to Britain, ready for clean running water and TV and my own bed. I was even ready to put up with prison's aggression and confrontation, ready for my canal runs through the centre of the city. I felt content. I knew my attempt on Ulta had been enough for me but I also knew it was just that – an attempt to reach the summit.

Walking through the cold streets of Huaraz late in the evening, the wind blew in from the mountains, lifting dust off the streets. It stung like hail. Dogs barked. Women selling grass for animal fodder or corn-on-the-cob or avocados lay in the dirt under alpaca blankets. Tomorrow would be just another day, much the same as the day before, which would be the same as the day after that.

Injured, I returned to work in the prison gym and the confined atmosphere settled around me once more. Bob McFadden shook his head and looked at me like I was crazy. At times I did wonder that he was right. Yet suddenly the normal, everyday things of life – grocery shopping, electric lights, clean water, sitting down to shit and working out in a warm gymnasium followed by a warm shower – no longer felt boring or routine. They felt special.

I felt privileged to be able to do things that people in Peru or India or Pakistan couldn't. Privileged, but not superior. Anyone could do what I was doing and I found it annoying when people at home complained their lives were not exciting. Or that a broken computer or maintaining a house could be classed as major problems. My lifestyle was easy and safe in comparison to many of the people I was now meeting and I felt embarrassed by my comparative wealth, although not embarrassed enough to give it away.

DETRITUS

"Buster's back," someone told me.

Immediately I left the gym, slotting a key to unlock the thick steel door and walking along the covered corridor unlocking and locking as I went. Finally, I unlocked, turned and opened the prison door and closed it behind me. The clatter and shouting of the inmates was almost overwhelming. I climbed the familiar cast-iron steps, one's landing, two's, and finally three's.

Stepping onto the walkway running around the warehouse-like space, the steel grate vibrates beneath my feet. I swing my bunch of keys on the short, knotted chain that keeps them joined to my body. Door after door after door. Arriving, I slide the small cell key into the cell lock. I push down on the polished brass handle and the bolt opens with a clunk.

The last time Buster and I had been together, we had worked out in the prison gym. He had been healthy and fit and talked about kicking the drugs and becoming an instructor in a leisure centre. He talked about a great deal. Now, sat on the bed in the dark of the cell, Buster looked up. He was pale and shaking and cowering, a sweaty disappointing, heart-wrenching wreck.

Welford Road, unlike Gartree with its serious offenders and lifers, was full of petty criminals: repeat offenders, drug addicts, gang members, thugs and bullies. Welford Road held the under-privileged, the poorly educated and even psychiatric cases. I found dealing day to day with many of the inmates depressing. I found it particularly depressing when an inmate came along like Buster, who was good fun to be around and to train alongside.

Buster was the sort of person I could teach about living in a healthy way. He was also the kind of person who, once released, would get no support and inevitably return to the same old crowd, the same drugs – and the same crime. Within a week, a month, a year perhaps, he would be back inside, a shadow of the man I had last seen.

I don't have an answer for this type of problem. I'm sure that, in fact, there is no solution, unless governments and society are prepared to put in more money, more resources, more training and more support. I find it deeply depressing if I dwell too long on how unlikely it is all that will happen.

"Get your gym kit, you're going to get a beasting," I told him. Buster perked up.

"Okay Nick. Brilliant, yeah, never again. Yeah, brilliant." I thought of Dipper, my golden lab.

John and Dean the gym orderlies were both brighter than the average criminal in Welford Road and also good fun to be around. Dean was a farmer. Not the kind with cows and sheep and chickens; Dean grew crops – crops of cannabis. In a good month he made £20,000 and the overheads were small. He ran high-wattage cables from a streetlight or a 'borrowed' fuse board into whatever disused building his latest crop was growing in. John was the salesman who marketed the produce.

In my time at Welford Road John changed dramatically from poacher to gamekeeper, successfully making the switch to drugs counsellor. Both John and Dean were great listeners, and they were trained to sit and listen to inmates who were suicidal. Most days we had a laugh but the day after the film *Sexy Beast* aired on TV was one of the funniest.

"Did you see that film last night?" Dean said.

I looked at John, Dean looked at me and in unison we shouted: "Plummy!"

Plummy was an inmate who regularly attended the gym. Don Logan, the character played by Ben Kingsley in the film, could have been modelled on Plummy, for both looks and character. Plummy had a shaved head, a goatee, and one eye, his other being made of glass. He had lost the real one in a fight.

Looking at Plummy was always difficult as you never quite knew if he was talking to you or someone else. This presented a dilemma, since you ignored Plummy at you peril. He took no shit from anyone and had absolutely no qualms when it came to smacking people, especially if he thought they were being disrespectful. Plummy was fine with the PE staff but he hated other inmates and officers. He was the type of person to dwell on something and then suddenly snap.

One day I followed him into the gym and as the class walked in ahead of me, someone said something to Plummy. There was no hesitation. He ran at the inmate and beat him to the ground and then stomped on his head. Personally, I quite liked Plummy, but I wouldn't want to upset him – or go to the pub with him.

"I'll see you on the out!" That was the threat shouted into my face one day after I refused an inmate entry to the gym. Welford Road was like that. Dealing with repeat short-term offenders from the local area meant I could be walking around the large outdoor market in the centre of the city and bump into someone who had been in the gym the day before. That was fine most of the time; they would say nothing or sometimes say hello. But I always felt tension, that next time it wouldn't be fine

Now on days off I began to avoid the city centre, somewhere I had once loved to walk. The scruffy wine bars with wooden floors where I would spend the evening were certainly out of bounds, especially after the night I walked to the front door of one wine bar, looked at the doorman and realised the last time I had seen him was while locking him up on B Wing at Gartree, where he had been serving a sentence for kidnapping.

In the evening we worked on our own in the gym and it was usually peaceful, but one night, walking with twelve inmates along the corridor between the main prison and the gym, one of them lost it.

"Get me out of this fucking place, I want out now," he screamed.

The inmate was shaking and sweating, and his eyes were red and bleary. I wasn't sure I could control the situation, especially as he resembled Mike Tyson from months of pumping iron. I was still broken from Jirishanca and running through my mind was how much it was going to hurt when we began fighting.

I managed to talk him down until we reached the gym and then called for assistance immediately. The assistance took an age, but I talked quietly and listened and he came down. After he was collected and returned to the prison I sat down and thought to myself, 'Get me out of this fucking place.' Leaving the prison that night I threw my keys down the slot, said goodbye to the gate staff, stepped outside and breathed in a lungful of exhaust fumes.

'Another one done.'

My plan to save money was going well. I now had enough to pay off my mortgage, but I still needed a safety blanket to see me through two years of full time climbing. Every day I thought about leaving and every day I was petrified that when it came to it, I wouldn't have the bottle to let go. I decided then to make a pact with myself, once I had paid the mortgage and saved enough to live on. I would start telling people my plan and in doing so I knew I would not back down.

My elbows were a worry. I was in constant pain with chronic tendonitis and I was no longer allowed cortisone injections, having received over twelve between both joints. The Voltarol had to stop as well, since it was making my stomach bleed. Before travelling to Peru for Jirishanca I made inquiries about the possibility of an operation on my elbows. I asked about the success and recovery rate, the length of waiting lists on the National Health Service and the cost of a private operation. When I got back, I had both elbows operated on, one privately, the other on the NHS. Both procedures were a complete success.

197

While I was off work recovering from the operations, I painted my house and began preparations for letting it out. I booked time off for a winter trip to Canada and a return to Jirishanca and in between painting and varnishing I fantasised about future climbing trips with my new elbows. Sometimes I wondered if my addiction was as bad as that of many of the inmates. I could still hear Dad's voice as we drove past Werrington Young Offenders Centre on the way to Hanley.

"That's where you'll end up."

THE SEA

The cold was a knife in my lungs. I felt my nostrils stick together. A stand of tall pine trees ran along the golf course road to continue up the steep hillside ahead. The full moon threw shadows onto the tarmac as we walked. In the distance I heard the distant trundle of a freight-train approaching Banff, the sound of its horn plaintive and sad in the freezing Rockies night.

We had missed the turning into the forest the first time, lost in excited conversation. I felt like I had been waiting for this climb all my life. I felt the same compulsion as I did with *The Bells! The Bells!* but on ice rather than Gogarth's crumbling quartzite. It was one of those climbs I knew I would have to try from the moment I first read about it. And, just like *The Bells!*, when I'd first read about *The Sea of Vapours* it had been far beyond my abilities. Maybe it still was, but life and time wait for no one.

The day before, returning from the Icefields Parkway, I had skidded the car, bumping onto the verge in a cloud of snow. A large logging truck, horn blaring, whisked past, a vortex of grey powder sucked in its wake. Once the powder had settled I twisted my camera's long lens, zooming in on Mount Rundle's Trophy Wall. I had definitely seen a continuous thread of ice. But was it thick enough? Solid enough?

Dawn lit the frozen river cleaving the valley. Above our heads, plumes of spindrift tore through the pines, raking the boulderfield and scouring the Trophy Wall. The grey rock was smeared with glistening stripes of glassy ice. The corners are choked with it, silver-blue.

Four hours after leaving the car, the pine trees, like curtains, parted on a vast cinema screen. We were presented with the grey seemingly impregnable base of the wall. It revealed itself, waiting silently, honed, for us to accept to the challenge. As brazen as a bare-knuckled prize-fighter. As violent as Charlie Bronson. As deadly as a *Blade Runner* android. The wind howled support for the favourite.

I looked up at the wall's oppressive weight, and for the first time on this trip I felt the hollowness of fear. Last night in the warmth of the Canadian

Alpine Club hut in Canmore, the staff had told tales of big falls, ripped pitons and the mortal combat that was the current season's only ascent of *The Sea of Vapours*. I realised standing beneath it, that I hadn't been listening properly.

The complete streak of ice I spied from the road is a route called *The Replicant*. The ice, a sheen smeared over vertical smooth grey rock, is broken only by a chandelier-fringe dangling from the overhang. It looks like it might go, but nowhere is the ice thick enough for more than a few teeth of an axe's pick. Certainly, there will be no protection.

I turn to my climbing partner, Dave Hunter. "Looks a bit thin. What do you reckon?"

He snaps back like a pine cracking with cold: "Death on a stick!"

Hunter is not one to hold much back. He is abrasive, opinionated, loud, aggressive and argumentative. I like him because I always know where I stand. Hunter can be trusted.

"Hmm, you might be right. Could give it a go, but if I run out sixty metres and there's no fixed gear for belay it might get a little interesting."

Hunter's ordinarily deep Scottish rumble turns falsetto: "A LITTLE INTERESTING?!"

"*Sea of Vapours* it is then."

"Aye," says Hunter, peering at me over the top of his small rectangular wire-framed glasses, "and what about that great empty space where the ice should be?"

"Climb the rock. The gap's not that big."

On the only occasion ice formed to the valley floor, climbers had flocked to Trophy Wall from around the world to complete the route in 'easy' conditions. The most usual way is via a seepage that regularly freezes to form a thick ice-pillar. This is *Postscriptum* and it's followed by a second pitch called the *Whipper Traverse*. This hard mixed line was climbed when no other way could be found to reach the thicker ice above. Subsequent lean winters have made climbing these alternative pitches the recognised way onto *The Sea of Vapours*.

Unfortunately, in this, the leanest of winters, *Postscriptum* has hardly formed. A thin sliver of ice running down the broad corner hints at bigger things. Where fat ice should froth from the overhang at the start there is only rock – and not the solid granite of the Cairngorms. This is grey Canadian limestone – dirty, brittle, smooth, loose.

The base of Mount Rundle bulges out, then fades into a maelstrom of snowflakes that trace the rock's contours like a murmuration of white starlings. Tier upon tier of grey limestone climbs into spindrift from above. We are small and alone with only the wind and snow.

We climb a mound of thick, vertical ice at the base of *Postscriptum*. I clip a tape, threaded through an ice hole. Above this, I manage to get an ice screw in about a third of its length and tie it off. Poised above this, I squeeze myself beneath a roof. By leaning out I can just see around an arête to where a smooth groove of limestone offers some hope. There are small cracks in which to torque the picks of my axes.

I inch my feet higher, front-points scraping on the rock. An icicle, like an inverted unicorn horn, hangs just out of reach, useless to me. I stretch and hammer in a blade piton. It goes into the rock but wobbles. So I place a wired nut in the same crack as the piton. All this effort forces me to lurch back underneath the roof. My head crackles with anticipation.

I face out and watch the trucks, snow ploughs, four-wheel drives, a yellow school bus moving along the distant scar of the Trans-Canada Highway. Further away the ground stretches into blurry whites and greys. My mind drifts a little too… I'm in the far distance, in a time tucked away at the back of my mind. I'm in my gamekeeping days and images accelerate towards me – images from the film that obsessed me then – *Blade Runner*. Instead of pillars of ice I see angle iron, alloy tubes, ragged electrical wires that crackle and spark and swing in the rain and wind. Shadows flicker across the grey limestone. A woman wails. Snow, rain, fizzling neon advertisements… and now… snow slaps my face. Another life, high above me, beckons through the spindrift.

We need more time. I need more time. I have done questionable things.

I remember watching Creepy Colin packing his bag to quit gamekeeping and the estate in North Wales to return to a life of unemployment in Scotland.

People unaware of the contest, of my contest, of my guilt are at this moment driving to work down the distant highway. They are being warmed by their car heaters, lulled by breakfast radio. Or perhaps not, perhaps some of them are chilled by the thought of a desk waiting for them where they will sit all day. Perhaps some of them fight with the thought of their lives spent waiting for weekends. I leave the security of the corner. Force myself out in the open. Will I be brave enough?

"No one resigns." Smooth rock soars into the white. I climb the small crack, crowded with the peg and wire. The picks of my axes twist, my feet scrape on the rock. I jerk around, like a bed sheet being shaken out. I reach the icicle, stab it…

… it breaks. Large lumps of cleanly fractured ice crash down and thump Hunter. He hardly flinches. He just goes on looking up, watching my every move.

I swing an axe, aiming for the remains of the icicle. It shears. Again – tap, tap. Two teeth sink into the remaining fascia. I gently weight it. The picks hold but the skin isn't strong enough. Confrontation is unavoidable. "What the hell have you done?" I stare into the inside of the mountain's flesh, and for a moment I see streaks of red and white, a hidden universe, a parallel life. I broke free… but can I really break free? "See you again soon dreamer."

Moving leftwards I pull myself into the groove. Fleece-covered fingers stick to cold rock and my front-points teeter on limestone flakes. There's no gear. I slot the pick of an axe into a crack then make two moves with the points balanced on edges, the point of one crampon teetering on a leaf of limestone. All of Trophy Wall towers above me, the rest of life sways into focus and blurs just as quickly…

… quickly as the foothold breaks…

… falling…

… the peg rips with a ping, a single note from a bell…

… falling…

… but my fall is so long and the rock so overhanging that the rope catches me softly. I hang level with Hunter.

"That was a big one!" I'm shocked by my trembling voice.

"Aye, could say that," Hunter's humorous tone calms me.

"Reckon it'll go with some jiggery-pokery. Glad I placed the wire – would've been spectacular if it'd pulled."

Before Hunter can reply, I quickly climb back up, protected by the rope above me clipped through that one small wire high in the groove above.

Beyond the wire I play some Alpine tricks. After some marginal pick placements, I hammer in another wire as a point of aid. I take a blow. Snow swirls. Then inching, inching, I poke my head through a window of ice dribbles and muddy limestone. Spindrift scours my face. A frozen elevator shaft of ice stands to my right. I struggle to escape through the window and reach its security. A high placement… I just need one placement… a howling wolf-like scream.

My head and shoulders, then my torso are through the window, but my legs dangle. I shudder with fear. A half-frozen replicant's cold hands could grasp my legs and pull me down. From above, some half-mangled but stupidly strong android hand could seize my arm and snap my fingers, one by one. I'm half in, and I'm half out the window.

But now I'm slowly slipping backwards. I gulp icy air into my lungs. Must slow my breathing. Must slow down. Life is so very short. I hang. Count to ten to steady myself. *Six, seven, go to hell, go to heaven.* Eight.

Nine. Ten. THUNK… my pick bites, and body tension holds me, the pick's vibrations running through my limbs. I pull up and through and release my feet from the window. *Proud of yourself, little man?*

I try to control my terror and the burn in my limbs. I kick a front-point above the overhang. *I've seen things you people wouldn't believe. Attack ships on fire off the shoulder of Orion. I watched C-beams glitter in the dark near the Tannhauser Gate.* I force my body against an ice streak to take the strain from my arms. I gasp deep. *All those moments will be lost in time… like tears in rain.*

From now on the climb is just vertical, no longer overhanging. I've escaped my imagination. But I still have to grovel from the top of the cleft. And reality is still just as dangerous and untrustworthy. Points pricking the ice's skin, I tie off a stubby screw, then tie another one… I inch up, take another gasp of air, reach for another life. But now there's a gap. It seems a whole universe of rock runs between me and the belay. I have to step off one form of solidity, solid water, and scrabble with metal points up rock made from the shells of ancient sea creatures. At last – I hang from the rusted ironware.

Hunter joins me and sets off almost immediately. I urge him on because of the pain in my legs from hanging and belaying. Cautiously he threads his way up the continuing ice-skin until the right-curving corner at the start of the *Whipper Traverse*. Rusty pegs appear regularly. Hanging in agony, I shout encouragement in an attempt to speed things up.

"Come on Dave, for Christ's sake, I'm dying here. We're running out of time. Just frig up the fucking pegs!"

"Not that simple – some of this old gear's crap."

"You'll be alright! Just do something – I can't feel my legs."

With my gentle powers of persuasion running up the ropes, Hunter launches out. He teeters, nearly comes off, screams and launches again, and wobbles horribly but just keeps it together, cursing my impatience. Finally he's onto thicker ice, that elevator shaft of ice.

"Well done. You'll be at that thread in no time."

"Maybe, but the ice isn't so thick."

"Just do your best. And do it quick… Please."

A fifteen-metre run-out over thin and rotten ice gives way to the second section of fat ice on the climb. Now we fly. The final two pitches are a steep soaring jet stream cleaving the cliff. Night is drawing in quickly. Hanging on the belay, exchanging gear, I watch the commuter traffic now returning from work. Headlights cut conical beams through the driving snow. I think of androids performing rituals. I think of me driving to and from the prison.

Feeling the exertion from the first two hard pitches, the last two long ice pitches are anything but easy. It doesn't help that I've left my headtorch in my pack at the base of the climb. But at last I pull alongside Hunter. And the climb is done. It's done, and I'm sated and content. Time to go down. *I guess you're through, huh?*

Not quite through. Things are never quite done, especially not when you assume they are. It takes us another four hours of plodding to get back to the car. We are both drained. The wind has dropped, but the quiet and the cold penetrate our exhausted bodies. We have to tug open the frozen doors and then crawl into the car. I turn the key and the engine fires. The dashboard lights up like the controls of a small spacecraft. The windscreen is frozen grey and it's as if the craft is surrounded by grey space. The digital clock blinks 00:30 – well beyond either of our wildest guesses. Eighteen hours for a four-pitch route – but eighteen hours burned brightly into our minds, never to be forgotten.

Fiery the angels fell. Deep thunder rolled about their shores… burning with the fires of Orc.

DETOX

I had only been back at work for a week when Cartwright phoned. "Fancy trying a new route in the Alps?" I did and the date Jules suggested coincided with a long weekend. I could make it.

Out of season climbing, or more accurately out of season and out of condition climbing, has certain advantages. The trouble was, we weren't out of season. An anything but easy easyJet flight brought us to the crowded Chamonix valley and we fought our way into the equally crowded bar La Terrasse in search of Guy Willett, the key to a free doss in a chalet. We found him easily, in luck for once, but that meant he found us too.

"Tequila!" Willet screamed. Cartwright too readily succumbed.

At seven next morning the chalet floor was strewn with bodies, burnt-out husks belonging to some of Britain's foremost mountaineers. We packed our rucksacks quietly to avoid disturbing the comatose and, more importantly, my accomplice's throbbing head. Raiding the kitchen to find some sustenance for the day's activities, we unearthed only stale bread. Cartwright didn't seem to mind though. His body appeared to function perfectly well without solid food.

Dressed for success, and after a quick trip to the supermarket, we joined the mêlée outside the Grands Montets cable-car station. We spent three hours snaking along the glacially slow queue fighting off the hordes of skiers hell-bent on squashing our newly acquired baguettes.

Another hour of flogging through deep snow eventually put us beneath the castellated ridge of the Sans Nom and our intended line. We were just around the corner from the Petit Dru and its dark north face where I had suffered three years before with Paul Schweizer struggling up its famous couloir. Cartwright pointed up. Our intended route followed a light grey rock scar – dust, dirt and loose rock marked the way. Jules knew it well having tried it once before in winter with Simon Yates and once more in summer with Guy Willett. This would be his final attempt; Jules was fed up with the face and the complex ridge above. He declared he'd give it one last big effort or people would start calling him obsessed.

Still hungover and stinking of alcohol, Cartwright started up the first pitch, a corner-crack line, not quite vertical, but still steep. The difficulty was in the footholds, or rather the lack of them. He started laybacking, bracing his feet against one wall and hanging off his arms for fifty metres of what felt too much like a tough gritstone corner. Having followed him to the belay, Cartwright pulled up both rucksacks on the spare rope hand over hand, and nearly threw up as they came within reach.

I took over the lead, marvelling at how climbing could transport me from an inner-city prison gym to the mountains of the French Alps, swapping sweat, attitude and tattoos for suntan lotion, sunglasses and Gore-Tex, and all within twenty four hours.

Smooth granite walls, sandpaper rough, towered above our heads, hemming us in. The air was sharp. Beneath the jagged peaks, I could see skiers swishing down brilliant white fields of virgin snow, carving huge turns from the Grands Montets in perfect powder. From where I stood, I could hear their edges cutting the icier snow in the shadow of the Dru's North Face and then the skiers emerged into the sun beneath the peak's elegant West Face. No doubt they stopped on occasion, savouring their awesome surroundings before racing on to the Mer de Glace and down to the comforts of the valley.

It was my lead, a continuation of the corner, twenty metres of absorbing climbing made all the more interesting by the odd loose block. It was still quite early but the third pitch looked hard. So with an hour of daylight left we decided to stay put. Our Colton-MacIntyre epic was still a vivid memory in both our heads. My half-numb toes were a permanent reminder that hanging on a rope all night is not fun.

A good spot it was too, especially after some digging gave us lying room. Cartwright, normally pushy and driven, was happy to settle in early. His hangover had abated to the extent, he wryly observed, that he might actually be able to eat something now.

The second day dawned clear.

"Sleep well?"

"Yep, how about you?" I replied between mouthfuls of cake, determined to lighten the weight of my sack by eating as much as possible.

"Crap, your bloody snoring kept me awake."

"Hmm, sorry, must have been all that food I ate for supper."

"Must have been. And hey, don't think I haven't noticed that I've got all the gas and the stove while you have the food."

Rumbled, I apologised, stuffing another lump of cake into an already over-filled mouth. Get over it, I thought. I still hadn't forgiven him for the route on Mount Hunter in Alaska.

Cartwright set about the fourth pitch, more delicate than the first pitches, and not as obvious. His previous encounters with this line no doubt helped, as he danced a delicate foxtrot across the near vertical unprotected slab. Miraculously, a number one wire sprouted from the grey rock, a silent witness to the previous summer's attempt. Clipping it made a necessary lurch back into the corner more secure. Then it was pure hanging-scratching-teetering-torquing-scrabbling to the top.

Reaching Cartwright it was my turn again but fortunately the slab eased off, turning into an open book corner with an off-width lying at its rear. There was no choice but to thrutch. My surgeon's words as he'd signed me fit after operating on my elbows that summer came to mind:

"Be guided by pain Mr Bullock. If it hurts don't do it."

Fat chance. After only a few metres, I ran out of gear – typical. Hating every grunted inch of this unprotected slither-fest I was distraught to find the angle increasing the higher I climbed until I made a final pull over a roof guarding the exit. Cartwright cruised it. But he didn't cruise the steep blank groove above.

Scratching, fighting, swearing, Cartwright fell once and then he fell once more, rattling down the groove to beneath a poor wire. Out of gear and exhausted, he offered me the lead, but I had to decline gracefully. Perhaps he had believed recent press reports branding me as "out of control and crazy." I wasn't that crazy. So instead he scampered rightwards, following a rising traverse toward a ridge-crest. It was the final pitch of new climbing before our line joined the route pioneered by Joe Brown and Tom Patey forty years earlier.

I had expected things to get easy at this point but after several pitches of exacting climbing I started to wonder what the hell was going on.

"Er, Jules? What grade did you say this climb is?"

"It's TD+."

"What year did you say this climb was done?"

"1963."

"And where do we have to go?"

"Around the gendarme, across that knife-edge ridge, around the big gendarme, abseil into the notch, through the gap, up that overhanging wall, past the last gendarme and onto the ice slope."

"That's okay then, I thought it was going to be difficult."

"It's not too bad, although we spent two days on it last time."

By 9 p.m. we'd done the final pitch. Easy climbing led to the great sweep of ice in the middle of the Aiguille Sans Nom's North Face. Exhausted and happy, we settled in on the best bivvy spot ever. Two great fins of rock balancing on the ridge's crest protected us on either side. The corridor of snow between the fins ran for twenty feet and was perfectly flat. Luxury was a harness-free evening. It was time to eat some more of that food.

Next day our ridge of retribution finally gave way to an iron-hard ice-slope of injustice. We moved together at first, confident of our abilities, out into the middle of a frozen, sixty-degree sea of icy nothing. Battered by winds and spindrift pouring from the face above, the exposure got to us and we started to pitch it. A frozen form of Chinese water torture plagued us. Our front-points, blunt from two days of grinding against rock, refused to penetrate the hard winter ice without repeated bludgeoning. My calf muscles were screaming in protest.

"Fucking ice-climbing. I hate this shit," Cartwright wailed, while angrily thrashing with his crampons.

"This isn't ice-climbing, this is self-flagellation," I groaned, desperately wishing he'd slow down to give me a longer rest. "We should've abseiled after finishing the new stuff. Why are we doing this shit?"

The trouble was, we both knew why. Driven, ambitious, some would say obsessed, the voices buried deep in our sub-conscious minds would have stirred the moment we reached the valley. 'You didn't take on the full challenge. You gave up when the going got tough. You were not good enough. You failed. You're a failure.'

There was no other choice. We had to go over the summit ridge.

"So is that why you abseiled from the top of the buttress on Hunter instead of going to the summit? You'd had enough? You decided you'd done enough?" "You don't let things go easy do you?" Jules replied.

He knew I was pissed off that my Alaska trip had been taken away from me. "No I don't. I know it's a fault of mine."

"Well I am sorry about that, but this makes up for it. And if it doesn't you'll just have to get over it?"

The distance to the top of the icefield reduced inexorably. We chose a steep gully of ice first climbed by the brilliant French Alpinist François Marsigny after his partner, Philippe Mohr, fell to his death, leaving Marsigny to finish their route alone. We had earlier thought to finish up the top pitch of a route climbed by Americans Mark Twight and Scott Backes dubbed *There Goes the Neighborhood*. But an epic at such a late stage would have been annoying. Another option, the top section of a climb done by Patrick Gabarrou and Philippe Silvy, was suddenly off-limits. As we crawled up the final section of the Brown-Patey ridge, we saw Guy Willett and Kenton Cool ahead of us. They had climbed an easier approach the day before and nipped in front of us. We didn't want to climb under them, exposed to falling debris in the confines of a narrow goulotte.

I was tired now and it felt as though steel fingers had wrapped around my calves and were squeezing the life from them. This easier gully had been a wise choice. But glancing to the left I couldn't help studying the *Neighborhood*. I even convinced myself, with the bravado of someone not planning to return in the near future, that it looked okay.

At the top, with such temptations thankfully beyond reach, we climbed down for a bit and then began the first of numerous abseils. Cartwright was now sponsored by DMM, a climbing gear manufacturer based in North Wales and it showed in the way he rigged the abseils. I threaded the ropes through one where he had left behind a nut and a brand new camming device.

"Bloody hell Jules, you feeling flush?"

"The amount of this sort of stuff I'm doing, Nick, it's only a matter of time before something happens. I'm not taking risks any more."

We reached the Charpoua glacier and eventually Cartwright led the way through the heavy door of the small hut balanced on top of a rock spur.

The hut was deserted, but the cooker worked, and with tons of fresh snow outside, our stay would be luxurious. I pulled the remaining food out of my sack and, in between rooting round the hut for other more exotic delights, prepared risotto sufficient for an army. I delved deep, but Cartwright, no doubt smelling the closeness of fermentation in the valley, returned to his liquid diet, drinking brew after brew. Nothing could go wrong now.

BANG. The bedroom door in Willett's apartment flew open and Cartwright, tall and rocking like a half-felled tree, was led inside. Steered towards the bed like an infirm grandmother, he was brought to the edge of the bed and abandoned. Jules swayed for a second and then toppled forwards. Landing face down on the mattress he gurgled contentedly in his alcoholic stupor.

For once everything had gone smoothly – good weather, luxury bivvies, abundant food, stacks of hard climbing and a new line climbed. But with mere hours left it was falling apart. The Prison Service wouldn't take my absence kindly, especially as I had needed to pull all kinds of tricks to get a couple of extra days in the first place.

Rudely awakened, I wearily slid out of bed. Someone had to arrange the bus back to Geneva. Reaching the airport for the return flight looked as though it could be the hardest part of the trip.

Jogging across town, I burst through the door of the bus company's office. The woman looked startled by this early-morning pink-faced apparition.

"Bonjour, parlez-vous anglais?"

"Oui, monsieur, what do you require?"

"Could you tell me when the next coach leaves for the airport?"

"Certainly, it leaves in thirty minutes," she replied coolly.

"And the one after?" I muttered while starting to panic.

"Two o'clock."

That was the same time as our flight took off.

"Give me two for the bus in thirty minutes please. Quickly."

Back in the chalet I was gripping Cartwright's shoulders and screaming in his inebriated ear: "Jules, wake up!"

"Eugh."

"Come on," I pleaded, throwing my belongings into my one giant bag, "the bus leaves in twenty minutes." Heaving it across my shoulders, buckling under the weight, I headbutted the door to make a final check on Cartwright. He was lurching across the floor, naked, unsure of what planet he was on and failing miserably to focus or locate a single piece of clothing.

"I'm going Jules. I'll try to delay the bus." A snail with an outsized shell, I stumbled into the street.

The bus driver glared at me.

"Please, un moment, monsieur," I said, struggling with my elementary French. "Deux…" I held two fingers. "Personnes…" I waggled them to indicate a running Cartwright, "…arrivent bientôt." I pleaded with him to wait a little longer while the other passengers checked their watches and muttered complaints. I got off the bus to stop him driving off, and looked longingly in the direction of the chalet. Finally he'd had enough.

"I go now!"

Admitting defeat, I stepped onto the bus but as I did so caught sight of a heavily laden figure struggling through the early morning crowds.

"Wait!" I screamed, jabbing a finger towards him.

The drunken Cartwright swayed into view. His blond hair was plastered with sweat to his forehead, his boyish good looks deserting him for once. His cheeks glowed bright red and his clothes were marked with damp patches that spread like fungus as he jogged towards the bus, puffing and panting, and clouting unwary tourists with his rucksack. His head drooped under the strain of its colossal weight.

"Good effort Nick. Didn't think you'd get him to wait."

STARS

Running beside the canal through the middle of Leicester, along the overgrown towpath, I feel behind the city's scenes. It passes in a blur, a blur of litter, beer cans and condoms ground into dirt. Life for me here, outside climbing, away from the mountains, is also a blur. It is life on the periphery, merging into the cloistering dark. Life is reduced to a pinprick of light in the distance. A single impossible star shining across wastes of empty space. My life stands still until I'm on the next climb – approaching the next mountain. Life outside the mountains will remain mere existence, until I walk through the prison gates for the final time.

"Nobody leaves."

Graffiti on brick road bridges preaches racial hatred. Drivers cross in their cars, ignorant of what's below them. I smell the traffic, the fumes of machines and people on the move. There are syringes and foil amongst the nettles and brambles. I run past the ragged shape of a drunk slumped on a bench. He's sobbing, head in his hands. A mile on and the drunk's moans – and the sight of his red scurfy ears – are still in my mind. A blurred group of kids blocking my way heckle me. I can smell fags and their smoke like ghostly threads. I think of the clean early morning mist in the mountains but the dim world here won't let me go. It pulls me back.

I pass the vague form of a girl pushing a pram. She screams into its void: "Shut up, shut up, shut up!" Her noise fades as I run away but my brain won't let go of her. The thick blur of scum on canal water. A dead cat bobbing on the surface, bloated, eyes open, unfocused, fur peeling from its pink corpse. A swan stands next to her destroyed nest, her angry hiss mixing with my heavy breaths. On I run, running against a sense of myself disappearing, lost, fading into this half-world.

"You won't go. Nobody leaves. A job for life."

For life. Out shopping, out walking the streets, people float around me, blurred outlines, pained expressions painted onto skulls. I walk the streets pretending to be carefree, but always I'm alert. Dried puke, a piss-stained doorway, a crumpled tin of Tennent's Super balanced on a bollard.

I pass a dark alley, at its mouth a fresh mess of used condom. I stroll along, feigning nonchalance, but I'm wound tight, ready to spin round, ready to protect myself against some hate-filled shape.

Climbing is calling me, a new, clean and safe way to challenge existence. Yet perhaps I'm just the same as the other poor trapped addicts. Life is running out. With every step along these streets I imagine the grating tick of some giant rusting second-hand grazing the vast cracked clockface of life … life … for life … that's life. You buy a one-way ticket to live one way. Living scared has to be faced, but living sick, living terrified doesn't.

How fate turns and twists our lives. One day everything is fine, yet so easily that same evening you are being kicked, kicked hard and repeatedly, curled in the road outside a nightclub, the smell from the drains in your nostrils, the smell of the sewer just beneath the pavement.

Arms and legs pulled in tight, blows coming, over and over, the crowd silhouetted fuzzily against the blur of orange streetlights, and the stars unseen and silent above the light pollution, the jeer and shout, jeer and shout, an execution crowd. But I know that the stars are there, above me. They are silent but I can imagine the clear, ringing, pin-prickling sounds they make on a clear night. I'm in a frosty valley. The stars' sounds echo amongst the precise silhouettes of mountains. Still…

… still … still afraid, I imagine the kicks and punches raining down. The stench of the drain in my nostrils is thickening but it reminds me I'm still living. And it reminds me of that exciting whiff of sea coves and open-mouthed zawns and guano-smeared ledges at the bottom of coastal crags.

Since becoming a Gogarth devotee, I have often stared longingly into the guidebook that describes its routes, reading the descriptions, absorbing its pictures. One photo stands out more than the rest. Paul Pritchard's eyes burn into the rock. He peeps from behind his duvet jacket, focused only on the solidity of his immediate future. Thin, black-striped Lycra-clad legs poke from the oversized jacket. The Lycra leggings are tucked into socks pulled high. Pritchard is literally clinging to life on a cold wind-driven day on Red Wall. The South Stack lighthouse shines in the background, lighting his way with methodical, mesmerising regularity. The sea below is in turmoil. Stare long and hard and be there with him. Listen long and hard – hear the gull's cry and the raw crash of the sea… listen to his heartbeat… feel your own heart beating.

… beating fists in my face, boots in my gut, a falling…

… a falling rock or falling from rock… life is impossible to fathom… what is this experience? This dream? This life? I ask myself, really ask myself… and I walk to the outdoor covered market…

…in the centre of the city. A multi-coloured striped hardwood roof. Wooden market stalls overflowing with bananas, peach, pear, melon, cauliflower, broccoli, carrot, apple. "Two bowls for the price of one!" I roll an avocado in my hand, the bustling…

…streets of Huaraz burst from it. The woman behind her flatbed push-bike stall, a small hand-written sign propped in the middle of her pile of avocados: *Tres aguacate para uno sol*. Her red wide-brimmed hat shades creased skin and dark eyes glistening with intelligence. Black plaited hair stretches the length of her back. She wears a blue-buttoned alpaca cardigan and a purple knee-length skirt covering her thick black woollen leggings. I walk on…

…walk through…walk through the crowded market in Leicester bumping into outlines that should be people. Stopping, I lift okra, in my hand its knobbled skin and…

…Skardu and sitting in a shed on the side of the dusty road opposite the K2 Motel. Jamie and Jules are eating greasy curry and drinking Coke and I look at the large dirty glass window painted with the menu partially covered by lace…

…just as quickly as a blur passing me along a canal, and I'm back. Back home from a PE officer training weekend with a swollen knee. One of my fellow trainees has slid feet first into me while I was in goal. Studs raked my knee cap gouging tramlines the length of my shin. Is this it then? Injured and put back? Or even out for good? Just because of one thoughtless tackle. Later. A nightclub in the centre of Leicester. I'm sitting on the floor, out of the way, it's late and I'm tired. A youth walks past me… he makes an effort to trip over my outstretched leg. Instantly he spins and kicks my knee.

"Get your fucking legs out of my way."

I grimace, say nothing. But as he walks away the wound that I am begins to fester, becoming more and more infected, angry, furious…mad for not standing up for myself…I hobble around the club inspecting faces, determined to find him…when I do I'll walk straight to him and punch him as hard as I can…punch him…

…punch him to the ground, kick him over and over, kick him till his bones crack and he bleeds, kick his head, over and over until all he can see…see before the final darkness is stars.

I search the club frantically but I can't find myself and so I leave, hobbling into the street.

And I vow never to return.

TRUTH

I'm falling, tumbling, cartwheeling, smashing into rock upside down. My body collapses, my knees smash into my face and chest. I can't breathe. The air has been driven from my lungs. My chest feels like it's being torn apart. I black out for a moment and then struggle back to consciousness.

I wake with a start and shake my head, attempting to clear out the nightmare of our doomed attempt on Jirishanca twelve months earlier. Any sane person would avoid repeating such an experience. So why am I now perched on the same rock-step, waiting to climb the same evil chimney with the same deadly face above? Powell, sitting at my side, looks thoughtful, his intense, dark eyes set deep in a gaunt face. Is he also wondering what has made us return to this mountain?

Jirishanca's South East Face had only had one ascent. In 1973, a Japanese team sieged their route over forty five days. Now several teams are coming this year to try their luck. Al Powell and I comprise the second team. The first, Alex Fidi and Julian Neumayer, two young guides from Austria, didn't make it beyond their warm-up climb. While attempting a new line on Jirishanca Chico in preparation for the main event on Jirishanca, they were caught in an avalanche. Both were killed.

We start soloing at 1 a.m. We have two days' food for the nine hundred-metre line. My stomach is playing up. I feel terrible. As we approach the start of the chimney my breathing becomes laboured. Turning the key, fighting the desire to run away, I open the door and begin the sprint, but on perfect névé. It's freezing cold, a welcome luxury not experienced the year before. The chimney's dark cell-like walls constrict my swings and kicks. Lumps of snow whoosh past me, the odd rock whirrs by. I desperately want to escape.

A crashing rumble breaks the black silence. Driving both axes into the névé, I pull in tight and wait. And wait…

Nothing happens. I swear at myself for being so stupid. It's a serac collapsing on Yerupajá Chico. My guts feel like rope creaking under load. I rush upwards until finally the rock surrounding me opens out, and I'm released onto a wide expanse of snow.

A large overhanging buttress to the right promises a haven. In my mind's eye I can see the picture of the face pinned above my desk in the prison gymnasium. I have stared longingly at it for two years. I can see the massive snow and ice gargoyles stuck to soaring towers directly above our heads. Why had Powell talked about earthquakes the day before? Where is he, anyway? I turn to look below. Yes, there he is. I can see a pinprick of light still in the confines of the chimney. He is still in danger. Still plugging away. Still moving as fast as his body will allow.

A final sprint across the wide, right-leaning snow slope deposits me safely under an overhanging buttress. I gasp for breath as I wait for Powell to catch up.

"Jesus, what were we thinking last year? This place must have been loaded with fresh snow." He mutters as much to himself as to me.

"It'll be one of the best ice routes in the world if we do it." I reply, trying to control the tremble in my voice while glancing above, to the left, to the right, below, behind.

"That chimney went on forever. I thought you said you were nearly at the ramp last year?"

"Yes, well. I did have other things on my mind at the time."

Powell now meticulously checks the pictures of the face he had blown up from slides taken last year. I wonder how he feels. What drives him? A partner at home cares for their newborn baby; how would that affect me? Thirty seven years old, single and likely to remain that way once I give everything up. There will be no distractions or complications to interfere with my climbing. Does Powell find this as scary as I do?

Chalk and cheese, Powell and me. My aggressive, impatient character forged by working in the prison is tempered by his quiet, laidback but solid approach. A partnership three years old now and already gnarled and knotted like an old oak lintel. I trust Al more than anyone.

Dawn highlights our spectacular setting. We cling to life in the middle of a great concave amphitheatre. Organ pipes of ice hang all around us in this cold cathedral; some are as thick as tree trunks. The mountains behind wake for another day, lit with a deepening red glow as the sun lifts above the horizon.

Suddenly the sun's warmth makes its presence felt. A large serac breaks free from the wall above the chimney. It crashes, scattering into a thousand pieces that are funnelled through the constriction below us. Minutes later a second one follows. We cower with every booming crash, insects in the bottom of an egg-timer.

Powell cuts right, aiming for a great swathe of sastrugi-rippled ice.

When he stops, I move toward him, crossing runnels furrowed by falling debris. We pitch the climbing now; the chance of something crashing from above and wiping us out is very real.

Setting the belay, two screws and two axes, I stand marooned between vertical ice above and below. Powell, obsessive about saving weight, has chosen to bring small fun-size chocolate bars for our food. But as I gaze up I realise that even that extra weight will slow us down on the difficult ground above. While Powell seconds the fifty-metre ice wall below, I study the East Face of Siula Grande across the valley. It looks like hell. I imagine Joe Simpson and Simon Yates down-climbing the ridge above it. I am amazed as I recall the epic of their struggle. My amazement turns into trepidation. If we are lucky enough to reach our summit, how will we get down?

A strained, serious face pops above the final bulge of the long pitch. Al has struggled with the sustained climbing, shouting repeatedly to be held. Maybe he has some full-sized Mars bars stashed in his pack?

"Shit, that is desperate," he says through clenched teeth reminding me of Clint Eastwood in a spaghetti western. "I'm really not fit for this sort of stuff."

A winter of skiing in preparation for his guide's test has seriously affected his climbing. But I'm not worried. With more gnarly first ascents around the world than anyone I know, I can't think of a better person to be with on such a serious face as this. Our partnership works because with every pitch I throw myself at, he will restore the balance with quiet control on the next. Even so, I sense the icicle fest above my head is about to be offered back to me.

The pitch looks innocuous enough except for the overhanging ice at the top of a gutter. However, I'm twenty metres out with only one screw between us. I really must learn to say no. It comes naturally enough in the prison gym – so why not when climbing? But of course I know why not – the feelings of not being good enough or pulling my weight are never far away.

Out of balance, I frantically scratch and scrape, looking for a placement. I clear powder from the rock and this allows me to hook my right pick on a rugosity. I gingerly weight my right crampon point on a sloping edge, and release my left foot from the good ice, shouting to Powell to watch me. I hold my breath as I match the left monopoint on the sloping edge. With both feet now in the middle of the gutter I can finally balance. I need to step up right, but there is only smooth rock and a thin blob of rotten ice.

"Why do I always get into this shit?" I yell, shaking.

Looking down, I spy the screw ten metres below, and Powell another ten metres below that. Maths was the class I most often skipped at school. I would rather be walking across the squelchy fields near our home in

Cheadle watching the lapwings and skylarks. Still, even I could calculate the distance I would now fall in a flash. Twenty metres to the screw and another twenty metres below. And a bit for the rope stretch. I regret not missing more maths lessons.

Insecure, frantic footwork, I'm fumbling and scratching for purchase. Eventually I find myself under a large cluster of icicles drooling from the exit. I place three screws into cruddy ice, one tied-off, the other two wobbling. Then I make another move up, and another. Feet kicking, lumps of crud fly, which Powell dodges. I swear as the higher axe rips. Lurching onto the lower axe, I reverse. Then I try again, I attempt to break free but fail – again. I can't get out from beneath the overhang.

"Any ideas?"

"Why don't you aid it?"

"On what? Everything is rotten."

"Just slap a sling on your top screw to stand in, and aid it on your axes."

The thought of aiding through rotten ice doesn't appeal. "I don't do aid."

After an hour Powell realises I'm not joking. "I thought aiding is supposed to be less strenuous than proper climbing?" I gasp, lungs heaving.

"It is if you know what you're doing," Powell replies.

As I grovel up the unconsolidated snow at the top of the overhang I vow never to scoff at aid-climbers again.

Powell starts to climb, quickly realising that the sensible option is to jumar one of the ropes. I belay him on the other, and watch television-sized blocks of ice bounce constantly down the steeple of rock on the other side of the overhang. Powell comes into view. He fixes me with his long gunslinger stare.

"You're a fucking nutter." This pleases me. Obviously, he also thinks it was difficult.

Two pitches of worrying, unprotected powder place us on a knife-edge arête beneath a vast tilting serac fringed with a vicious grin of sharp, icy teeth. For the first time since day broke we can see down into the valley, the place we have spent so long waiting for this chance to climb. Our tent is a dot nestled among the capillary system of streams pouring from the tumbling glaciers that spew from Yerupajá Chico, Yerupajá and Siula Grande. The dark rocky peaks of the Huayhuash extend beyond for miles.

For the last hour I have watched a storm track across the range. We go to work cutting a ledge from the snow. It won't be long before the bad weather hits. An hour and a half of daylight remains.

The storm lashes the mountain with snow and hail. The wind gusts and the views disappear. Night arrives, and we are shrouded in our vertical world.

I squeeze alongside Powell, shoulder to shoulder inside his home-made bivvy bag, The Coffin.

"I suppose we can sit it out for a day if this keeps up."

For once I don't have to strain to hear his whispered reply "No need. We can climb through this."

I think of the slopes above loaded with fresh snow, and how little it took to knock me off last year. I think of us being trapped, unable to reverse the chimney as avalanches thunder through it.

"Yes, I suppose we can."

During the night the clouds pass over us, and much to my relief the sky clears. As we ease the stiffness from our aching limbs, the sun comes out and the mountain begins its morning song.

We climb six pitches, weaving and grovelling through rotten snow and ice. Climbing vertical unprotected mush eats into our precious time, though moving together for a while claws a little of it back.

Moving together is a part of mountaineering that doesn't usually worry me. In fact, most of the time I prefer it. The ground is covered quickly, and there's no messing with belays. This face is different. The uncertainty of the ground taxes my nerves. The high chance of being hit by falling debris taxes my nerves. The weather and snow conditions tax my nerves. All our hard-earned progress so unfairly taxed. The simplest formalities on this mountain are serious. I watch Powell kick a stance beneath another vertical, rotten wall of despair and I force myself to get on with it.

Tunnelling through a wafer-thin cornice I crawl onto the East Ridge, first climbed by Austrians Toni Egger and Siegfried Jungmair in 1957. A panoramic vista opens in front of me: new valleys, intense blue lakes, grass, unseen mountains. I feel alive and relieved that the dark and foreboding face has been left behind.

Dropping down from the overhanging cornice, I traverse to belay at the side of a large ice umbrella. The sight of Jirishanca Chico tempers my joy. A growing sense of guilt begins to threaten my contentment. The Peruvian police left the area yesterday – we heard their chopper blades thudding in the early morning, mingled with the sound of crashing ice. The bodies of the two Austrians have finally been found. From where I am I can see the holes in the snow where they had lain. Had they been pushing too hard in questionable conditions? Were they trying to get acclimatised to beat Powell and myself onto this route? Was it worth it? Is any of this worth it?

We had helped in the search for the Austrians' bodies, leading the police through the icefall on the first attempt. The policemen were a happy bunch, just doing a job. Pointing to the South East Face, we told

The massive South East Face of Jirishanca, Peru. Not a place to have a picnic.

them that we were going to try to climb Jirishanca. They looked at us as if we were aliens beamed down from Planet Pointless.

"You should go to the beach and meet women," one of them said.

After the last two days, I start to think that maybe he has a point. For the first time I have witnessed the pain of loss and the devastation for those left behind. Am I selfish to pursue a life of satisfaction for myself? Perhaps. But an existence of work, warmth, comfort, and mundane regularity simply doesn't give me enough reward. Truth be told, I feel safer in the mountains than in a city.

How would people view my demise if it came now? "He lived life to the limit and died doing what he loved." I hope that's what they would say. A cliché, I know – but true. The reward from climbing will always be worth more to me than a life lived waiting for retirement.

Powell traverses to join me, disturbing my thoughts. He continues up the slope until beneath the wildest umbrella of ice. There he fixes a belay. "You're going to love this!" he calls. As I climb up to meet him I just know that 'loving it', whatever 'it' is, is not what I'm going to be doing.

Belayed underneath the umbrella, formed by erupting ice at the rear of the cave, Powell sits like a fly in the jaws of a Venus flytrap. At his feet is a hole, giving a direct uninterrupted view down the face. I now begin to traverse a wall of thin, corniced snow that hangs over the hole.

"Careful!" Powell yells at me quite loudly. "You haven't seen how far that overhangs."

I haven't, but as I balance around the hole to join him, it suddenly becomes obvious.

"Why is nothing on this mountain normal?" I whine. "Everything has to be bigger, steeper, scarier, more rotten."

Powell ignores my moaning and sets about digging a five-star bivvy ledge. Soon, we have a pulpit overlooking a fine congregation of mountains. The night draws in, and for the first time in three days the afternoon bubbling of cloud hasn't resulted in a storm. "The weather looks to be settling again – just in time for our summit bid, eh? Couple of hours, maybe?"

"Hmm," Powell whispers his reply, "still a long way to go, I reckon."

Bastard! I think. Why does he always have to spoil my illusions with the truth?

Seven in the morning and I'm tiptoeing across the knife-edge ridge. I cross a thin bridge of icicles shining in the sun. Multi-coloured prisms of light dance as though through a stained-glass window. I'm petrified. Staring at the bridge all night has freaked me out. It's so thin, and the whole face drops away so drastically beneath it. Finally on the other side of it, I whoop a yell of relief.

The climbing above continues in a vein similar to the day before; never as hard as the first day, but sustained, uncertain and always serious. We cut slots, crawl over crumbling rock and pull up on overhanging ice. Mid-morning finds me tackling a steep buttress head on. It isn't until I'm in trouble that I realise that a snow slope to the right is running straight up the ridge. "There's a fucking simple slope there!" I yell to Powell. "Didn't you think to check around the corner before sending me on this death pitch?"

I'm not really that angry. In the three years I've known him this is his first error of judgement. It is good to realise he is human after all. Still, throwing a little tantrum gives me a smug feeling of satisfaction.

A careful sideways shuffle to escape the buttress deposits me gratefully on the slope. Climbing it indeed proves to be easy, apart from the effort of pushing, kicking and swimming at nearly 6,000 metres. There is no protection, but that is par for the course.

Powell swims to the base of a second rock buttress, to which I am now attached. The rock is a pile of crumbling corn flakes. Rusty pegs sprout from lumps of congealed mud, and rotting slings hang forlorn, blowing in the wind. The angle of the buttress looks amenable for the first few feet, but bulges higher up. I point to a line to my left. It looks more in keeping with everything we have already done, and will give us more new climbing. Powell sets off around the corner to check it out.

"It looks like it'll go," he mumbles.

My ears struggle. "Eh?"

"It looks okay as long as the ice isn't rotten."

"Oh, it'll be desperate then," I whisper.

The morning sun dazzles me as I belay at the base of the buttress. Around the corner Powell, squeezed into the dark confines of a typical Scottish gully, is in a different world. Chockstones, overhangs, thin rotten ice covering compact rock; it is the Ben's *Minus One Gully*, only at 6,000 metres. No queuing here, then.

After fifty five metres of sustained climbing, Powell escapes the confines of the gully, pulls through an ice overhang and belays at the base of a great dollop of snow balanced on the crest of the ridge. I join him with a deepened sense of respect. It's easy to forget the skill and determination that brings you and a close partner together in the first place.

Powell points me towards the third, vertical, unprotected death-fluting-excavation-pitch of the climb. I dig through it with surprising ease, emerging onto the steep summit ridge. With each kick in the rotten, sun-bleached snow I sing hallelujah, each step bringing us nearer to our goal.

I make a long traverse left, passing above Powell, who is hidden beneath the whipped-cream dollop twenty metres below. I now start to burrow through Simpson-esque flutings of despair. Halfway up one fluting I dig out some ice and belay. Above looks to be the final ridge leading to the summit. Below my crampons, the runnel drops dramatically for thousands of feet. I picture falling now, without a single piece of gear between us. We would hang in space over the headwall without a chance of pulling back onto the face. Powell won't have a clue if that's about to happen; he is tucked away out of sight and sound. I don't fancy emulating Simpson's Siula epic, even if it would make a good story.

Powell follows my weaving steps to join me at my confined spot. It's a tight fit hemmed in by snow walls. Continuing directly up the runnel he chops through the top of the fluting and follows a steep icy slope. The afternoon of cloud has started earlier than normal and now it's spitting with hail. Spindrift falls in great clouds, blowing across the hundreds of fringed icefalls hanging from the headwall to my left. Soon I am covered.

"Come on Al, it can't be far now."

I'm impatient; the weather has started to concern me. I just want to be up this thing, though the thought of getting off it scares me stupid. I picture all the white shit thundering down the chimney, and before I can stop it my head starts to list climbers I knew who have been killed by falling debris. Sod that. I have Powell to get me down safe. I know he won't take any risks getting us off.

The summit is close. Taking the gear, I quickly scurry off before the clouds come in and block the view completely. The mist clears for a second and I can see a flat ridge and a tower less than a pitch away. It has to be the summit. But what I now see scares me. The ridge looks deadly. On the right a curling cornice overhangs the North West Face, and on the left a perfect avalanche slope waits to be set off.

I belay off my rucksack buried in the snow. Powell grovels back from checking the tower. Leaning close and shouting in my ear he delivers the bad news. "It'll go with a lot of digging. There's no gear, and getting back will be interesting. Maybe we can get down the other side?"

I didn't like the idea of blindly forcing on in the teeth of a storm.

"How about digging a ledge to bivvy and waiting for the weather to pick up? At least we'll be able to see what we're getting into."

"No, we're strung out now. And if this weather continues we could get stuck here."

He's right. We have no food left and even less energy. Getting down is going to be exhausting enough as it is. The line has dictated we move light and fast. We have no fixed rope to slip back down in times of trouble. There is no de-stressing, relaxing and eating before our summit push. My mind flashes to the scene that would greet me on my return to work. The detox class would come into the prison gym fresh from the street, pale, rattling and drug-addled. Taking one look at me, they would smile and wink recognizing a fellow sufferer. Little would they know the drug of my choice didn't come wrapped in foil. If we bivvy up here now, I am going to make the worse crack addict look healthy.

All we want is to stand and rejoice on the tip of the summit, shake hands and celebrate. We have paid our taxes, but the weather is now robbing us. Battered by large snowflakes, hoping for a miracle, we stand there for half an hour. But our prayers are not answered.

"We should start getting down – it'll be better down climbing if it's light," announces a stoical Powell.

I don't want to leave. Neither does he. We want the summit. It just doesn't feel fair. Fair is for dreamers, though; fair isn't real. Life isn't fair. Kicking angrily, I turn, facing in toward the slope and begin the long scary way back down to normality and the prison.

TURN

———

As soon as I got back from Jirishanca I paid off my mortgage. I also looked at the prison with fresh eyes. I couldn't help scrutinising the stairs, the doors, the bricks, the bars, the alarm bells, the lights, the locks and the gates. It felt strangely as though I'd never really seen them before. I worked out as usual with Buster, and as usual I ran beside the canal. But it wasn't 'usual' any more. Already I could feel a new sense of freedom, and a fluttering in my stomach.

Now as I ran on the towpath I was constantly planning. I could resign now and climb full time, living off savings and the rent from my house for at least two years. Then again, if I continued to work for just another ten years I could retire for good with enough money to live comfortably.

'Comfortably,' I said to myself. The word circled my brain. 'Comfortable' meant, to me, calm, quiet, stillness, being fixed in one place, static, inert – lifeless. Comfortable meant the death of uncertainty. It would kill the thrill of not knowing where next, who with, how and for how long. Comfortable is nice parties, full plates, TV straight after getting home, walking well-lit streets knowing what's around the next corner. Above all, comfortable meant routine, and routine was what I needed to leave behind.

As I ran along the muddy banks I saw myself climbing golden, sun-bleached rock in northern Spain, or busting a gut approaching a dark north face in the depth of winter, or jumping on a plane heading out on expedition to Nepal, Peru, India, Pakistan, Patagonia, or wherever. I saw crumbling rock at Gogarth and bristling ice in Canada, I saw myself running crisp sawn steps of slate in the quarries near Llanberis.

I saw my escape route, but I also felt scared to take it. I felt scared of losing the very things I needed to escape. The thought of having no systems and routine or even a regular place to sit and eat and sleep and call my own was frightening me, holding me in my place. Even so, eventually, after lots of running and a great deal of thinking, I built up the courage to let go of it all.

I can still remember the date. On 21 August I wrote my letter of resignation. The next day I handed it in.

One part of me felt relief, huge, overwhelming relief. And yet it seemed a bigger part of me screamed: 'What the fuck are you doing?' I could hear the voices of others too.

"It's a job for life – good money, good pension."

"No one resigns."

"Just another dreamer."

During the first week I moved into my house, I bought a picture of an old dilapidated Citroën, crumpled and rusting in a pine forest, grass growing through its bodywork. The picture had hung in my living room ever since. I took the picture from the wall and wiped away the dust. At some point in the past that Citroën had been brand new.

"Nothing lasts forever. Move on. Comfort is the killer of dreams."

I wrapped the picture in brown paper and taped the seams, carried it upstairs, climbed up into the attic, and placed it with many of the things I'd lived with and that were part of my own house: my books, my records, magazines, cutlery, and the china I'd eaten off.

As the weeks passed, the jobs to be done became fewer. My house had been inspected, the electrics rewired, the chimney swept. The old sofa on which I had sat and iced my knee, my elbows, neck, ankle, shoulder, the same sofa that had I collapsed onto during nights of sleeplessness, the sofa I had made love on – I put it on a trailer and took it to the dump. It felt like I was abandoning an old friend. The yellow 'Klingon' fingerboard above the toilet door where for hours, even when injured, I'd hung and pulled and hung was taken down and put away.

The yucca I had given to my parents when I had worked at Alton Towers, only to be given it back when my parents retired and moved to live on a canal boat, was carried from the bathroom and planted outside in my small garden. It would wither and die, but who wanted a giant yucca? At least planting it outside gave it a chance. And all of us, I decided, need to be given a chance.

Every evening during my final week in both the prison and my home, I walked around the village, past the old horse chestnut, its leaves yellowing, crispy conker shells scattered beneath it along the road, leaf skeletons and stalks layered over each other randomly like the sticks of some intricate Chinese game. The tawny owls would soon be squeaking and looking down at me from between the branches.

I passed the village green and the thatched post office, the pub, the house with warped walls and a tin roof, the grazing sheep and the telephone box I had burst from celebrating Tim Neill agreeing to climb with me at North Stack. Then past St Andrews, the humble medieval church built from ironstone, the same yellowy stone I climbed on at Slawston Bridge.

I reached my usual stopping place, the rusty metal gate beneath a mature oak. I leant on the cold bars, the gritty rust under my forearms. I leant as I had leant, on and off, for nearly fifteen years. I looked across the field to the grazing cows, the hawthorn hedge, the rabbits, the rooks and also a solitary lapwing.

"No one resigns."

On the phone wires, swallows lined up like soldiers, their black silk shoulders squeezed together as they chattered to each other.

Driving to work on my last day in the dark, I switched on the radio and heard Ian Dury's Essex drawl: *I could be the catalyst that sparks the revolution/ I could be an inmate in a long-term institution/I could lead to wide extremes, I could do or die/I could yawn and be withdrawn and watch them gallop by.*

The small prison door at the side of the wooden gates was, as usual, lit yellow. The same yellow today as it would be tomorrow, the same as it would be next year and the year after that. The door slid open. There was still time.

"Changed my mind Governor. All a big joke. Nobody leaves, I know that."

Sliding one of my keys into the first lock of the day I thought of Ian Dury, Sid Vicious, Jimmy McCausland killed on his proper punk motor-bike, Malcolm Owen... and Jamie Fisher... and Terry Jones, the prison officer I met in my first week at Gartree. He had been working in the Emergency Control Room, and I could still see him laughing and joking. Terry had always been friendly and funny, he was one of the good guys. When I started work at Welford Road, there he was again, the same friendly laughing, unaffected person who I had met years ago.

I shut the door and walked towards the gate in the fence, walking across the same tarmac where Terry had lain the week before, dead before he hit the ground. I could still picture the prison officer pumping his chest, pink lips meeting pale lips. To comfort myself, to keep on the track I was now walking, that I mustn't now step off, I sang, almost silently, just under my breath: *A voice shouts loud, we'll never surrender, a voice in the crowd, never surrender.*

For the first time in my working life, a thirteen-hour shift in the shadow of the walls passed quickly. I walked around the prison meeting officers and inmates for the final time. All of them were supportive. So many times over the last few weeks I heard someone say: "I wish I had the balls to do what you're doing."

I wanted to shout: "But you do!"

Of course, I didn't, I just commiserated with them and agreed that their life choices had been different to mine.

At lunch I didn't go for the usual run alongside the canal; I wanted to spend the whole thirteen hours behind walls. I wanted to do the time. It wasn't because I was going to miss the place. It was more to remind myself how much I hated it. Bob wasn't in. He'd said his goodbyes already. It was just Tony and Rich and me. And at five they left.

At quarter to eight, just after I'd supervised my final evening class, I opened the door of the main prison. I was taking the evening class back to the cells including the two gym orderlies John and Dean, and the effervescent Buster. I stepped in, pulled the air into my nostrils, and then stood aside to allow the inmates to file past me. I breathed deeply again. I wanted to draw as much tainted air into my body as possible. I wanted the atmosphere to fill my lungs and enter my blood and flow through my body – for the last time.

I climbed the iron stairs, metal rattling around the building as other officers and inmates climbed up to the landings and the cells. I unlocked John and Dean's cell. I noticed the key, and watched it as I slowly turned it in the lock. Dean shook my hand, always more reserved than John, who hugged me and wished me all the best.

"Likewise mate."

Other officers were locking up the rest of the inmates from the class, except for Buster. I followed him along the landing until I stood outside his cell. Once more, I inserted the small cell key, and pushed down on the handle. The door clunked as it opened; it sounded like something being released.

"Right mate, you take care of yourself and stay off those dirty drugs."

"Nick, never again, never again. You've shown me the way – this is it, I'm going to be the next Bruce Lee. Wha-ha!" He feigned a chop and laughed.

We both knew it wasn't true. Buster was the typical habitual drug-using criminal for whom prison had become a way of life.

"Yeah, and where's Bruce Lee now Buster?"

We hugged, shook hands turning the handshake into a thumb grasp, a finger lock and finally a knuckle bump. "Now get in your cell. I'm out of here."

Clunk, the door closed on Buster – on a prisoner – for the final time in my life. Doors clunked shut all around me. I walked the landing, and down the metal stairs. Clunk after clunk, reverberating through the empty central space of the prison, somehow louder than they'd ever been before. For the first time I noticed the texture of the sound, the short curtailing echo after each door connected with its frame.

I walked away to the abrupt sound of human lives being locked away.

Returning to the gymnasium, I packed the few things I had left after clearing my desk the day before. I unpinned pictures from the corkboard of Tengkang Poche, the mountain in Nepal I would be heading for with Al Powell and Jules Cartwright in a week's time. I unpinned the picture of Jirishanca, a line drawn up it that stopped just short of the summit. Finally, I took down the black and white photograph of Paul Schweizer, Cartwright, Jamie Fisher and me at K2 base camp.

I pushed the pictures into my rucksack and left the office turning the lights off. Then I locked the door. I was the last in the building, which was now almost silent. The corridor where the inmates changed smelt musty. A few sweaty blue vests had been left lying on the wooden bench. I grabbed them, stuffing them into the white laundry bag. Then I took one final look before opening the building door and walking away. I walked past the sandstone turrets, through the inner fence and the gate, then across the tarmac, and through the wooden door and into the gatehouse. I threw my keys down the shoot.

"Keep my key tally. I don't need it any more."

"That's it then? You're done?"

The officer behind the Perspex hit a button and the metal door slid and creaked open.

"Lucky bastard."

I stepped out and the sounds changed. There was the distant rumble of a lorry, and now a snatch of a police siren far away. Cars swished down the Welford Road, cutting furrows into the wet tarmac. I could hear the high dull whine of planes descending into East Midlands airport. I could hear the wet air in the trees. A few pigeons, huddled in the shadow of one of the prison's turrets, briefly mumbling to each other. I turned my face upward to feel the rain, and I imagined the stars beyond the sodium lights, fixed in a slowly spinning sky. The acidity in the rain felt cleansing. The exhaust-fumes in the air smelled of freedom. I breathed in deeply. I listened to the air enter my body.

Then, as I breathed out again, I turned and started walking.

Me, at home in the trusty green Berlingo. Cataluña   *Photo: Rich Lucas (aka Boy Wonder)*

ACKNOWLEDGEMENTS

After nine years on the road, in the van, and staying with friends, this list is long. I know I will have missed people and for this I apologise profusely. I would like to say I will buy you a beer to make up for it, but generally being skint means I possibly won't …

The order of the list of names, like a graded list in a rock climbing guide, bears absolutely no relevance to anything.

Mark 'The Pretentious Poet' Goodwin (the reason I began this long and arduous literary journey so blame him) and Nikki Clayton (whose narrow boat has become the usual stopping off point and site of much writing rant); Tim, Lou and Esme Neill (who's house has become nearly a second home and watering point), Graham 'The Hippy' Desroy (who owns my third home and office and, when he's awake, is my regular belayer. I would say climbing partner but belayer is more appropriate I think!); Paul Pritchard, Lesley (my long suffering sister and drop off point for expeditions) and David, Al Powell, Paul Schweizer, Ken Wilson (there from nearly the start and nearly the publisher of this book), Libby Peter, Zoe and Ruby Wood, Clothile and Jake Stone, Noel and Ali, Katie Ives and everyone at *Alpinist* Magazine, Lindsay Griffin, Alex Messenger, Miranda and her Mum, Michael Tweedley, Iain McKenzie, everyone at The Tower Climbing Centre in Leicester, Bruce French and Andy Evans, Clive Taylor, Rob Cooper, Dr Jon Reid, Stu Lorrie, Gordon Everard, everyone at DMM (thanks for the internet and a place on rainy days), everyone at Mountain Equipment, Boreal, Adam Wainwright, Mick Greenslade, Rich Sawbridge, Bob McFadden, Lou Hale, Nige Masters, Stu McAleese, Jude Spancken, Lukasz Warzecha, Jack Geldard, Rob Greenwood, Alastair Lee, Dave Reeves, Chris Rowlands, Ian Burton, Henry Iddon, Baby Dave Rudkin, Matt Stygal, Dave Evans, Keith Ball and

Rachael (owners of fat cat), Rich Cross, Michelle Blaydon (Samsung), The Climbers' Club (unofficial landlords and publishers of my writing and feeder of food), The BMC, The MEF, The Nick Estcourt Award, The Welsh Sports Council, Neil Pearsons, Gill Kent, Ian Parnell, Ed Douglas, Andy Houseman, Kenton Cool, Jon Bracey, Matt Helliker, Pete Benson, Lozzie Benson, Jonny Baird, Katie Moore, John and Pat Horscroft, Bernard Newman, Ian Smith, David Simmonite, everyone at Vertebrate Publishing, Andy Kirkpatrick, Chris Bonington, Richard Wheeldon, Bill Mennel, Tony Buckle, Phil Preece, Dave and Llynwen Brown, Jon 'The Hobbit' Ratcliffe, Steve Mayers, Gill Lovick and everyone at The Beacon, Katie Forrester, The Chris Walker Memorial Fund, Lyon Equipment Award, Shipton Tilman Award, James McHaffie and Sophie, Pete and Rachael Robins, Dan McManus and Sophie, Plas y Brenin, Martin Chester, Rob Spencer, Kath Goodie, Ric Potter and Kate Potter, Joe Simpson, Loben Sherpa, Ian Wall, Doug Scott, Mark F. Twight, Mick Fowler, The Alpine Club, The American Alpine Club, Kelly Cordes, Freddie Wilkinson, Kev Mahonie, Ben Gilmore, Will Gadd and Kim Csizmazia, Steve House, Owain Jones, Jen Olson, Max and Zoe Turgeon, Ian Berry, Dave Noddings, Dave Harrison, Steve Goodwin, Andy Benson, Dave Hunter, Steve Ashworth, Woody, everyone at V12 Outdoor in Llanberis, Catrin Thomas, Boz Morris, Jonny Garside, Becky McGovern, Nico Favresse, Seán Villanueva, Ray Wood, Simon Panton, Chrissy and Nige Shepherd, Nick Colton, Dave Turnbull, Scott Titt, Rab Carrington, Rich Lucas, Robin Richmond, Wojtek Kozakiewicz, Rebecca Dent, Neil Cowburn, Ray Saunders, Johnny Dawes, Neil Brodie, John Redhead, Guy Willett, Ioan Doyle, Steve and Alison Dyche, Sue Westwood, Sheila Salt.